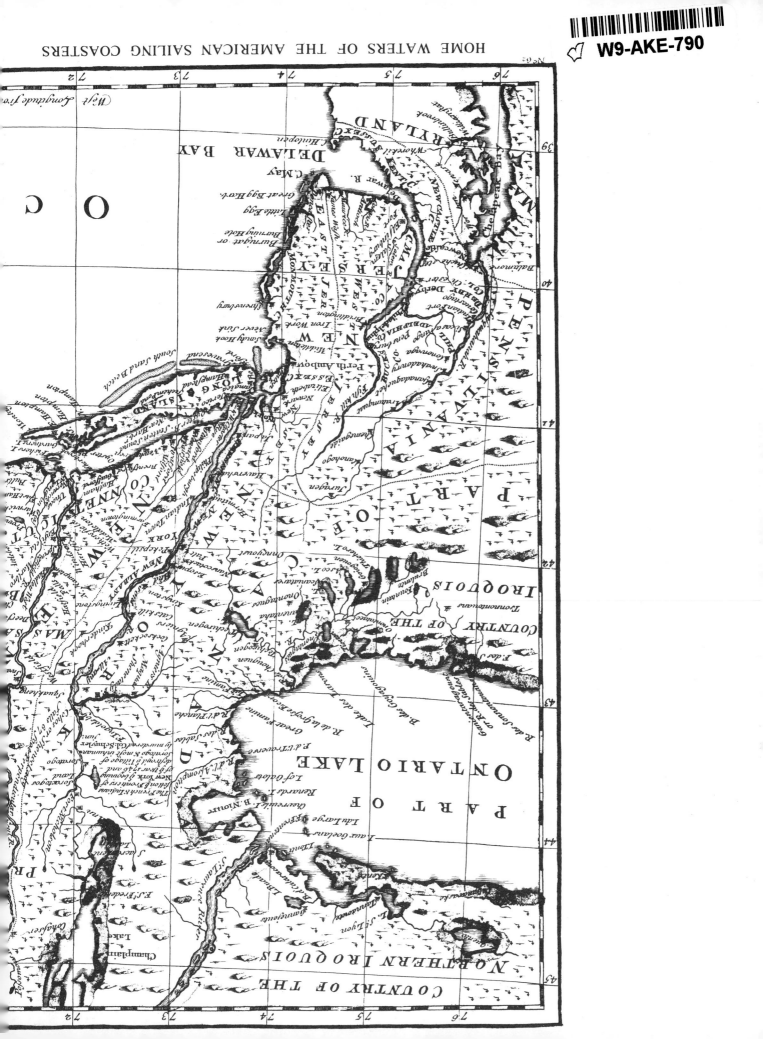

# AMERICAN SAILING COASTERS
## OF
## THE NORTH ATLANTIC

A BRIGANTINE RIGGED GALLEY

**AMERICAN KETCH OR "CATCH" BEATING TO WINDWARD**

AMERICAN TOPSAIL SCHOONER OF THE MID 1700S WITH A
SQUARE TOPSAIL ON THE FORE TOPMAST

# AMERICAN
# SAILING COASTERS OF
# THE NORTH ATLANTIC

By

## PAUL C. MORRIS

WITH A FOREWORD BY
### EDOUARD A. STACKPOLE
Director of the Peter Foulger Museum, Nantucket, Massachusetts
and
Former Curator of Mystic Seaport, Mystic, Connecticut

146 ILLUSTRATIONS
*Original Photographs and Reproductions of Pen and Ink Drawings*
*Produced with Special Reference to the Text*

## BONANZA BOOKS
## NEW YORK

This edition is published by Bonanza Books,
a division of Crown Publishers, Inc.,
by arrangement with Bloch and Osborn Publishing Company.
a   b   c   d   e   f   g   h
BONANZA 1979 PRINTING
Manufactured in the United States of America


Library of Congress Cataloging in Publication Data
Morris, Paul C.
    American sailing coasters of the North Atlantic.
    Bibliography: p.
    Includes index.
    1. Schooners—United States. 2. Coasters (Ships)—
United States. 3. Coastwise shipping—United States.
I. Title.
VM311.F7M67   1979        623.82′2        79-333
ISBN 0-517-26190-1

*This book is dedicated with thanks to my father*

PAUL C. MORRIS, SR.

*whose encouragement and many, many hours of help in the darkroom account for some of the photographs used herein.*

SHALLOP FITTED WITH GAFF RIGGED FORESAIL
AND MAINSAIL. THE SHALLOP WAS OFTEN OPEN
OR ONLY PARTIALLY DECKED.

## FOREWORD

From the very beginnings of Colonial America until well into the 19th century the major highway connecting the major ports along our coasts was the sea. Despite the competition with the advent of the railroads, fleets of sloops, schooners and steamboats continued to provide transportation for goods and people for nearly a century after the iron rails ran their spidery connecting links. In the bulk carrying trade the schooners became the "work horses" of the coastal commerce, supplying a humble occupation for many sailors.

The schooner has become the last representative of commercial activities under sail. In terms of maritime history the schooner eras are but a short space of time, but their contribution to the development of our country is remarkable. Many of them were long-lived, escaping a variety of dangers as they reached and tacked and drifted into harbors alongshore and to the West Indies. Others made but few voyages and then met disaster. A number made whaling voyages into the Arctic and to tropic seas, proving durable and able.

They came in a variety of designs, being graceful under full sail or ugly and stubborn in a tide-way. Many performed incredible feats in clawing off a lee shore, or racing before a smoky sou'wester. They could carry amazing loads of lumber, coal, ice or clay, and they created marine history as they fought winter gales, or navigated through thick fog, or bucked icy straits, in the accomplishment of what their skippers reckoned was just another voyage.

We may find accounts of some of these individual schooners in a number of excellent books. However, a wider treatment of them as types, and in a more or less chronological manner, is what Paul Morris is presenting in his study, and this is welcome, indeed. The vital statistics may be located in various registries and in marine columns of contemporary newspapers, together with reports of voyages and "trips". In this volume we have the schooner displayed on the broad canvas of her accomplishments.

We have seen the passing of them in our own lifetimes. A few of them linger as members of the "windjammer fleets", providing much pleasure for vacationists. But commercial trade no longer includes them. The schooner has become a legend. One or two handsome replicas have been built but, for the most part, they are now recalled by the paintings, photographs, and old quarterboards that serve as relics of their days of service. Only a handful of men remain of what was once a goodly number of schooner men.

In his pages, Mr. Morris presents the development of a marine type, so that it may occupy its proper role in maritime history. In following his story we become aware of the careful use of detail without losing the narrative. The evolution of the schooner has a natural sequence governed by the commercial demand. The addition of more masts, increased beam, added rails and counters, centerboards, lengthening of hull, and refinement of bow — all become intriguing details. This evolutionary process brings to the book an excellent dimension, aiding the reading as it carries the narrative forward.

Of special interest are those chapters devoted to the three, four and five-masted schooners. Here there is a wealth of detail concerning masting, sail plan, hull development and deck lay-out. When the first five-master made her appearance in 1888, one of Nantucket's veteran mariners wrote, that having sailed in many types of craft:

"My poor old head can't figure by dead reckoning or lunar
What kind of looking vessel is this new 5-masted schooner."

However, they were built to a number of half hundred or more, and proved quite successful — one even rounding Cape Horn and reaching San Francisco.

These great schooners were able to carry tremendous cargoes, and they lasted well into the twentieth century. In carrying bulk cargo they were in a class by themselves, surviving long after the fate of the schooner type was sealed as an economic maritime factor.

In this book Paul Morris brings out the important role of the commercial schooner. He will intrigue with the variety of their building and the wide range of their adventures. Here are accounts of the men who owned them and sailed them. Their successes and their failures; their rewards and their disappointments become the chronicles of a vanished marine age. The wealth of detail demonstrates that the true facts of maritime history are as gripping as the legends and eminently more satisfying in the long run.

*Edouard A. Stackpole,*
Nantucket Island, Massachusetts

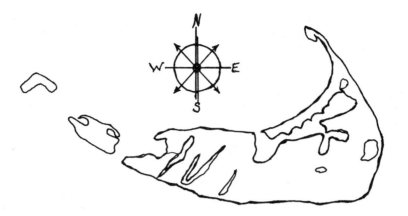

*Nantucket Island, Massachusetts*

## PREFACE

Vessels of the coasting trade have claimed my interest since boyhood days on Long Island Sound where my father and I used to photograph passing schooners. This interest has continued since I moved to Nantucket in 1958. Shortly thereafter I became aware of the role that the little island had played in the history of American shipping, particularly with regard to the coasting trade. The "Little Gray Lady of the Sea", as the oldtimers used to call Nantucket Island, lies roughly 30 miles off shore, southeast of Cape Cod. While justly famous for its early history of whaling, this sandy outpost and the surrounding area were justly infamous among seafaring men as a place to beware and to be approached only with caution. Together with Cape Cod and Martha's Vineyard, Nantucket forms part of a barrier stretching out into the Atlantic Ocean, around which our north and south bound shipping has to pass. Not only were these exposed areas in the way, but Nantucket in particular is surrounded by shoals and these, together with the island, have accounted for over 700 record shipwrecks. The bulk of these wrecks proved to be coasting vessels of one type or another.

Nantucket today is a tourist haven and in as much as there is no other industry here, a visitor to the island finds it very little changed from the days when the sailing coasters prevailed. The town is still permeated with "salty atmosphere", and there are also a few of the old timers around who remember the schooners that used to pass by and occasionally "fetch up" on the sands. When one learns how truly numerous were the multitudes of coasting vessels, the wonder is that more were not caught and lost. The majority of the laden coasters that went by the island did so in Nantucket Sound, which is to the north of the island, between Nantucket and Cape Cod.

An island resident named Nelson O. Dunham, who was in the old Life Saving Service, before it became part of the Coast Guard, once told of being on a four hour watch in 1912, at the Madaket station, which is located on the west end of Nantucket.

"I was substituting there at the time and during that watch we counted 92 vessels going through the sound under sail. This included some barges in tow, which had their sails set, but by and large most of those vessels were schooners. The bulk of them were two and three masters, but there were larger ones as well."

I mentioned this story one day to Everett Chapel, who also lived on the island. He smiled and said: "Why, I can top that. One day I counted over a hundred."

Neither of these men is given to exaggeration and both have had long associations with the coastline in this area. Everett was on hand when the mighty "Wyoming" went to pieces off Pollock Rip in 1924 and salvaged some of the lower sections of her tremendous masts.

"Olney" Dunham was around many schooners in his days with the service, both on Nantucket and at Cape Ann, and the integrity of each man is unquestionable. Nevertheless, pondering the thought of so many sailing vessels in sight at one time did give rise to some doubt.

My family and I have often gone to Dionis on the north side of the island and from the sand cliffs we can look out over the calm, blue-green waters of the sound. Usually the only vessels we ever see are the steamers that run between Nantucket and the mainland, and during the summer an occasional yacht. As a rule, the sound presents the same scene; it's nice to look at, but it's empty.

It's indeed difficult for today's visitor to the island to imagine the vast amount of traffic that once passed by its picturesque shoreline. However, the number of people and vessels once engaged in the coasting business was truly tremendous and if one is inclined towards digging into the past, a bit of investigation and searching of maritime records begins to bring forth a most fascinating history.

P.C.M.

# CONTENTS

# ILLUSTRATIONS
## Line Drawings

# PHOTOGRAPHS

# PHOTOGRAPHS (Continued)

EARLY COLONIAL PINNACE WITH SPRITSAIL AND
JIB. THE PINNACE WAS USUALLY FULLY DECKED
AND LARGER THAN THE SHALLOP.

*A Topsail Sloop*

## Chapter I

## THE COLONIAL PERIOD

The story of the coasting trade begins with the early days of the American colonies. In colonial times, roads connecting towns were few and far between and in most cases little more than muddy paths. Travel by land was hazardous and uncertain and positively not suited to the moving of produce. Consequently, all freight in any amount was shipped by water. It was for this reason that practically all the early settlements were located on rivers, bays or inlets. For over a century after the "Mayflower's" voyage in 1620, for example, one finds that few Massachusetts farms or settlements were more than 30 miles distant from the sea or tide water. The colonies' very existence was dependent upon their trade with the mother country. However, the small size and scattered locations of the various farms and villages made it difficult for them to gather cargoes for foreign trade and to transport those cargoes over land. Therefore produce was sent by small boats to a more favorably located port which gradually grew in size as an export and import center. Hence the beginning of coasting. At the export centers the cargoes were combined, loaded on British vessels and shipped over seas. These ports, quite naturally grew in size and importance and as they did so, they gradually drew produce in larger quantities and from greater distances. As a natural outcome of this enterprise it followed that many of the small boats carrying freight to these ports were built in the colonies.

Early ship and boat building in the colonies, however, did not become a really active industry until after the middle of the 17th century. Most of the early vessels that were built were small and included such types as the shallop, pinnace[1], sloop, ketch or "catch", pink, galley and skiff.

1

The inconsistent naming of many of these colonial types of craft makes a clear understanding of them difficult, as the type names at that time were loosely applied. In "The National Watercraft Collection", by Howard I. Chapelle, is found a very concise explanation of most of the various colonial craft:

"A shallop thus might be anything from a small open ship's boat fitted to row and perhaps to sail, to a sizable decked coasting craft or fishing boat. Large shallops sometimes had one mast fitted to carry a jib and a gaff or sprit mainsail, but gradually the typical shallop rig became a two masted one having two gaff sails, the fore the smaller, and no jib. Most shallops were square sterned; those having sharp sterns were commonly called double shallops. The lateen rig, it is believed, was also used in the shallops, but rarely in boats working in unprotected waters.

"The pinnace was either a ship's boat, long and narrow and built to row fast, or a decked craft designed to sail and row and often fitted with the two masted shallop rig. The pinnaces were sometimes the English equivalent of the Spanish "brigantine". The name pinnace was also applied to galley-ships in the 16th and early 17th centuries, but by the beginning of the 18th century this application of the name ceased.

"At the end of the 17th century colonial shipbuilders were constructing for the North Atlantic run between the New England colonies and England, galley-ships and galley-brigantine-rigged vessels both called "gallies" or "galleys." These vessels were required in the unprotected colonial trade, the British Navy then being unable to furnish adequate cruisers for convoy guards. These galleys were flush-decked ships armed for war on one deck and with a rowing deck below; they were sometimes called "runners."

"The ketch was a square-sterned sailing vessel having two masts; the type was used for trading and in the Banks fisheries. Colonial records indicate that these vessels had very small crews, so they could not have been very large. It is very doubtful that they ever carried a square rig similar to that of the naval bomb ketch, since their crews would have been inadequate to handle such rigs; probably they were fore-and-aft rigged, with fore and main gaff sails of approximately equal size and with one or more jibs. This supposition is supported by the fact that, early in the 18th century the ketch or "catch", previously very numerous, suddenly disappeared almost completely from colonial records, being replaced by large numbers of "scooners". This suggests that there was merely a change of type name rather than that the "scooner" was a new rig or hull-type. It is noticeable that the "scooner" appeared all along the coast within a very short time.

"Sloops were commonly employed in coasting or in the West Indian trade and were usually craft of some size, up to 60 feet in length, having one mast, a gaff mainsail, and two or more jibs. The larger sloops were decked and fitted with bulwarks. Large-size sloops, 60 to 65 feet long were built in the West Indies by the last half of the 17th century and the fast sailing "Jamaica sloops" produced at Jamaica were popular with the buccaneers and piratical gentry in those waters.

"The small craft constructed in the colonies included "boat-canoes", dugouts shaped to resemble ships' boats and usually square sterned. Except in Eastern Maine and in the Canadian Maritime Provinces, the birch-bark Indian canoe was seldom employed on salt water.

"Skiffs" appear to be merely small rowing craft and were not usually fitted to sail.

"The rigs of colonial boats in the 17th century were those employed in England and included the leg-of-mutton, a triangular sail fitted with a boom; the shoulder-of-mutton, which was similar but with a very short gaff; the hoy sail, which was a gaff-sail with a long gaff, rarely lowered; and the lateen sail. These rigs and sail forms were quite well developed in Britain by the middle of the century when colonial ship and boatbuilding became very active. Large vessels were rigged as ships or brigantines, in the English manner, of course."

The sloop rig was indeed very popular in colonial America. Sloops varied in size from 20 to 50 feet as early as 1690 and were used in all manner of trading. As its popularity spread, the building of the fast sailing Jamaica sloop was not long confined to the island of Jamaica. The same type of vessel was built at Bermuda and eventually on the mainland. The larger sloops often carried, in addition to their fore-and-aft canvas, one or two square sails, the upper-most, or square topsail being set upon a topmast. They needed fairly large crews and often were employed in deep-water work as well as in the coasting trade. One sloop, the 60 foot, 89 ton "Union" of Boston, began a voyage in 1794 which took her completely around the world and lasted almost two years. The rig persisted on deep-water until the 1820's and in coastal work until well into the 1830's. Thereafter, sloops were confined largely to river and estuary traffic. However, when looking into the period between the late 17th century and the early part of the 19th, one soon realizes that the sloop was one of the "work horses" of the American coast.

The schooner rig, so called, came into being, as stated before, in the early 18th century. As a rig it was basically a two masted vessel, fore-and-aft rigged on each mast, with the foresail slightly smaller than the mainsail and carrying one or more jibs. The evolution of the schooner rig and its name have occasioned much discussion among historians and not a little disagreement. One thing however, seems to be agreed upon by most modern historians and that is the fact that the rig was not invented here in America. Unfortunately, in times past, one of the often accepted accounts as to the origin of the schooner is the fable of its invention by Capt. Andrew Robinson in Gloucester, Massachusetts in 1713. According to E. P. Morris in his book "The Fore-and-Aft Rig in America", factual evidence proves that the rig was in use in Europe before that date, notably in England, where pictures imply its existence as early as 1690. It is even possible that the rig was used by the Dutch at an earlier date. Where the name "schooner" comes from is even more difficult to trace. The verb "scoons" has never been in the English language. It is given, of course, in various dictionaries, but only as quoted from the Robinson story wherein a bystander, upon seeing the new vessel sailing, cried, "Oh, see how she scoons". Robinson was supposed to have replied: "Then a scooner let her be". This story being unfounded leaves us with little to go on. In truth we do not know the origin of the word schooner any more than we know the origin of the words catboat, ketch or bugeye. The rig itself was first portrayed here in America in a view of Boston rendered in 1725. Previous to 1760 it was employed usually in its pure fore-and-aft form, most probably having evolved as Mr. Chapelle suggests, from the earlier colonial ketches or "catches".

By 1790, if not earlier, the schooner had become the national rig of the United

3

States and Canada. At that time the larger sea-going schooners were usually rigged with square topsails on the fore-top mast and frequently so rigged on both the fore and main topmasts. Around the turn of the century the term "schooner" implied the square topsails, while those rigged without them were called fore-and-afters. Many of the early schooners had booms on their gaff fore sails, but these went out of style when the over-lapping, or lug fore sail came into general use sometime after the Revolution. I don't mean to imply that all schooners around the later part of the 18th century had square topsails. It's probable that the fisherman and many coasters were more often rigged without them, especially if they were small in size.

---

[1]In 1607, the "Virginia", a pinnace of 30 tons had been built at the Sagadahoc Colony at the mouth of the Kennebec River at a place known as Popham's Beach. There appears to be authenticated historical evidence that this was the first vessel of such size to be built in New England. According to Captain Harold G. Foss, of Hancock, Maine, the "Virginia" sailed from Maine in 1609 bound for the Virginia colonies for which she was named. She made four round trips between Virginia and England and was lost on her fifth trip during a gale off the west coast of Ireland. At the time of her loss the "Virginia" had reached the age of 20 years.

COLONIAL SLOOP OF THE EARLY 1700'S ENTERING PORT

*A Double Topsail Schooner Chasing A Brig*

## Chapter II

### PIRATES

(Some Effects on Commerce and Design of Sailing Vessels)

The civil war in England in 1641 did much to disrupt commerce to and from the colonies and by the end of the 17th century the colonists were looking elsewhere for trade. Their search culminated in the building up of the West Indian trade. Trade with the West Indies, although not confined to the actual American coastline, was to grow and persist as an important factor in American commerce for over two centuries and was to have an effect on design of coastal sailing vessels and development of a special U.S. naval squadron.

The 18th century saw a great increase in American shipbuilding and as the vessels increased in numbers, the demand also arose for an increase in the speed of these vessels. Because of piracy in the West Indies from the 1500's to the 1830's, trade there was dangerous and a fast ship was the best insurance for a man's continued success in business. While sloops, schooners, ships and brigantines were all used in the early West Indian Trade, notably fast vessels whose design evolved from that of the old Jamaica sloops, were built in the Chesapeake Bay area. These vessels were divided basically into two types. The smaller, or pilot boat type and the larger type which developed into the famous Baltimore Clipper. Both types were schooner rigged, with extreme rake to their masts, rather deep aft and did not have much freeboard. While they were fast, they did not have the ability to carry a great amount of cargo. A few of these vessels were rigged as three masted schooners, thus making them the first of this type. Those that were rigged in this manner were not, however, rigged in the same

5

way as the later day three masted schooners. The mizzen mast, for example was considerably shorter than the fore and main masts and had more rake. The fore and main sails were both loose footed and without a boom, the mizzen being the only sail to carry such a spar. Usually the larger vessels carried square topsails forward and frequently carried them on the main as well. Generally speaking, however, it was the two masted rig that was usually found on these Baltimore schooners. Baltimore Clippers, as the larger variety eventually were called, did yeoman service for the United States, particularly during the war of 1812. After this date, when more burdensome vessels were required, the Baltimore type of vessel gradually lost popularity. Only in the more odious seafaring such as slaving and pirating was it to remain in favor. As a type it disappeared completely following the abolition of slavery.

The northern colonies also contributed a fast vessel type which became known as the Marblehead Schooner. Both the Baltimore and Marblehead varieties were used as privateers and small war vessels as well as commercial carriers.

Trade with the West Indies proved most lucrative for a great many daring enough to engage in it. However, although large profits could be quickly made, it was not always fair weather and easy sailing. An individual in this business risked either his fortune or his person against some very real and uncompromising dangers. Besides shipwreck and unsettled governmental conditions, the specter of the skull and bones hung over every trip to the south.

The first cargoes to go to the West Indies from the thirteen colonies were mainly salt fish, but as the trade grew, farm produce, building materials, manufactured goods, hardware, horses, and everything and anything was shipped south. Goods sent north included sugar, salt, molasses, coffee, special woods and dyes and materials for shipbuilding. It was the custom to take along specie, or money, to pay for some of the return cargoes even though barter, bills of exchange and three cornered trade with Africa were also prominent ways of settling accounts in the West Indian trade. This specie was usually brought aboard the vessel and secretly stowed just before she sailed. It was also common for the captain, who generally owned an interest in the vessel, to be given charge of the final disposition of the outward bound cargo and also the selection and purchase of return cargoes. Sometimes an agent, or supercargo, was sent along for this purpose.

It was only natural, therefore, that these valuable loads of merchandise, plus the good chance of finding loose cash aboard, would attract the more unscrupulous members of the seafaring brotherhood. Pirates were all along the Atlantic coast in the 1700's. The heaviest concentration of these sea bandits was in southern waters, to be sure, but they ranged in some cases as far North as Nova Scotia. As a result, honest merchantmen, even the smallest, were obliged to carry arms to defend themselves. Most merchantmen, however, preferred flight to fight and speed was therefore a desirable quality in any vessel, especially those used in the West Indies trade.

In the early days of West Indian piracy, sailors from the Netherlands, France, and England were enjoined in the plunder of the Spanish vessels returning home with loot filched from Spain's colonies in Central and South America. Many of

6

the islands in the West Indies were occupied entirely or in part by the hated Spaniard. There were, however, literally hundreds of unoccupied islands that gave a perfect refuge to the pirate bent on raiding Spanish treasure fleets. As piracy increased, the vessels of any nation began to look Spanish to some pirates and finally no one in the area was safe from attack.

Pirate methods varied from time to time, but for the most part, followed a fairly consistent pattern. Usually a pirate vessel was a schooner, brig, or brigantine and quite fast. If a likely looking prize was spotted, either from a hiding place behind some headland on an island, or while cruising the high seas; the chase was on. If the pursued looked rich and easy she was ordered to heave to either by command or by warning shots fired across her bow. Pirates usually tried frightening their victims into submission without a fight. The legendary skull and bones (the Jolly Roger), or some equally terrifying banner was, in fact, frequently used as a battle flag and was run up after an approach had been made, often under false colors. Sometimes if the vessel surrendered without a fight, the crew would be spared and in some cases the ship itself was let go, but of course, not before it had undergone a thorough sacking.

If a pursued vessel chose to put up a fight and lost, then things were different and usually it went hard for the ship and crew. Many pirates were firm believers in the theory that "dead men tell no tales" and often whether they had resisted or not, both prisoners and vessel were destroyed after being plundered. Occasionally prisoners were given the opportunity to close ranks with their captors and join the happy family. In some instances captives were forced to join the pirate bands against their will. However, when an opportunity of this sort was given to the crew of a captured vessel, the officers, serving as the butt for the past hatreds, real or imaginary, often suffered indignities and tortures so terrible, that the mere recounting of them leaves one sickened.

A great many vessels listed as missing from 1600 to 1830, were probably victims of piratical action, but as Billy Bones wasn't one for keeping an accurate written account of his wrong-doings, the number can only be guessed at.

As late as 1800, Edward Stevens, the U. S. Consul-General at Santo Domingo, in a letter dated in January of that year, estimated that there were no less than thirty-seven barges (rowing barges waiting to attack becalmed ships) on the coast from Cap Carcasse to St. Marc and at least fifteen thousand pirates. Few escaped who fell into the hands of Rigaud, leader of those pirates who infested the bight of Leogane on Haiti, where our ships were continually passing to and from the coffee and sugar ports.

One of the last recorded acts of piracy was on the brig "Mexican" of Salem in September of 1832. While this voyage was not a coasting voyage in the strictest sense, it is still worthy of note as part of the final act in a great history of sea going thievery. The "Mexican" left Salem on a Voyage to Rio de Janeiro with only a light cargo. However along with this, she carried on board a fair amount of specie for the purpose of purchasing a return cargo at the South American port. On September 20, she was overtaken and boarded by the pirate schooner "Panda".

After the usual roughing up was administered to the crew and the money on the "Mexican" taken aboard the "Panda", the crew of the "Mexican" were forced below decks and the hatches battened down. After this the brig was set afire. The pirates left the "Mexican" and her crew to what they supposed was a certain fate and sailed away. Fortunately for the men aboard the burning brig, they were able to escape from below and keep the fire under control. They were afraid to extinguish the blaze completely until the "Panda" had sailed out of sight. Once she had disappeared over the horizon, the crew of the "Mexican" then put out the fire and headed back home for Salem.

This act of piracy raised a great cry of indignation in the shipping world of the 1830's and it is interesting to note that the "Panda" was subsequently caught and several of her crew taken to Boston where they were tried and convicted. Six of these rogues were hanged in 1835, the last to be so rewarded for piracy committed on the Spanish Main.

There were some governmental efforts to stop piracy; notably by Britain in the 1700's, but this met with only partial success. Later, during the revolt of the Spanish American colonies (approximately 1810-1824), many small revolutionary governments were set up. These new governments hired so-called "privateers" who in fact were little more than pirates. At this time piratical depredations increased to such an unprecedented scale that the newly formed American republic was finally forced to take action. Acts of Congress were passed in 1822 establishing an appropriation of $500,000 to fit out an expedition which was to wipe out the West Indian pirates.

Commodore David Porter resigned his office as Navy Commissioner to take command of the expedition. It is interesting to note that one of the vessels in this squadron was a steam vessel named "Sea Gull". The "Sea Gull" earned the distinction of being the first steam propelled man-of-war to engage in actual combat. This naval force was very effective in protecting shipping in the area and also in destroying many nests of pirates. It was largely due to its' efforts that the piratical plague was finally stamped out in the 1830's.

*A Topsail Schooner Packet*

## Chapter III

## THE RISE OF THE PACKETS

The early 18th century saw the coastwise business steadily increase as commodities from north and south were exchanged and as the West Indies trade continued to grow in importance.

Early in the 1700's, Oxford, Maryland, for example, was trading with such ports as Boston, New York, Philadelphia, Salem, Falmouth (Portland), and Nantucket as well as with ports overseas. Outward bound shipments included such products as tobacco, furs, and black walnut lumber. Later, grain, livestock, hoops, shingles, staves, bricks and sassafras were added to the list of exports that were shipped north.

The early coastal trade among the Chesapeake states, as elsewhere, followed much the same pattern as did their foreign trade. Local produce was sold or exchanged for needed commodities not locally obtainable. Virginia began by sending tobacco to New England in trade for salt fish. Maryland also traded for the same commodity, sending Indian corn north in exchange for salt fish. Both of these southern states were soon trading with the Dutch at New Amsterdam and the Swedes on the Delaware.

Sloops and schooners were gradually emerging as the two predominant carriers of freight along the coast, with square rigged vessels also being used on trips to the West Indies. After 1740 the average size of coasting vessels began to increase, many of them being designed to fit into the lumber trade which was then becoming a more active industry.

Unfortunately, when the Revolutionary War came along, it was as disastrous to coastal shipping as it was to our deep-water craft and many vessels, fearing capture or wanting cargoes, were laid up and went to pieces during the seven year period of hostilities. However, five years after the surrender of Cornwallis, shipping in America was back on a prosperous course. Trade from Halifax to New Orleans was booming, with every port on the coast sending or receiving goods in vessels large and small. All possible manner of merchandise was carried. An examination of the cargo manifest aboard the sloop "Polly", of Eastham, Massachusetts, which sailed from Boston in the year 1783 in command of Captain Simeon Higgins, graphically illustrates the "general" nature of many of the cargoes carried during that period.

The "Polly" had on board the following items: 1 crate, 1 tierce of crockery ware, 2 boxes of pipes, 4 chests of tea, 2 tons of steel, 1 bundle of frizzing irons, 4 bags of shot, 5 boxes of chocolate, 5 crates of nails, 5 barrels, 1 trunk, 1 ton of hollow ware, 1 hogshead of brandy, 1 bag of Indigo, 1 bag of pepper, 2 kegs of spirits, 1 box of glass, 6 looking glasses and 3 tierce of "goods".

By the year 1800, it was becoming apparent that the schooner was taking over as the basic coastal cargo carrier in America. Also at this time, a new classification of vessels termed coastal packets could be found sailing regularly from many tidewater villages to nearby larger ports. A packet, as the term was understood before the Civil War, was a vessel whose owner or owners advertised its sailing to designated ports on schedules, as regularly as weather permitted. Packets carried passengers and freight supplied by the public rather than produce shipped on the owner's account.

Shipping or commuting on these packets however, being dependent on the whims of the wind, was upon occasion, exasperatingly slow. The trip of the sloop "Mary", which left Boston on Nov. 7, 1800 and arrived in Philadelphia 31 days later, would make the fast traveling businessman of today wonder how they managed to show a profit in the old days. Admittedly 31 days for such a trip was slow even then. An average of many trips to and from the same ports during the same year indicates 13 days as the normal time required. This is still rather a long time when compared to modern methods for getting things moved about.

Going from Philadelphia to New York in those times might take only two days or might last as long as two weeks. Regardless of the length of the trip, goods and people did arrive and business was transacted. People of that era accepted the fact that the footsteps of progress occasionally dragged. During the year of 1800, Philadelphia had over 400 arrivals from other coastal ports. New York, Boston, Portland, New Bedford, New London, Providence and many more large ports were also daily receiving vessels that were doing their utmost to maintain bi-weekly, weekly and daily service from smaller out-lying ports. From small packet sloops to larger packet schooners, these vessels were the great grandparents of the commuter trains, buses and trucks of today.

Plymouth, Massachusetts, in 1830 had a population of less than 5,000, however, the town had six sloops of 60 tons each, which were in the Boston packet run, two schooners of 90 tons, which went regularly to Nantucket, New Bedford and New York, and three other vessels which brought lumber from Maine. "Constant traders" as many of these packets termed themselves, were regularly advertised as taking freight and passengers from Boston to points south on fixed schedules.

Square rigged packet vessels were generally preferred by passengers who were engaging in long coastal trips in the early days of the trade. However this preference gradually changed as the years went by and eventually the longer coastal trips were made in steamers. Schooner packets, none the less, gave sharp competition and continued to operate in the late years in the less important routes.

A typical schooner packet was usually built for that specific purpose or was brought in from some other trade as a result of her having earned a reputation as a fast sailer. She was two masted and in most cases carried slightly more sail than the average coaster. Most of these vessels were under 100 feet and if engaged in a run that was fairly long, the after cabin was fitted out to sleep her passengers. The accomodations on these packets were usually the best the times and money could afford, however, things like flush toilets, bathtubs, proper heating, ventilation, etc., were unheard of. You paid your money and took your chances. In most instances, when sailing on the smaller vessels, passengers had to supply their own food. Many packet schooners had hatches fitted with removable ramps so that horses and carriages could be safely stowed below. Although all of this may seem very inadequate by todays standards, traveling by water in the early 1800's with all its difficulties, was still more comfortable than traveling by stagecoach and usually faster.

There were some packet lines which worked in conjunction with various stagecoach lines and frequently the packets carried the mail. Prior to 1844, for example, the mail and most of the passengers coming to Nantucket arrived by way of a packet. As with other important ports of the period, there were many packets running to the island from various cities on the mainland. Boats from New York, Boston, Albany, New Bedford, Baltimore and other places, each carried passengers and a sack of mail and their arrival was quite a unique and important event. As soon as a packet docked, some person who could make himself heard, would grab the mail sack, climb to a place of advantage and as he hauled forth the mail, cry out the name of its recipient. In those days the cost of sending a letter to Boston was 12 cents, so the mail to and from the island was never terribly heavy.

After 1884 the packets no longer carried the mail to Nantucket on a regular basis, the steamboats being used from then on for this purpose. The old sloop "Tawtemeo", which ran between New Bedford and Nantucket under the command of Captain John Ray, was the last of the packets to run to the island, having replaced the old sloop "Portugal". The "Tawtemeo" was built in Pierpont, New York in 1850, and was listed as 43.82 gross tons. She measured 61.6 feet in length, 23.2 feet in breadth and 5.4 feet in depth. She was owned for a while by the Nantucket Steamboat Co., but was sold by them to Capt. Ray in 1855 for $2,300. The "Tawtemeo" continued in service as an island packet until May 1881, when she was sold shortly after the death of her skipper and left Nantucket. During the later years of her packet career, she would occasionally bring over the mail when the regular steamers were not in service.

Even though traveling by packet was more comfortable and frequently the quickest way to travel the coast, there still remained the uncertainty as to time of arrival and also the bone chilling possibility of no arrival at all. Added to the constant worry of storms, fog, lack of wind, etc., was the over-riding fear of shipwreck.

Most people going on a coastwise trip usually searched for a vessel which was specifically fitted out to carry passengers. Some packets were large and could accomodate many people, while some were small and had space for only a few. From time to time, travelers were able to book a passage "on the spot", with a vessel which was not a regular packet but happened to be going in the same direction and had room. Regardless of the boat one chose to travel on, the possibility of the trip ending in disaster was always present, and often dependent on the whims of nature. Storms or squalls could seemingly come from nowhere, and frequently while a vessel was making her way through a tricky passage, fickle winds would blow in a blinding fog. In "Wrecks Around Nantucket", compiled by Arthur H. Gardner, one finds entries covering a long period of time which typify some of the dangers encountered by travelers while making a coasting passage under sail.

"1774, Oct. 30th, a small sloop, bound from Nantucket to the mainland, with eight people on board, was lost on Horse Shoe shoal, and all probably perished, VIZ: David Folger, master and owner, his son, Richard Swain, and another white man, two Indian men, a squaw and papoose."

"1803, Feb. 4th, the New Bedford packet "Aurora" in coming over the bar, struck and bilged. The crew and passengers came ashore safely in their boat. The vessel was stripped of sails, rigging, etc., and sold at auction as she lay for $158. An unsuccessful attempt was made by the purchasers on the 8th to raise her by lashing two vessels down to her at low tide. On the 11th, she drove from the bar towards Brant Point in a gale from the north, and went to pieces."

"1819, Oct. 10th, the mail packet, which left here for Falmouth, had proceeded as far as the Horse Shoe shoal, wind S.S.E., when she was struck by a squall of wind, hail, thunder and lightning from the northward. The mast was struck by lightning, and shivered to pieces, and the bowsprit injured and several on board knocked down and stunned. They let go the sails and run before the gale, expecting every moment to founder, but got back here all right."

"1823, Sept. 29th, sloop "Iris", of this port, Capt. George W. Luce, bound to East Haddam, was struck by a squall from the northward at 7 p.m., and upset. At the time Cape Poge Lighthouse bore S.S.E., two leagues distant. It being west tide, the vessel drifted down towards the cape. The captain and three men who were on deck at the time were taken off by a boat from a vessel nearby, at 2 o'clock the next morning. At 7 a.m., a boat from Edgartown took Capt. Luce from the vessel that had rescued him, proceeded to the wreck, which lay with only a small portion of her quarter above water, and rescued the captain's wife and one other woman from the after cabin by cutting a hole through a false window. One woman, named Eliza Cone, who was in the same cabin, had drowned before assistance reached them. A Methodist preacher named Crandall and one other man, who were in the forward cabin, were also rescued at the same time. The sloop was subsequently towed back to this port and repaired."

The passengers of the packet sloop "David Porter", going from Sag Harbor, Long Island, to New York, in 1827, finally arrived at their destination, but not in the manner in which they had planned. The "David Porter" was only two years old at the time and made regular weekly trips from Sag Harbor to Peck Slip. She had sleeping quarters for 22, the trip one-way often lasting three days, but as was common, the operators of the sloop supplied no food for passengers. Loaded with whale oil and happy travelers, she left Sag Harbor on the afternoon of Sept. 19, 1827. That night she ran into a real Long Island Sound snorter, which disabled her. After consultation among the passengers and crew, it was decided the next day to try to beach the sloop. This was done near Eatons Neck, amazingly enough, without loss of life in spite of driving rain, rough water and nearby rocks.

Fortunately for the men, women, and children aboard the "David Porter", and even though she broke in two after striking, they were able to scramble ashore up a steep bank and reach the shelter of a house which was close at hand. The next day, after drying out, they were able to salvage some of their baggage. They then proceeded to New York in wagons, which had been kindly offered them by sympathetic people who lived in the vicinity of the wreck. Their bedraggled and salt stained appearance attracted a good deal of attention upon their eventual arrival.

The fate of those aboard the schooner "Patriot", which left Georgetown, South Carolina for New York on Dec. 30, 1812, was in many ways more unusual than any of the preceeding. Although it is generally assumed that the "Patriot" drifted ashore at Nags Head, North Carolina, in January, 1813, there is no real proof of this, nor is there any proof as to the fate of her crew and passengers. They simply sailed away into oblivion. The "Patriot" had been both a pilot boat and a privateer before she entered into the business of carrying passengers, and must have been a fairly fast and able schooner. The beautiful Theodosia Burr Alston, daughter of former vice-president Aaron Burr, was one of the passengers aboard and when the schooner failed to arrive in New York, a full scale and far reaching investigation was carried out. All of this proved unsuccessful and the vessel was assumed lost at sea with all hands. However, in later years, a deathbed confession added to several other accounts, gave rise to the suspicion that the "Patriot" had been boarded by pirates, all aboard murdered, and the schooner allowed to go ashore at Nags Head. None of this subsequent information seems to have been conclusively proved and to this day the disappearance of the beautiful Theodosia and her fellow passengers, remains a mystery.

Lost with all trace was not a fate confined only to those who went deepwater sailing. There were many who set forth on a coasting voyage, either as passenger or crew, who were literally swallowed by the elements and never heard from again. It was not infrequent for vessels upon arrival in port, to tell of having sighted a derelict, floating bottom up, or with decks barely awash, which they were not able to identify. Even when the vessel was identified, the fate of the passengers and crew often remained a mystery.

Captain Worthington, bound from New London to St. Vincent, is reported in the Gazette of the United States, May 5, 1800, as having sighted in Lat. 34 N., Long. 68 W., the wreck of the pilot-boat-built schooner "Eagle", of Baltimore. "Her foremast was ripped, hanging over the toprail. There was so Nausceous (sic) a smell issuing from the vessel that no one could venture on board her. It is supposed that part of the crew must have died on board."

That they did not go aboard, is not surprising. Sailors, besides being a superstitious lot, had reason to fear diseases which might lurk aboard a vessel, particularly if coming from a tropical port. So they sailed away and the fate of the crew of the "Eagle" goes down as another one of the many unsolved mysteries of the sea.

*A Carronade*

## Chapter IV

## THE EARLY 1800's

As prosperity started to return immediately following the end of the revolution in 1782, the American coastal trade really began to grow, and some national effort was made in an attempt to protect this trade. The fear of foreign shipping encroaching upon our domestic routes, led to the Third Act of the First Congress, in 1789, which provided that American coasting vessels should pay the duty declared once a year and that foreign vessels should pay duty at each entry at a United States port. At this time it was not thought wise to completely exclude foreign shipping from our coasting trade.

During this period the United States was experiencing a great deal of difficulty with both Great Britain and France. These two countries, while waging war upon each other, drew the United States, very much against its will, into the middle of their struggle. Each warring nation forbade trade with the other by way of any neutral and our vessels, both deep-water and coastal, were being seized, goods confiscated and crews impressed or imprisoned.

The Philadelphia Gazette of July 21, 1800, reports that, "a gentleman from Guadalope, informs that in 16 days there were 42 American vessels captured and brought in there." French privateers were to be found all through the Carribean and English men-of-war were everywhere and no less troublesome to American ships and crews.

On Dec. 22, 1805, President Jefferson, thinking he could force the warring factions to cease their restrictive actions on the United States, placed an embargo on all American shipping, hoping thereby to coerce France and Britain into letting our ships sail undisturbed. Any vessel that left a United States shore enroute to a foreign country was henceforth liable to seizure, fine and confiscation. Even coasting vessels were required to put up a bond in order to proceed with their business. The embargo immediately became very unpopular in the states and went far towards ruining certain segments of American commerce. Many deep-water-men were laid up with the unemployment of many American sailors resulting.

In a letter dated June 4, 1808, one T. Selby,[1] a merchant seaman who felt that he had had enough of the infernal embargo, did what many Americans still feel compelled to do when things aren't going right. He sat down and wrote a letter to the President. This letter not only gives an idea of how Mr. Selby felt, but reflects the general attitude of many of his countrymen toward the embargo and to its perpetrator.

"Philadelphia, June 4, 1808

Dear Sir:

I wish you would take this embargo off, as soon as you possibly can, for dam my eyes if I can live as it is. I shall certainly cut my throat, and if I do you will lose one of the best seamen that ever sailed. I have a wife and four young ones to support and it goes damned hard with me now. If I don't cut my throat I will go join the English and fight against you. I hope, honored sir, you will forgive the abrupt manner in which this is wrote as I'm damn'd mad. But still if ever I catch you over there, take care of your honored neck.

Yours

T. Selby

No. 9 Pine St., if you wish to see him, you damn'd rascal."

President Jefferson duly endorsed the letter. "Selby T. Phila. June 4, '08 rec'd. Aug. 25," with no additional comment.

The embargo, besides restricting regular trade, created another unfortunate condition on our coast. Smuggling erupted on a wide scale in many ports and the government was forced to maintain revenue vessels in an attempt to enforce the hated law.

Despite the fact that our deep-water commerce was hurt, it seemed in large ports such as Boston, that our coastal trade was little diminished from normal time. Here, many sloops and schooners were employed carrying the cargoes brought in by foreign ships, to coastal ports from Maine to New Orleans. Boston's coastal trade during this period was divided mainly into four parts:

1. To New England and New York went farm produce and most important of all, imported goods.

2. To the middle coastal states, vessels were sent for flour.

3. To the southern states they went for cotton and tobacco.

4. Last of all, shipping was sent to the newly acquired city of New Orleans.

Frequently on the southern leg of these voyages, Massachusetts vessels carried fish, as at that time, Massachusetts, which also included Maine, owned five sixths of the nation's fishing fleet.

With this large amount of coastal shipping going on, vessels leaving on apparently simple coasting trips, frequently and unaccountable wound up in British ports, or managed to transfer their cargoes to foreign ships waiting offshore.

The sympathies of the citizenry were, for the most part, very much on the side of the smugglers and the government was sorely tried in its efforts to make the embargo effective. In the Act of April 1808, which was a supplement of the Embargo Act, foreign vessels were finally excluded entirely from our coastwise trade. However, when Jefferson removed the embargo in 1809, just three days before the expiration of his term of office, the coasting trade again was left open to foreign shipping. Jefferson's embargo was completely unsuccessful and failed to bring either France or England into line. While England no longer was trying to impress our seamen, Napoleon's decrees kept our ships from going to British ports.

In spite of the fact that France had actually done more damage to our shipping and Great Britain was easing up on the impressment rule, the United States declared war on England on June 18, 1812. Again as in the revolution, our coast-wise trade was almost paralyzed by the English blockading vessels. Men refused to sail, fearing capture and imprisonment.

Fortunately, the War of 1812 did not last long and following its conclusion by the Treaty of Ghent, on Dec. 24, 1814, our coastwise shipping headed into a period of steady increase and prosperity.

On March 1, 1817, under President James Monroe, the United States permanently closed its coast-wise trade to foreign vessels with the Navigation Act of 1817, section IV. This law has never been rescinded and was one of the important factors which aided in the build-up of our coasting business. American coasting tonnage in 1789 amounted to 68,607 tons. This increased steadily until the Civil War in 1860 and during the preceding 71 years the only important setback that occurred commenced in 1828.

In 1829 our entire merchant marine diminished by 27.6%. Fortunately, this situation did not last long and soon the tide started to flow in a more favorable direction. During the early 1850's, our great clipper ships were constructed, which forever won for the United States the distinction of having built the swiftest and most beautiful square-rigged vessels ever to sail the seas. The life span of the clippers, however, was not destined to last long. In 1857, our country fell into the depths of a depression, which was closely followed by the Civil War. This lead to a decrease in shipping tonnage from 2,496,894 tons in 1861 to only 726,213 tons in 1898, a slump from which our deep-water merchant marine was never to recover.

Our coasting trade, on the other hand, continued to grow during this period finally reaching its peak in 1932 when it boasted a grand total of 10,727,565 tons, which was a net increase of 8,082,687 tons since the Civil War.

It was in the 1830's that American tonnage in the coast-wise trade eclipsed that which was engaged in foreign trade. New England's trade to the south for coal, cotton and grain was largely responsible for this. In 1822, four coasters left the Delaware River bound north with coal. Five years later, in 1827, 397 vessels are listed as carrying 3,900 tons, and in 1837, Philadelphia is credited with shipping 350,000 tons of coal in 3,225 vessels. The vessels employed in this trade very often on their south bound trips, carried lumber, ice, apples and fish to Philadelphia and Norfolk, which were the principle coaling ports at that time.

In the cotton and corn trade with the states further south, we find cargoes of ice, stone and newly manufactured clothing carried from the north. The recently established mills in the north were much in need of cotton from Charleston, Savannah, Mobile and New Orleans, plus cheap food to feed the mill hands. Boston's import from New Orleans alone totaled $3,334,000 in 1839 and was steadily increasing. From Sept. 1, 1841, to May 1, 1842, one quarter of the lard, over one quarter of the flour, almost half of the pork and over half of the corn shipped from New Orleans went to Boston. In 1855, 175 vessels cleared from Boston bound south to New Orleans. Of course, this lucrative trade was completely ruined during the Civil War and never was to revive in quite the same way. Following the Civil War, railroads cut heavily into businesses that had formerly been handled by coasters.

During most of the pre-war period, and not to be overlooked, our trade to the West Indies had remained a most important factor. Following the revolution and the subsequent struggles with France and England, this trade as did the others, showed a continuing rate of growth. After 1820, commerce to this area was carried almost entirely in topsail schooners and brigantines. These vessels were large carriers for the times, usually averaging over 80 feet on deck, sailed fairly fast, and carried general cargoes. Some were fitted with guns as late as 1855. In appearance they had a marked sheer, or graceful sweep, running fore-and-aft along decks and rails, and had short quarter decks combined with high main-deck bulwarks. The deck, or floor, of the after cabin being flush with the main deck allowed all the space below the main deck to be used for the stowage of cargo. Larger vessels often carried a small deck house located at or just abaft the foremast. This cabin served as a galley and occasionally quartered the crew, although the larger vessels usually carried the forecastle below decks foreward. Smaller vessels usually housed their crew in part of the trunk cabin, aft. Some of the Maine built West Indiamen had quarterdeck bulwarks, while others had the turned-stanchion and capped rail, aft, which was eventually to become a popular feature on the larger coasting schooners and some deep-watermen. The West Indiamen of the 1820's and '30's were often roughly and cheaply built but lasted through amazingly long and profitable years of trading.

[1]Mr. Selby's letter is in the collection of Jefferson Papers at the Missouri Historical Society, St. Louis, Missouri.

*"Eckford Webb"*

## Chapter V

## FROM A TWO MASTER TO A THREE MASTER

After 1825, New England schooners engaged in the regular coastal runs were simply rigged two masters, not much over 70 to 75 feet in length. They were rather full ended vessels possessing quarter-deck rails similar to those found on the West Indiamen. The schooners owed their increase in popularity to three basic factors. They were much cheaper to build than square rigged vessels, were more weatherly than the square rigger and could be handled by much smaller crews.

These schooners usually carried a plain fore and aft rig, although a few still had square topsails on the foremast. The most common rig was that of the fore and aft foresail and main, two headsails (the fore-staysail or jumbo and jib), with gaff topsails on fore and main. Frequently only a main topsail was carried in winter months, many vessels dispensing with the fore topmast during this time, lessening the necessity to go aloft in freezing weather.

Vessels of this type frequently had high hatch coamings and were often loaded until their maindecks were nearly awash. Figureheads were seldom carried, the bow being more likely to be decorated with a billet head and trailboards. A typical stern on the early schooners was in the style of the old round tuck, with wide upper and lower transoms. This style gradually changed as the two-master evolved; first to a flat raking transom with round tuck and then as it finally appeared, with a short counter, a raking transom, curved athwart-ship and usually elliptical on New England Vessels.

As the clipper ships become popular in the 1850's, their influence on design was often reflected in the hulls of many of the coasters built during the same period. The round fantail counter of the clipper, was incorporated in some coasters, but was not to become as popular as the clipper bow which was used in various forms on many of those vessels built during and after the '50's. An average two-masted schooner trading between Philadelphia and New England in the 1850's, was somewhere in the neighborhood of 150 tons. However, upon the conclusion of the Civil War in 1865, there was a marked demand for increased size in coasting vessels which arose from the need for carrying ever larger cargos in bulk.

Two-masters as large as 100 to 135 feet on deck were built following this period. The largest two-master was the "Oliver Ames", a two decked, centerboarder of 435 tons, built in Berkley, Massachusetts in 1866, for the Taunton coal trade. The "Oliver Ames" was 124.4 feet long, 33.2 feet beam and 17.2 feet in depth. While this vessel was not the longest of the two-masted schooners, her great depth plus her length, accounts for her rating as the largest of her type. Two masters of this size earned the reputation for being man killers as they were brutes to handle requiring large crews and therefore proved expensive to operate.

Eventually, as the package trade, passenger trade and general cargo trades were gradually taken over by steamers, the only thing left for the schooners were bulk shipments, and vessels which were able to handle larger and larger quantities of bulk cargo were in demand. Finally the hulls required were just too large to be practical with a two-masted rig.

The period involving the greatest use of the two-masted coasting schooner lasted from around 1825 to 1885, at which date it had reached its peak in development. However, one should not infer from this that two-masters were no longer built after this date, for in fact, many were built after 1885 and continued to be built until well into the 1920's. The last two-masted coasting schooner to be launched was the little "Endeavor", built in 1938 at Stonington, Maine.

Many special types of two-masted schooners were built during the heyday of this rig and there were many variations in design intended to perform in certain specialized fields, such as carrying stone and brick. Two-masters were popular in the lime trade and a great many carried coal and lumber. In spite of the inroads made by the steamers in the general coastwise trade, there were many out of the way ports and places along the coast of Maine, Florida and the Chesapeake where the little two-masted schooner continued to haul general cargos until well into the 20th century.

At the time of its greatest development, the two-masted schooner really fell into two catagories. One was a shallow model, often fitted with a centerboard and the other had a deep hull which in design was reminiscent of the deep-water hulls of the square-riggers. As the two-masters increased in size, the number of headsails, or jibs, was increased as well; first to three and then to four jibs. Many had the wooden bowsprit with jibboom and dolphin striker, or martingale, which was the typical timber bowsprit found on most wooden vessels, although some were built with a single pole or "Spike" bowsprit. Some of the larger two-masters carried a topmast staysail between the fore and main, in addition to the sails mentioned earlier. These vessels were well finished, had good capacity, could sail well and were extremely attractive from a nautical point of view. Although popular both in Eastern United States and Canada, the two-master, as mentioned before, could not be built beyond certain practical limits in size. The next step, obviously, was the addition of a third mast.

The building of the first three-masted schooner however, was not occasioned by a desire for increased hull capacity. As stated earlier, the first three-masted schooner appeared in the Chesapeake Bay area about 1795. These were not large vessels, being perhaps about 75 feet in length and were of the Virginia pilot boat model. Some of these early three-masters were sold to France and one of them, the "Poisson Volant", eventually fell into English hands. Her lines were taken off and sent to Bermuda in 1808, where six vessels for the British navy were built from these plans. As a result of these six schooners the Bermudians adapted the type to their own use, with various modifications; one such being the use of the leg-of-mutton, or three cornered sail. The Bermudian schooners, thusly rigged, very soon acquired a great reputation for their speed.

The Americans, unlike the Bermudians, retained the gaff rig on the few three-masted schooners built in this country. Around the year 1800, vessels of this rig were favored only in a limited area near Baltimore. From this time until the need for increased hull capacity was felt, which was around the middle of the 19th century, three-masted schooners were built only sporadically.

All through the history of seafaring, the customs, styles and traditions found therein were slow to change. Sailors were a superstitious lot and "sot" in their ways. Anything as unusual as a three-masted schooner was bound to be met with a good deal of suspicion and resistance and was not used to any great extent until it had thoroughly proved its worth.

In the United States, early three-masted schooners were called "tern" schooners, meaning a series of three. This name was used both here and in the Canadian Maritime Provinces as the popularity of the new rig spread. The term "tern" schooners eventually was dropped in the United States, but continued to be used in Canada until the disappearance of the three-masted rig.

The sharp model three-master of the Baltimore type was not successful in the coasting trade as it could not carry a large amount of cargo and was consequently altered. Not only were alterations made in the hull, but they also were made in the rig as well. Most of the early three-masted schooners carried square topsails and had masts of varying height, the mizzen mast being the shortest of the three. All of these characteristics were soon to disappear as the three-master evolved. The exact date of the building of the first three-masted schooner, as we think of it in its final stage of development, is rather difficult to pin-point. Many little Down East ports have laid claim to the honor of having launched the first three-masted schooner, but it seems as though the honor may belong to those further south. In "The American Neptune", Vol. 1, No. 2, published in Salem, Massachusetts, are listed 18 three-masted schooners built before 1850; the earliest being "Harmony" built in 1799. Among these, the

"Ferrata", outfitted at Baltimore in 1827, the "Aurora" or "Amora", 147 tons, built at Ellesworth, Maine, in 1831, the "Magnolia", 83 tons, built at Blue Hill, Maine, in 1833, and the "Zachary Taylor", 250 tons, built at Philadelphia in 1849, have all been listed as "firsts" in various historical accounts.

R. B. Forbes states that the "Magnolia" was the first three-master to have purely a fore and aft rig, but she still had the short mizzen mast. The "Zachary Taylor", has often been designated as being the first true three-masted schooner, however W. L. Parker, in his history, "The Great Coal Schooners", gives credit to the "Kate Brigham" for being the first three-master built with all her masts equal in height. The "Kate Brigham" was built in Greenport, New York, in 1853, by Webb and Bell and measured 546 tons.

The firm of Webb and Bell also built the three-masted schooners "William L. Burroughs" and "Eckford Webb" in 1855. The "Eckford Webb" registered 495 tons, somewhat smaller than the "Kate Brigham", and was considered a very smart sailer. The "Webb" subsequently made a voyage to England which she accomplished in 21 days time and upon her arrival created a sensation in that country due to her unusual appearance. A woodcut, printed in the "American Neptune Pictorial Supplement V", shows the vessel to be rigged very much like her later day sisters. There is some difference in the arrangement of the headsails, or jibs, but in the main, her appearance varies little from later vessels. Her rig included two topmast staysails, one being set between the fore and main and the other between the main and mizzen. In addition to these she carried regular gaff topsails and lowers, plus four jibs. The fore staysail, instead of running inboard of the bow, runs just abaft the cap of the bowsprit, making for a rather large sail. The other 2 headsails lead from just below the cap on the foremast and it is known that she set a jib topsail over these although one is not shown. Her hull has a solid bulwark with marked sheer and there seems to be an indication of a solid rail about the long quarter-deck with a boat carried astern on fixed wooden davits. The solid rail was probably built over her turned stanchion rail for the Atlantic crossing. The bowsprit is typical of the later vessels with a long jibboom and dolphin striker. There appears to be the usual trunk cabin aft and another cabin on the main deck between the fore and main masts.

By 1864, there were only 39 three-masted schooners registered in the United States and of these only four registered over 500 tons. However, after the conclusion of the Civil War, the three-masted schooner had proven her worth and the numbers of this type of vessel began to increase at a steady pace. By 1875, as had happened with the two-masters, the three-masted schooner hulls were divided into two categories. One was the shallow type, fitted with one and sometimes two, centerboards; the other being the keel variety akin to the Down East square riggers. Very often in the former type, the centerboard, the main mast, or both, were set off center when only one board was used. The centerboarders had graceful sheer, carried a large rig, and were quite fast, however they could not carry as much cargo as the keel or deep variety. The keel schooners, on the other hand, had the disadvantage of being difficult to handle when light, so a compromise in hull design was evolved. The new hull had the advantage of both hulls with few disadvantages, combining therein a moderately deep hull with a centerboard. Although it is surprising to many who are accustomed to thinking of them as something only found in small boats, centerboards were used in the building of schooners with as many as four, and in one case, five masts.

The combining of the centerboard with the deep hull occurred in the late 1870's and produced a schooner that reached the ultimate in design for the three-masted rig. These improved schooners were better sailers than the later, more modern three-masters because of their finer lines and the centerboard. Their construction was better also, their builders having a better choice of timber available and they were generally stronger in proportion to the later, larger, five and six-masters, holding their sheer well and having longer careers on the average, than did the later vessels. Many of the early improved three-masters had long quarterdecks, running forward of the main mast. There was a very short well deck, or main deck, forward of this, which was protected by a raised deck on the forecastle. The long quarterdeck eventually went out of fashion and was replaced with a shorter one, running, as a rule, to a point just forward of the mizzen mast. This new style continued in use until the end of the sailing ship era.

There were many three-masted schooners built with flush decks, but these were not as prevalent as those possessing a quarterdeck or poopdeck. Many small three-masted schooners had a quarterdeck and no raised deck forward. However, if one were asked to describe a typical three-master at the end of its evolution, probably the best choice would be that type with the raised forecastle-head-deck, long main or well deck and a short quarterdeck. Centerboards lost their popularity in the larger vessels around 1890 and after that date few were built with their inclusion.

The improved three-masters built in the '80's were very popular vessels in New York and New England and were the backbone of the coasting fleet. Besides being well built, these schooners were well kept, owners and officers taking great pride in the appearance of their vessels. The majority of the New England three-masted schooners had turned stanchion rails running the length of the quarterdeck, the stanchions and rails being painted white as were the cabins and frequently the inside of the main deck bulwarks. Hulls were painted black, white, bottle-green with a black waist and sometimes gray on later vessels. Most schooners had one or two stripes which ran the length of the vessel and did much to accent their sheer. These stripes were often white or yellow and in some cases green and red were used. The Billet Head and vine pattern on the trailboards were usually gilded and a scroll work, a vine pattern, or a carved rope or molding, painted white, yellow or gilded, was generally to be seen on the transom. Not infrequently the compass and square was placed on the transom between the vessels name and her port of registry. The lettering on the bow and stern was painted in white, yellow or gilded or in some cases black on white hulls. Quarterboards carrying the vessels name were placed on each side, between the stern and the after chainplates. The masts were unpainted, except for the trucks, the doublings and the area between the saddle and the deck, which were white in most cases. The ends of the spars were often painted white as were the areas around the jaws on gaffs and booms. The bowsprit and jibboom were either painted white or black or both inside the cap, with the remainder of the jibboom frequently left natural or painted buff. Sometimes the end of the jibboom was given a white tip. On the forward side of the bowsprit cap, under the jibboom, was often seen a star or an American shield. When trailboards went out of style, the vine pattern was run part way down the stem, however the effect was less pleasing to the eye than with the trailboards.

Deck arrangement was fairly consistent, starting with the forecastle-head on the larger vessels, upon which was often found a capstan and on either side of this were the catheads running inboard on the deck. Under the forecastle-head-deck, on the main deck, was located the anchor windlass immediately aft of the Samson Post. On the forward side of the Samson Post was butted the after end of the bowsprit. On small schooners the forecastle-head-deck was either very small or there was none at all, leaving the windlass open or uncovered. The forward cabin or house, was located on the maindeck, aft of, or in some cases, in line with the foremast, so that the mast passed through the cabin. This housed the galley, the crew and in later vessels, the donkey engine used for hoisting. The three-master "Charles A. Briggs", a big 758 tonner built in Bath, Maine in 1879, was the first schooner to have power hoisting, being fitted with a steam donkey for the windlass in the year of her building. In later schooners the cabin was frequently found to extend forward to touch the forecastle-head-deck and the anchor windlass and hoisting gypsies were connected to the donkey through a system of geared sprockets and chain drivers. Running athwartship, through the sides of the cabin, was a shaft on each end of which was fixed the wildcats and gypsies used for warping, hoisting sails, cargo, etc. These went far in reducing a tremendous amount of back-breaking work and materially aided in the reduction of the size of the crew. On the main-deck there was a hatch located between the fore and main masts and another hatch between the main and mizzen. The quarterdeck, or poop, held the trunk cabin, which was the largest cabin wherein were quartered the officers and also the crews on very small vessels. Aft of the trunk cabin was the wheel. A very few of the later schooners had wheel-houses, the first to carry such a structure being the three-masted "Wilson & Hunting", launched in Alexandria, Virginia in 1883. Generally speaking, however, wheelhouses were the exception rather than the rule on coasting vessels.

In addition to operating as general traders, three-masted schooners largely monopolized the lumber and for a while, the coal trade. Large three-masters were also used for the carrying of New England ice to southern and foreign ports, a trade arising from Kennebec and Penobscot ports which grew to great proportions in the last half of the 19th century.

The handiness, low operating cost, comparatively low initial investment and general efficiency of these vessels, enabled them to persist and survive longer than any other type of commerical sailing craft on this coast. They were built all along the Atlantic coast, with the greatest number coming from New England, the Chesapeake region and the Canadian Maritime Provines. There were approximately 1,500 three-masted schooners built on the Eastern and Gulf coasts of the United States and about 750 built in Eastern Canada.

Canada has the distinction of having launched the smallest working three-masted schooner on the east coast. In 1902 the little tern "Maple Leaf" went overboard at Welford, Nova Scotia, and she was tiny to say the least. She measured only 21 net tons, was 48 feet in length, 15 feet beam and five feet in depth. It's rather doubtful that three masts in a hull this small could be worked to advantage and she probably would have been better off rigged as a two-master.

The largest three-master was the "Bradford C. French", built in 1884 by David Clark in Kennebunk, Maine. The "French" measured 968.62 gross tons, 920.29 net tons, was 184.3 feet in length, 37.5 feet beam and 9.2 feet in depth. She was built for Taunton, Massachusetts owners and could carry 1,700 tons of coal. She was larger than many four-masters, having in fact, greater tonnage than the little five-master, the "Elvira Ball". When she was about 25 years old she was taken to Nova Scotia and retopped above the waterline. She continued in service until July, 1916, when on a voyage from San Juan, Puerto Rico to New Orleans loaded with molasses and alcohol, she ran into a hurricane. In the words of Captain O. R. Farrell, the old "French" just dissolved:

"She lasted through the hurricane with ten feet of water in her. The midship house was smashed; the mainmast partners all broken and the mast waving around; the molasses leaked and clogged the pumps. Oh, she was a physcial wreck! We abandoned her in the yawl boat after the hurricane passed and using a blanket for a sail, we sailed about 250 miles and landed five days later at Panama City, Florida.

Another large three-master was the "Mary B. Baird", built in 1890 at Camden, New Jersey by Morris and Mathis. Between 1896 and 1898 her registry changed from Camden, New Jersey to Philadelphia, Pennsylvania where it remained until June 27, 1912. On that date, in Lat. 33.15 N, Long 74.24 W, the "Baird" foundered; fortunately with no loss of life. She was a "back breaker" in size, measuring 908 gross tons, 811 net tons, 170 feet in length, 36.4 feet beam and 19.1 feet in depth.

Vessels such as the "Bradford C. French" and the Mary B. Baird", of necessity had to have extra heavy gear as sails and spars were so large that only the toughest, biggest and heaviest of material would hold out in a blow. Naturally, when handling such gear, especially without the aid of a power winch, or wrestling with the necessarily huge and heavy sails in the teeth of a gale, any crew would be wearied to the breaking point. It was not uncommon, under adverse stress of wind, sea or freezing rigging, for the vessel to take charge and run away with tragic consequences.

This was the case with the "Louis V. Place", a big three-master built in 1890 at Kennebunk, Maine by George Christenson. The "Place" measured 735 gross tons, 698 net tons, was 163.7 feet in length, 36.5 feet beam and 13.9 feet in depth and was owned in New York. In the latter part of January, 1895, she sailed from Baltimore with 1,100 tons of coal bound for New York. Upon entering the open Atlantic on February 4, 1895, she soon ran into a violent winter gale and her rigging became encased in ice, making her practically unmanageable. After issuing a terrific dusting the weather showed signs of moderating and the tired crew of the "Place" beat off a bit of the ice and reset a few of the sails, which of course had been reefed during the storm. On February 7, the wind again increased and once more she was reefed down. The next day, the wind suddenly shifted, making a violent cross sea which tumbled the vessel about in a fearful manner and caused her to be swept fore and aft by every sea again encasing her in more ice. The running rigging froze, the sails became unmanageable and her crew was worn out from four days and nights of bitter cold, frozen clothes and no sleep.

Not being sure of his position because of the blinding snow and believing himself near land, her master, Captain William Squires, ordered a sounding taken. They found themselves in only eight fathoms of water. To add to this misfortune, the mate, Claus Stuvens, informed Captain Squires that the "Place" was beginning to open up and was rapidly taking on water. Realizing he was too close to land and hoping to halt his shoreward progress, Captain Squires then ordered the anchors overboard, but the exhausted crew found them frozen to the deck and could not free them. The halliards were cut in an effort to lower the sails, but they were so ice encased, they would not fall. The men on the lunging coaster were thus being carried ever closer to shore on a vessel that had many of the aspects of an iceberg and there was little they could do to alter their destinies.

As a last resort it was decided to try to beach the schooner head on and accordingly, after passing out a ration of whiskey to each of the hands, she was headed for the shore which was hidden in clouds of swirling snow. Within minutes the laboring "Louis V. Place" thundered in among the breakers and smashed onto a bar about 300 feet from the beach. She commenced pounding immediately and with the surf making a clean sweep over her hull and crashing into and splitting her icy sails, the crew did the only thing possible and climbed into the rigging in a vain effort to prolong their lives.

They were wrecked near a stretch of beach close to the Life Saving Station at Lone Hill on Long Island, New York. A man on beach patrol had seen the "Place" heading for the surf just before she struck and had immediately gone to inform his already busy teammates. As soon as they were able, the Life Saving Service arrived to render whatever assistance they could and found themselves faced with an almost impossible task. The surf between the vessel and the shore was filled with a grinding mass of porridge ice, two feet thick and there were huge cakes of ice all along the beach. This was surely no place to attempt the launching of a surfboat. A line was fired across the stricken vessel and another and another, but the crew of the "Place", having already spent many hours in the frozen rigging, was in no condition to aid in setting up a breeches buoy. Gradually, in between snow squalls, it was seen by those watching on shore that the men in the rigging were beginning to fall. As the hours dragged into a second day, the gale continued without let up and those on the beach could do nothing. Fires had been kept burning during the night and the Lyle gun had put lines aboard the schooner but those on board were too numb to do anything about them. Finally, the would-be rescuers could discern only two men remaining in the rigging who showed signs of life. Two more could be seen frozen to death, still secured to the vessel by their lashings. One hung head downward and swung grotesquely in the wind.

About midnight of the second day, the surf began to calm and there was a favorable shift in the wind which began to blow away some of the ice between the dead schooner and the beach. A boat was successfully launched and both men, horribly frozen but alive, were with great difficulty brought ashore. One was the mate Claus Stuvens, who had joined the "Place" only a month before and the other was Soren J. Nielson, a Dane who died shortly after his rescue in spite of all the medical aid given him at the Marine Hospital on Staten Island.

**THREE-MASTED SCHOONER OF THE 1890'S**

*"Weybosset"*

## Chapter VI

## THE EVOLUTION OF THE FOUR-MASTER

By 1885 more schooners were being built in a single year than all the other rigs put together. However, by 1880, the three-master had reached its practical limits in size and to capitalize on freight rates, a still larger hull was needed. Experimentation with the four masted schooner rig on the East Coast started shortly after the Civil War. The wooden gunboat "Osceola", built in East Boston in 1863, was sold by the government in October 1867 and in 1868 made her reappearance as the "Eliza", a 643 ton, four-masted schooner. Unfortunately she did not last long following her conversion. The 630 ton "Weybosset", a sound steamer built at Mystic, Connecticut, in 1863, was converted in 1879 to a four-masted schooner at East Boston. Working as a collier, she lasted until August 13, 1890, when she stranded at Pollock Rip, off Cape Cod, Massachusetts. In command of Captain Town, she was bound south with paving stones from Portland to Philadelphia. Her crew was rescued by the fishing steamer "Benj. Church".

The first schooner actually built as a four-master was the "William L. White", launched at Bath, Maine in 1880 by Goss, Sawyer and Packard. This vessel was built for the famous coal merchant Jacob B. Phillips of Taunton,

Massachusetts, who managed the big "Bradford C. French" and seven other big three-masters. The "White" was of course intended for the coal trade and proved a successful experiment. Henry Hall's government report on the shipbuilding industry in 1880, gives an interesting description of this schooner.

"The hull of the vessel is large enough for a Californian. She is 205 feet long on deck, 40 feet in beam, and 17 feet deep in the hold, being 309 feet overall from the end of her jibboom to the end of the Spanker boom. She registers 996 tons and is able to carry 1,450 tons of anthracite coal . . . To have fitted her with three masts would have required such large lower sails that the strain upon the masts would have been destructive, and she was therefore fitted with four, the after spar being called the Spanker Mast . . . This divided her 5,017 yards of canvas into smaller sails, and made her a good schooner, sailing well, easily handled, and requiring a crew of only five men before the mast, besides her mates and captain".

It is interesting to learn that the first Captain of the "William L. White" was Captain Henry Babbett, whose son Captain Emmans Babbett, was later to become master for a while of the huge, illfated "Thomas W. Lawson", about which more will be related.

In addition to the "White", three more four-masters were added to the fleet managed by Jacob B. Phillips. According to B. B. Crowninshield, in his book "Fore and Afters" the first five of the four-masted schooners were launched in the following order. The "William L. White" in 1880, the "Frances C. Yarnall" in 1881, the "Elliott B. Church", the "Charles E. Balch" and the "Augustus Hunt" in 1882. The second vessel, the 496 ton "Francis C. Yarnall", built in Wilmington, Delaware, was one of the smallest four-masters ever built and was nowhere near the size of her predecessor, nor most of the subsequent down east vessels launched with the same rig. The third four-master, the "Elliot B. Church", built in Bath, Maine, owned in Taunton, Massachusetts, and managed by J. B. Phillips, was a vessel of 1,137 gross tons and the first schooner to exceed the 1,000 ton measurement. Following the building of the "Church", the four-masters tended to steadily grow in size as they increased in number.

Schooners possessing such large hulls and having so few in the crew to handle the heavy spars and canvas, were soon fitted with donkey engines. This great boon to the coasting trade soon became standard equipment on most of the later vessels, both large and small and saved much time and money. Although an extra hand was required, namely the engineer, over a period of time his salary was more than offset by the number of hours saved in getting under way, pumping and hoisting as the vessels became larger. Those schooners not equipped with a "donkey" were referred to as "hand pullers" and were generally shunned by experienced seamen. Most of the vessels that fell into this catagory were usually old two and three-masters which were not felt worth the investment by tight-fisted owners and captains. During the latter days of the trade, these vessels had considerable difficulty in rounding up competent crews.

Practically all of the early four-masted schooners were built with centerboards in them, but as with the three-masters, and even though their inclusion made them easier to handle when light, the centerboard was discontinued in the later vessels. This was because of the additional cost in construction, loss of valuable cargo space, difficulty in maintenance and because tugs were available in almost every port and cheap to hire. In the years between 1880 and 1889 inclusive, there were 68 of these four-masted schooners built; one in 1880, one in 1881, four in 1882, three in 1883, three in 1884, one in 1885, seven in 1886, ten in 1887, ten in 1888 and twenty-eight in 1889. Of those listed, 48 were built in Maine; Bath alone launching 35. Three were built in Massachusetts, five each were built in Connecticut, New Jersey and Delaware, and one each in Virginia and Maryland. In 1890, the year of their greatest production, 41 of these vessels were built and in 1891 there were 32 set afloat. According to B. B. Crowningshield, there were 311 four-masted schooners built between 1879 and 1910. Following 1910, the demand for shipping produced by World War I, again occasioned large numbers of four masted schooners to be constructed; 31 being launched in 1917, 39 in 1918, and also 39 in 1919. At the time the final four-master had been set afloat in 1921, a total approximating 450 of these vessels had gone down the ways in the eastern United States.

The last four-masted schooner to be documented in the United States was the "Laura Annie Barnes", launched during the year of 1921. There were three other four-masters launched that year, namely the "Josiah B. Chase" the "Phoebe Crosby," and the "Atlantic Coast", and all four came from Maine yards. The "Laura Annie Barnes" was built at Phippsburg, Maine, by F. S. Bowker & Sons and measured 698 gross tons, 635 net tons, was 181.2 feet in length, 36.8 feet beam, was 15.3 feet in depth and carried a crew of nine. She received her first registration on Sept. 6, 1921 and was owned in Marblehead, Massachusetts. She was eventually sold in 1932 to Captain James L. Publicover of Dublin Shores, Nova Scotia and was lost January 17, 1939 on Tuckernuck Shoal, Nantucket Sound. Her loss thus made her the last commercial sailing vessel to be wrecked in this dreaded area. She was carrying baled pulpwood from Lunenburg, Nova Scotia to New Haven, Connecticut at the time and was under Canadian registry.

A very unusual four-masted schooner was the "Haroldine", launched at North Weymouth, Massachusetts in April, 1884. The "Haroldine" measured 1,361 gross tons, 1,293 net tons, was 209.8 feet in length, 40.5 feet beam, 18.7 feet in depth and at the time of her launching was the biggest of her rig afloat. She was built at the yard of N. Porter Keen in North Weymouth, and was owned in Providence, Rode Island. The most unusual aspect of the "Haroldine" was not in great size, but rather in her hull and rigging characteristics. She had originally been intended as a square rigged deep waterman, but was never finished as such, being rigged as a four-masted schooner prior to her launching. Her high freeboard, high maindeck bulwarks and large foreward house set well back from her raised foc'sle-head-deck would give any seafaring man a ready clue as to the original intent for this vessel. Her rig was also unusual for an east schooner in that she carried a yard on her foremast. Although this characteristic was fairly often found on west coast schooners, the "Haroldine" was the only four-master built on the east coast to be rigged in this manner. She further distinguished herself by going to Melbourne, Australia on her maiden voyage on Nov. 10, 1884. She made this trip in good time, taking 106 days and then proceeded from

30

New South Wales to Hong Kong with coal. From there she came home; a voyage which took her completely around the world. Upon her return to New England she entered the coasting trade, carrying coal with the rest of her sisters. Eventually she was stripped of her foreyard and during her coasting career was called upon three times more to make deepwater trips to the River Plate. These occurred in the years 1887, 1890 and 1891. She was finally lost at sea in 1898. During her 14 year span of operations, the "Haroldine" proved to be a most profitable vessel for her Providence owners, paying for herself many times over.

According to many historians, the biggest of the four-master schooners was the "Frank A. Palmer" launched at Bath, Maine, on March 18, 1897 by Nathaniel T. Palmer. Instead of using traditional rum, she was christened at her launching with a bouquet of roses by Miss Grace Palmer, niece of the builder. The "Palmer" was intended for the coal trade and was a huge vessel, measuring 2,014 gross tons, 1,831 net tons, 274.5 feet in length, 43.0 feet beam and 21.0 feet in depth. She was very heavily built, being three feet through the bilge and her 'tween deck planking was 14 inches square. She was fastened with 1¼ inch iron, was edge bolted every two feet with 1⅜ inch iron and was the first of Nathaniel T. Palmer's vessels to be rigged with rigging screws, or turnbuckles.

In 1901 the "Frank A. Palmer" was sold by her builder to J. S. Winslow & Co., of Portland, Maine. On May 25, 1902, while following the five-masted schooner "Arthur Seitz", during thick weather, both vessels stranded on Skiff Island Reef, five miles S.W. of Muskeget Island, Nantucket Sound. The "Palmer" was about a mile behind the "Seitz", but Captain E. J. Rawding still did not have time to bring the "Palmer" about and followed the "Seitz" ashore. Their predicament was sighted by the Muskeget station crew and by the steamer "Petrel" of Nantucket, both of which went to their assistance. The "Seitz" was finished, and although only a year old, eventually split in two; however the "Palmer", loaded with 3,350 tons of coal was freed and towed leaking, into Boston. Her career from this point on was short, for seven months later, on Dec. 17, 1902, the "Frank A. Palmer" sank following a collision off Cape Ann, Massachusetts.

There is little doubt that the "Frank A. Palmer" was the biggest of the four-masters as far as length was concerned, however she was smaller than the tremendous four-masted schooner "Northland", as far as gross tonnage was concerned. The "Northland", built by Cobb, Butler & Co., in Rockland, Maine in 1906, measured 2,047 gross tons, 1,568 net tons, was 242.2 feet in length, 44.1 feet beam and 22.0 feet in depth. She was originally built as an auxilary, being the first of the big schooners to be equipped with a gasoline engine. She was built for the Northern Maine Power Packet Company, as an experiment to carry paper from Maine to New York for the Great Northern Paper Company. She was flush decked with a turned stanchion rail encompassing her deck from bow to stern. Her six cylinder, 500 H. P. engine turned a propeller which was seven feet in diameter and which was supposed to give her a speed under power of between five and six knots. She also had two smaller gasoline engines aboard to generate power for two cargo elevators and an electric light system. As far as her rig was concerned, the "Northland" was a true schooner in all respects, complete with topsails and five jibs. When her auxiliary engine was removed in 1910, the power experiment having proved unsuccessful, she continued for 11 years to operate as a sailing vessel. She was lost by foundering off the coast of Brazil in 1921.

The three largest of the four-masters, with regard to their length, are as follows: The "Frank A. Palmer" is first and is followed by the "William B. Palmer", of 1,805 gross tons, 257.2 feet in length, which was also built by Nathaniel T. Palmer in Bath, Maine in 1896. The "Marie Palmer" is in third place, measuring 1,904 gross tons, 253.4 feet in length and was built in Bath in 1900 and was pioneer vessel in the fleet of Mr. William F. Palmer of Boston.

There were at least eight four-masted schooners built that were 235 feet or more in length and at least 27 that exceeded the 1,600 gross ton measurement. Among the nearly 485 or more vessels launched with this rig on the east coast, about one-third were over 200 feet in length and those in this category were launched not in one period alone, but all through the 41 year span in which four-masters were built. The "Josiah B. Chase" and the "Atlantic Coast", previously mentioned as being among the last of the four-masters to be built, both exceeded 1,600 tons and each were well over 200 feet long.

Although Maine built a great many schooners, she did not have an exclusive on the production of all the large four-masters built in the United States. The 1,547 gross ton "Virginia Pendleton", for example, was launched at Mystic, Connecticut in 1919 and was 222 feet in length. The "Anandale", a 1,630 gross ton vessel measuring 227.0 feet long was launched at Sharptown, Maryland in 1919. The "Hauppauge", measuring 1,394 gross tons and 228.0 feet in length, was set afloat in 1918 at Wilmington, North Carolina and the list could go on. The records show, in fact, that there were quite a large number of four-masters built outside of Maine, especially as a result of the building boom in shipping stemming from World War I.

An examination of these vessels would show that the four-masted schooners were rigged similar to the three-masters with the addition of one more mast, the fourth being called the Spanker. It should be mentioned here that coasting men had the habit of calling the after-most sail the "Spanker" on any schooner larger than a two-master. They also named the five jibs in the following order, from inboard, out; fore staysail, jib, flying jib, outer jib and jib topsail. Another way of naming these sails might go: Fore Staysail, inner jib, outer jib, flying jib and jib topsail, however it is understood that the former method was the most acceptable to coasting sailors. In addition to the jibs, the four-masters carried the lowers, topsails and topmast staysails found on the three-masters.

The hull developed for the four-masted schooners became almost standardized in form. It had a strong sheer, nearly vertical post, a short counter and a raking, eliptical transom. The entrance was sharp and convex, the floors usually quite flat and the run fairly short and well formed. These hulls could sail rather fast when conditions were right, however due to the flat floors, they were also prone to change the direction of a roll in a seaway with a vigorous snap, a fault which could cause damage to spars and rigging in light airs or in a calm.

Most of the four-masters, as well as the big three-masters, were built with two decks, although occasionally the 'tween decks were only a tier of beams.

Some of the larger four-masters had three decks, which were called the upper, main and lower decks respectively. In cases where the three decks were used, the lower deck would be completely planked and the main deck was just a tier of beams at the load waterline. This arrangement was used in the later five and six-masted schooners and was of absolute necessity in helping to strengthen the hull in the very large schooners.

There were many four-masters built with flush decks, or hurricane decks, as they were sometimes called. Some were almost flush decked, but had a small well deck just abaft the foc'sle head. There were also many built with the short quarterdeck, or poopdeck, and the overall deck arrangement was much like that of the three-masters. The four-master "Mary Manning", built by H. M. Bean, at Camden, Maine, and launched on Nov. 15, 1894, was one of the first vessels to change conventional design by extending the forward cabin to the forecastle. This was regarded as a decided improvement, as it protected the windlass and facilitated its operation in foul weather.

In the latter days of coasting it was found that flush decked vessels were not as satisfactory as other types. Most of the flush deckers were fairly large and intended for the coal trade and when this business began to decline for them, they had to look elsewhere for cargos. It was soon found that flush decks were not well suited to the carrying of deck loads and to operate profitably in those waning days, deck loads had to be carried. As a result the large flush deckers were laid up and the smaller vessels which offered the protection of a raised forecastle head and a quarterdeck, found work to do.

Most four-masters had a hatch located between masts, so that bulk cargos, such as coal, could be easily handled. There were a few, intended for differing work, which were built without a hatch between the main and mizzen. Those schooners built to carry lumber had rectangular lumber ports cut into the bows just below the hawse pipes, where long timber could be easily loaded and unloaded. These ports had to be tightly closed, fastened and caulked before proceeding on a voyage. It was said by some, that because lumber was often loaded in fresh water rivers, the lumber ports were frequently the places where rot would first show itself in the hull.

The rail arrangement on the larger schooners varied according to the type of hull. Those with flush decks had turned stanchion rails often running the length of the vessel. On those which were almost flush decked, but had a raised forecastle-head-deck forward, the rail would often run to the break in the deck, with solid bulwarks, even with the rail, running from there forward. Others with a raised deck forward would gradually increase the bulwarks from a point near midships, so that the sheer from the outside was unbroken and the turned stanchion rail rested on top of this, running the length of the vessel, or to a point abaft, or even with, or just beyond, the break in the deck. On those vessels with large well decks the bulwark and rail arrangement was the same as on the three-masters.

Practically all schooners carried a boat on metal davits hung over the rail at the stern. On smaller, earlier schooners, clumsy looking wood davits stuck out abaft the transom. On later vessels, many of the yawl boats carried astern had power in them and could be used for pushing or towing if the schooner were not too large.

As far as decoration was concerned, the four-masters closely followed the three-masters. Black, white and gray hulls were popular, with black predominating on vessels involved with the coal trade. One notable exception to this were the vessels belonging to Mr. William F. Palmer of Boston, whose fleet of predominately five-masted coal schooners were painted white. Many schooners were painted white when first launched, however this proved a difficult color to maintain and very soon most of them changed; usually to black.

The Canadian Maritime Provinces built in addition to a great many two and three-masted schooners, a total of 36 four-masted schooners in a period ranging from 1889 to 1920. The first vessel of this rig to be built in Canada was the "Uruguay", a 726 net ton craft launched at Windsor, Nova Scotia, in 1889. She measured 170 feet in length, 36.8 feet beam and 17.4 feet in depth. The "Uruguay" did not last long, for on October 24, 1891, on a passage from Windsor to New York with a cargo of gypsum, she struck a shoal at the mouth of the Bay of Fundy. She was subsequently sighted bottom up with her crew missing.

The largest number of Canadian vessels of this rig were launched as a result of the shipping boom produced by the First World War. During the two year period of 1918 and 1919, there were 25 Canadian four-masted schooners set afloat, with the largest Canadian vessel of this rig being launched during this time. This proved to be the "Jessie Louise Fauquier", launched at Hantsport, Nova Scotia in 1918. This vessel measured 939 net tons, was 201.8 feet in length, 39.2 feet beam and was 18.5 feet in depth. She was equipped with two small auxilary engines, but depended almost entirely on her sails. She was under the command of Captain R. A. McLean of Chatham, New Brunswick during most of her career. She was renamed "Avon Queen", which is the name under which she was best known and was in command of Captain McLean.

The last four-masted schooner to be built in Canada was the "Whitebelle", a vessel of 572 net tons, which was launched at Parrsboro, Nova Scotia, in 1920. She measured 172 feet in length, 37.4 feet beam and 13 feet in depth. The "Whitebelle" was a pretty little schooner, as were most of the Canadian vessels, however she lasted for only ten years, foundering off West Quoddy Head on May 22, 1931.

In most cases, Canadian four-masters were smaller than the United States' vessels of the same rig, the U. S. schooners ranging on the average, from 180 to 240 feet in length. Toward the end of the sailing coaster era, many three and four-masted United States schooners were sold to Canadian owners. Those of the four-masted rig are not included of course, in the 36 listed as built in that country. According to Captain Harold G. Foss, there were also six Canadian built four-masters that came under American registry. It should be noticed that although they started building four-masted schooners later than did the United States and built nowhere near as many, still the overall period of Canadian building closely paralleled ours and except for size, the vessels they built were very similar to those built in this country. The four-masters proved to be the largest of the schooner rig ever to be built in eastern Canada.

34

*Five-Masted Schooner Getting Under Way*

## Chapter VII

## THE MAGNIFICENT FIVES

It remained for the United States to increase the size of schooner hulls to a point where five masts were eventually required. The first five-master built in the United States, or anywhere for that matter, was a "laker" named the "David Dows", built in Toledo, Ohio in 1881. At the time of her launching, and as was the case with many lake built schooners, she carried yards on her foremast. These yards were removed after a year or two of service, leaving her with a plain fore and aft rig. The "Dows" measured 1,418 gross tons, was 265.4 feet in length, 37.6 feet beam and 18.1 feet in depth. She was owned in Toledo and never saw service on salt water. She was, for her day, a very large schooner.

The first five-masted schooner built on the east coast was the well known "Gov. Ames", launched at Waldoboro, Maine, on December 1, 1888. Mr. Albert Winslow, of Taunton, Massachusetts, one of the ablest designers of big schooners, made the model of this vessel for Captain Cornelius Davis of Somerset, Massachusetts. The "Ames" measured 1,778 gross tons, 1,597 net tons, was 245.6 feet long, 49.6 feet beam and 21.2 feet in depth and was listed for a crew of 10 men. She was the only five-masted schooner ever to be equipped with a centerboard, it being 35 feet long, set off center and dropping 14 feet.

Due to the large size of the vessel it was decided to rig her with five instead of four masts. Her masts were stayed in the old fashioned manner, the backstays and shrouds being set up with dead eyes and lanyards. It was due to the stretching of this new rigging, during the night of December 9, 1888, while on her maiden voyage, that she ran into trouble.

Bound from Waldoboro to Baltimore, she ran into a stiff southwester causing her to pitch and roll violently and as a result of this her lanyards became slack. Although her crew did their best to try and set up the lanyards again, their efforts were in vain and her masts went overboard near Georges Shoals. Captain Davis anchored his crippled vessel, hitched a ride to Gloucester from a passing fisherman and went to Boston where he arranged to have his new schooner towed to that port. She was rerigged at Boston at a cost of $20,000 and because of this financial handicap and the business depression prevailing in the '90s, the "Ames" for a long while was regarded as an unsuccessful experiment.

In 1890, Captain Davis, in an effort to find higher freight rates, took the "Gov. Ames" from Baltimore around Cape Horn to San Francisco in 143 days. She then operated in the Pacific for the next four years and finally came back to the east coast of the United States by way of a 139 day voyage from Port Blakely, Washington, to Liverpool and from there to Norfolk, Virginia. She arrived at Norfolk in August, 1894 and from then on operated in the coal business for which she had originally been intended.

The "Ames" was well built and was a tremendously strong vessel, part of which was undoubtedly due to the stiffening supplied by her centerboard trunk and also to her unusual hatch combing construction, which ran continually from the forward to the after hatch. At the time of her loss, she showed little of the hogging which was so often seen in many of the later, large vessels. The "Gov. Ames" was tragically wrecked on Wimble Shoals, December 13, 1909, near the Chicamacomico lifesaving station, Cape Hatteras, North Carolina, resulting in the loss of 11 lives.

It was felt by many that the "Gov. Ames" was a bit ahead of her time and it was not until 10 years after her launching that another five-master was built on the east coast. This was the big "Nathaniel T. Palmer", constructed by her namesake at Bath, Maine, in 1898. The "Nathaniel T. Palmer" was the sixth and final vessel that "Nathaniel T. Palmer" had built for his fleet and measured 2,440 gross tons, 2,244 net tons, was 295.1 feet long, 44.4 feet beam and was 22.2 feet in depth. There was a nip and tuck race to see which five-master would have the honor of being listed as the second such vessel launched on the east coast and the "Nathaniel T. Palmer" beat her rival, the "John B. Prescott" by only a few weeks. The "Palmer" was much different from her predecessor, the "Gov. Ames" in an interesting number of ways. Whereas the "Ames" had a hull that was very wide and flat, with a centerboard that reduced her carrying capacity, the hull of the "Palmer" was 50 feet longer, 672 tons more in gross tonnage and nearer in design to the conventional large schooner hulls. She was more full in the ends, had greater capacity for cargo and of course was without a board. The "Ames" had a large main, or well deck, while the "Palmer" had a deck that was almost flush, possessing only a very short well deck between the forecastle head and a point just forward of the main-mast. From this point a turned stanchion rail was erected which ran the rest of the length of the deck aft.

The "Nathaniel T. Palmer" was a fairly lucky vessel, although on March 11, 1901, she managed to get herself ashore at Beach Haven, New Jersey and for a while it was touch and go as to whether they'd get her off. However she was

36

finally hauled off by the Merritt and Chapman Derrick and Wrecking Company. All the Nathaniel Palmer fleet was eventually taken over by the J. S. Winslow Company, of Portland, Maine. The "Nathaniel T. Palmer" then stayed with this firm until she had to be abandoned at sea on December 1, 1911.

The third five-master was the "John B. Prescott, and she was launched in January, 1899, at Camden, Maine. She was slightly larger than the "Palmer" and was the first of the five-masters to carry a wheelhouse.

The five-masters that were built following the "Palmer" and the "Prescott" continued generally to grow in size with respect to their gross tonnage, until a peak was reached with launching of the 3,138 gross ton "Jane Palmer". This vessel was the largest of the five-masters and was launched at East Boston in 1904. After this date schooners of this rig showed a tendency to decline in size. The "Edna Hoyt" and the "Mary H. Diebold", both launched in 1920, the last year in which vessels of this rig were built, were each barely over 1,500 gross tons.

The "Jane Palmer" was one of the few east coast five-masters built outside of Maine and her dimensions were truly great for a vessel of this rig. She measured 3,138 gross tons, 2,823 net tons, 308.6 feet in length, 49.0 feet beam and 22.4 feet in depth. Originally she was supposed to have been launched as a six-master named the "Edward Burgess" and to have been fitted with an auxilary steam engine, but none of this came to pass. She was designed by W. Starling Burgess and was to have been built for M. A. C. Crandall at the yard of J. M. Brooks at East Boston. Although her construction was started by Brooks, the original promotion failed before she was completed and she was bought by Mr. William F. Palmer for a reportedly "very low" figure. Mr. Palmer completed her and rigged her with five masts instead of six. She and the "Elizabeth Palmer" were the only two vessels in the Palmer fleet not designed by William F. Palmer himself.

The "Jane Palmer" lasted for 16 years, although she came very near being lost in the $100,000 waterfront fire that ravaged East Boston in 1907. Before being pulled clear, her rigging, cabins and deck were burned and part of her cargo was on fire. The fire was put out, she was repaired and went to sea again until 1920. Then on December 18th of that year, she had to be abandoned in the Atlantic in Lat. 36.06 N, Long. 65.31 W, while in command of Captain Malvin J. Marston. This was most fortunately accomplished with no loss of life.

The second largest of the five-masters, again measured in gross tonnage, was the "Grace A. Martin", built in 1904 at Bath, Maine. The "Martin" measured 3,129 gross tons and was 302 feet long. The third largest was the 3,060 gross ton "Fuller Palmer", built in Bath, Maine, in 1908. Oddly enough the length of the "Fuller Palmer" was greater than either of the others, being 309.4 feet long, making her the longest of any of the five-masted schooners. In all there were six of these five-masted schooners that measured more than 300 feet in length.

As mentioned earlier, the five-masters did not steadily increase in length throughout the period of their building. There were six of them built after 1900 that were under 240 feet in length. These were the "James Pierce", 236 feet, built in 1901, the "Magnus Manson", 223 feet, built in 1904, the "Elvira Ball", 200.8 feet, built in 1907, the "Courtney C. Houck", 218.9 feet, built in 1913, the "Mary H. Diebold", 223.5 feet and the "Edna Hoyt", 224 feet, both built in 1920. If one compares these vessels to some of the larger four-masters, it is readily apparent that there was considerable overlap in size between the two rigs.

It is also apparent that the little "Elvira Ball" was the smallest of all the east coast five-masters. She was launched at Mystic, Connecticut, on August 24, 1907, and was valued new at $39,800. She was rigged by Captain William J. White and was in command of Captain L. B. Stanton. Her deck arrangement was very much like that found on smaller coasters, having a large well deck with raised forecastle head and a short quarterdeck, with a turned stanchion rail around the quarterdeck and solid bulwarks on the main deck, or well deck. She was a single decked vessel and during her brief career was owned by the Gilbert-Transportation Company of Mystic. On February 8, 1909, less than two years after her launching, she had to be abandoned 130 miles east of Cape Charles, Virginia. The elements then took charge of the "Ball" and her lumber laden wreck became a wandering derelict of the Atlantic which drifted completely across the ocean to the coast of Africa before being totally destroyed.

There were a total of 58 east coast five-masted schooners launched from 1888 to 1920, the year in which the last one went in the water. All of these, with the exception of six, were the products of Maine shipyards. Of the six not launched in Maine, one was built in Massachusetts, one was rebuilt from a four to a five-master in Puerto Rico and four went overboard in Connecticut.

The vessel rebuilt and rerigged in Puerto Rico is one schooner many historians have missed, for her career as a five-master is one of the shortest on record. Originally built and launched as a four-masted schooner on Nov. 24, 1904, at Milbridge, Maine, she was named the "Myrtle Tunnell". The "Tunnell" was a 1,498 gross ton schooner, very handsome in appearance, but one of those vessels which had misfortune and bad luck dogging most of her career. She had been in service only a year when she was abandoned in an easterly gale near Frying Pan Shoals. She was later picked up and towed into Savannah, Georgia where she lay condemned and unused for a year. While lying there she attracted attention of some business interests in Savannah who bought her and who had her thoroughly repaired. They also renamed her the "Forest City" in honor of the port of Savannah.

With a new name and new paint she sailed under the command of Captain Rines in October, 1907, and entered the New York to Savannah trade. For the next eight years she enjoyed a period that was relatively free from trouble.

In 1915, due to the shipping shortage, her Savannah owners sold her for a handsome profit to business interests in New York. She was then chartered to carry general cargo to the Gold Coast of Africa and from there to return to Boston with palm oil. She was placed under the command of Captain Allen who had been on the ill-fated "Paul Palmer" when it caught fire and burned to the waters edge north of Race Point, off Cape Cod.

The "Forest City" made the outward voyage without incident, loaded her return cargo and while homeward bound, put into the port of San Juan, Puerto Rico. On January 1, 1916, while lying at the dock in San Juan, fire struck the schooner and destroyed all her top hamper. Again she was discarded and lay unused.

About a year passed with the insurance company unable to dispose of the badly charred vessel, then along came Captain William J. Kennerly, who with some friends, bought the "Forest City" and began the difficult job of repairing her. All the materials had to come from the United States, which made it a tremendous and most expensive undertaking. Instead of equipping the schooner with four masts, they rebuilt her as a five-master and again renamed her, calling her the "Charles E. Dunlap." She loaded a full cargo for New York and on July 10, 1919, the 224-foot, five-master proudly set sail. On July 22, 1919, this very unlucky vessel ran ashore on Fire Island and was a total loss. The "Charles E. Dunlap" had a life span of 12 days at sea making her career the shortest in the history of the five-masters.

During the 15 years of the schooner's existence, almost half of her time was spent laid up or being repaired. She was declared a total loss three times, had four sets of owners, three different names, four home ports and two different rigs, truly a chequered career.

Of the four vessels launched in Connecticut, one was rebuilt in 1918 at Mystic from the old sidewheeler "Mohawk", ex "Penobscot", and it too did not last very long as a five-master. The history of the "Mohawk", as a sailing vessel, is best described in a letter received from Captain Foss.

"At Mystic they rigged her into a single decked five-masted schooner of 804 tons. Painted her white for eye appeal and nailed a few boards around her top. She towed to New York and loaded tankage for Charleston, South Carolina in 1918. Then she went to Gulfport, Mississippi and loaded lumber for New York. She arrived all right and then sailed from New York for Gulfport, empty. She has never been heard from since. All this happened in 1918 and Captain Jim O'Toole was her only master. I knew him fairly well and he was a decent fellow. He took this tub because he had just lost the "Blanche H. King" on Cuba and needed a job."

The six years from 1899 to and including 1904, saw the greatest production of five-masters, four being built in 1899, six in 1900, eight in 1901, five in 1902, five in 1903, and nine in 1904, making a total of 37, or well over half the entire number built. After 1904 the building of these vessels considerably decreased, only eight being built between 1905 and 1916. The war boom which occasioned an increase in the building of schooners of various sizes, also saw the launching of 11 more five-masters between 1916 and 1920.

The largest producer of five-masters was the company of Percy and Small of Bath, Maine who launched 15. H. M. Bean of Camden, Maine launched 8; G. G. Deering of Bath, Maine launched 7; George L. Welt of Waldoboro, Maine launched 6, and the New England Company of Bath, Maine launched 4. These five builders therefore were responsible for the building of 40 of the 58 eastern five-masted schooners.

Most of the five-masters built on the east coast were intended for the coal trade, were flush decked, or nearly so and therefore not suited to carrying deck loads well. The large vessels of this rig were designed primarily to compete with the barge lines, which by 1903, had begun to cut heavily into the business of carrying coal. As a result of this competition, many of the big schooners sacrificed fine lines for increased capacity, as at this period it was not always the swiftest vessel that earned the biggest profit.

As they increased in size, endeavoring for larger capacities, these wooden vessels began to feel the effects of the tremendous weights placed on the hulls at the bow and the stern. The large after cabin and the over-hang of the counter astern and the high bows with the weight of the massive anchors and accessories carried thereon, combined with the lengthening of the hulls, created the tendency for the big schooners to become hogged. This hogging, or sagging at the ends of the vessel, was often not readily apparent due to the great amount of sheer originally built into many of them. Frequently some builders gave their vessels a rocker or reverse curve in the keel during construction in anticipation of the hogging and to help offset it. Many of these long, big schooners were inherently so weak in the hull that they could not be sailed hard and their potential speed was unfortunately, seldom realized. Many leaked badly when fully loaded and under way in a stiff breeze.

Captain Charles A. Drew of the tug "Piscataqua", in Portsmouth, New Hampshire summed up the opinion which was held by many regarding the very big schooners around 1910 when he said that they were, "built of hoop poles and caulked with eel grass — limber as a snake".

It is said that the big Brooks built "Jane Palmer" had this snake like quality and that her forward house rose and fell a good two feet every time her bow climbed a steep sea. In heavy weather, when the scarfs in her rails started to open and shut with a snap, she had to be nursed along carefully and of course was troubled with increased leaking. So great was her draft when loaded with coal, that she usually had to anchor off Nobska to pump out before trying the trip over Nantucket Shoals. If it had not been for the donkey operated pumps, some of them would have been almost impossible to manage with the small crews they carried.

Very often when loading or unloading they would touch bottom, or "take the ground" at low tide and the strain then placed on the hull was tremendous, especially if only one section of the vessel was aground. The tendency to hog even further and to leak was in this way greatly increased.

The story involving the end of one big five-master, amply demonstrates the weakness found in some of the large schooner hulls. This weakness was discovered in the "Samuel J. Goucher" which was built in Camden, Maine in 1904. She touched and became firmly hung up on a ledge off Portsmouth, New Hampshire on November 6, 1911. The tide was high at the time, but the weather remained calm and there was every reason to think that she might be floated off with little or no damage. However, when the tide went out so did the bottom of the "Goucher", depositing her entire cargo of 4,000 tons of coal on top of the ledge, finishing her then and there.

In an effort to overcome some of the faults in wooden hulls, several iron and steel hulled schooners were built in the United States and one three-master was launched in Canada. One of the last of the metal hulled schooners launched in the United States was the steel hulled "Kineo", built in 1903 by A. Sewall & Company in Bath, Maine. The "Kineo" was rigged as a five-masted schooner, complete with top-masts and a spike bowsprit that was typical of the type used on the big Sewall built steel square riggers which preceeded her. She also had the protection of a wheelhouse aft, was equipped to use water ballast and had the latest labor saving devices for working the vessel and handling cargo. She was expected to carry approximately 3,000 tons of cargo on deep water passages and around 3,500 tons on coastal trips, making her potentially, a most versatile schooner. Her cost estimate was $120,000.

She was launched on April 16, 1903, and was the 50th and final vessel built by the Sewall firm. Her dimensions were: 2,128 gross tons, 1,867 net tons, 259.5 feet in length, 45.3 feet beam and 22.9 feet in depth. Although she was built primarily with the coal trade in mind, the "Kineo" made one deep water voyage around Cape Horn in 1905-06, that did much to discredit the large fore-and-afters as capable deep water vessels. The effects of this voyage on the "Kineo" were much the same as those on the "Gov. Ames" when she made her Cape Horn passage, both vessels suffering severe damage to the sails and rigging due to the slatting and banging of the fore-and-aft sails in heavy seas. According to Captain Frank W. Patten, who was master on this discouraging voyage, there was not a mast hoop left on the "Kineo" after this trip and she lost 14 sails.

The "Kineo" was sold to the Texas Co. in 1916 along with the "Edward Sewall", a steel four-masted bark also belonging to the Sewall fleet. The "Kineo" was eventually converted to a motorized tanker, was renamed "Maryland" and was still afloat in the 1940's.

With the exception of the "Sintram", which was a wooden Ferris steamer hull rigged at South Freeport, Maine in 1920, the last five-master launched on the east coast was the "Edna Hoyt". Not only was she the last five-mast schooner built and launched as such, but the "Hoyt" was the last of the schooners of this rig to be in operation. She was also the next to the smallest of the five-masters in gross tonnage and this undoubtedly had much to do with her successful career, for while the larger vessels of similar rig were being laid up for want of filling cargos, the smaller, handier, "Edna Hoyt" continued uninterrupted for 18 years, never being laid up once.

The "Hoyt" was built in 1920 in Thomaston, Maine by Dunn and Elliott. She measured 1,512 gross tons, 1,384 net tons, was 224.0 feet in length, 41.1 feet beam and 20.8 feet in depth. She was built at an approximate cost of $280,000. This may sound high when compared to the estimated cost of the "Kineo", but it must be remembered that the two vessels were launched 17 years apart and labor and material costs had risen considerably in the intervening time.

The "Edna Hoyt", like so many of her sister five-masters, was intended for the coal trade and was for some time operated by her builders. She was sold in the early or mid 1920's and was then owned by the Superior Trading and Transportation Co. of Boston, under whose management she operated for several years. Her owners sensing a decline in the availability of coal charters, sold the "Hoyt" on October 20, 1929, to Foss & Crabtree of Boston, a sister Company, who wanted her for use in the fertilizer trade. She continued with this firm, carrying sheep guano from Venezuela to North American ports and bringing down general cargos to the West Indies in return. Occasionally she would deviate from this pattern during hurricane season, at which time she would carry Florida lumber to northern ports. The "Hoyt" was in command of Captain Robert Rickson during most of the time that she was owned by Foss & Crabtree. Around 1936, due to the pinch of foreign competition in the West Indies, she went back into the coal trade. In 1937 a new captain came aboard named George H. Hopkins and arrangements were made for the "Hoyt" to make a deep water voyage to Belfast, Ireland.

Prior to her Atlantic crossing the old five-master was hauled out at Boston and made as ship-shape as possible. In her 17 years of trading the "Hoyt" had become somewhat hogged, as had many five-masters and although her strength wasn't what it once was, she still was tight and appeared in reasonably good condition. Her deck arrangement was not typical of most five-masters, in that her quarterdeck ran to a point just forward of the jiggermast. The masts on a five-masted schooner, going from forward, aft, were named in this manner: fore, main, mizzen, jigger and spanker. There was a turned stanchion rail that ran along the quarterdeck and a solid bulwark that protected the main deck, with a raised forecastle head forward. She had no catheads, using patent stockless anchors which were hauled up into the hawes pipes and she carried only four jibs.

On August 9, 1937, in command of Captain Hopkins, she left Halifax, Nova Scotia and headed across the Atlantic on a voyage from which she was never to return. Her trip across made her the last of the five-masted schooners to cross the ocean. With her cargo of lumber, she arrived at Belfast on September 23, 1937, after a somewhat rough passage which had shifted her deck load.

Three weeks later, after discharging her cargo of lumber, she left Belfast for Newport, Wales, where she was to pick up a load of coal briquettes bound for La Guayra, Venezuela. While loading at Newport she "took the bottom", which caused her to straighten out, snapping several of her stays and placing a terrible strain on her hull. Captain Hopkins wisely refused to finish taking on cargo and had her moved to Cardiff, where the loading was completed. She could remain afloat at Cardiff during all the stages of the tide, but unfortunately more damage had been done than was realized by the grounding at Newport.

On November 2, 1937, the "Edna Hoyt" left Cardiff for her trip back across the Atlantic. In the Bay of Biscay she ran into a real "screamer"; the type for which the Bay had earned an ugly reputation among seafaring men, and the poor old "Hoyt" began to work herself to pieces. The strain put on her hull at Newport, augmented by the heavy seas, caused a portion of her 'tween decks to collapse and her cargo shifted. Her hogging suddenly increased and she began to leak, taking on water almost as fast as the pumps could bail it out of her. The only sail she was able to carry was her fore staysail and a reefed fore sail and with these she ran before the gale as best she could.

42

The storm seemed to the men on the laboring schooner to be one without end and day after day it continued to driver her farther out to sea, out of the regular steamship lanes. Distress signals had been set but no help came. On several occasions steamers had been sighted way off on the lumpy horizon but they slipped over out of sight, either not having seen her plight or pretending not to.

Finally, after being battered about for 21 miserable days since leaving Cardiff, the "Hoyt" was sighted by the Norwegian steamer "San Amigo", which stood by her until the gale began to abate. The "San Amigo" then took the helpless "Hoyt" in tow and hauled her into Lisbon, Portugal, where she arrived fittingly enough, on Thanksgiving Day, November 25, 1937.

She was surveyed in Lisbon and condemned as unseaworthy. On February 1, 1938, she was bought from Captain Foss by J. Vasconcellos of Lisbon, for $3,500 for use as a coal hulk, thus ending the sailing career of the "Edna Hoyt", the last American five-masted schooner to hail from the east coast.

*A Six-Masted Schooner at Anchor*

## Chapter VIII

## THE BIG TEN PLUS ONE

In 1899, when Captain John G. Crowley, of Taunton and Boston, Massachusetts, ordered the building of a six-masted schooner, people wondered at his wisdom. Nevertheless, on April first of that year, the keel for this huge vessel was laid and work progressed on her hull at a rapid pace. The new schooner was being constructed at the yard of Holly M. Bean at Camden, Maine and was destined to be the only six-master to be launched from the yard of this famous builder of sailing vessels.

She was built under the supervision of John J. Wardwell who also had fashioned the model for her hull. Wardwell was one of the leading designers of schooners in his day, having evolved plans and models for over 150 vessels; on 83 of which he personally supervised construction as master builder. Wardwell said later it took him only three or four days to make the model and plans from which this revolutionary six-masted vessel was built.

Work on the huge new schooner went so well that she was ready for launching on August 4, 1900. On that day she was christened the "George W. Wells", by Miss May Wells, the daughter of the man for whom the new vessel was named. In front of an estimated crowd of 10,000 people, Miss Wells, in a unique ceremony, scattered white roses on the bow of the vessel as it started down the ways and then quickly released a flock of white pigeons.

44

The building of the "Wells", the first of the six-masted schooners, had attracted tremendous publicity prior to her launching, no single sailing ship having received so much attention since the days of the tall clipper ships. At the time she was set afloat, the "Wells" was the biggest sailing vessel in the world, containing material estimated in value at $120,000. Her dimensions were truly great, measuring 2,970 gross tons, 2,743 net tons, 319.3 feet in length, 48.5 feet beam and 23.0 feet in depth, with a cargo capacity of 5,000 tons of coal. She had two full decks, with an upper deck that was almost flush, running from the stern forward to a point just ahead of the main mast. From this point forward, there was a small well deck which extended to the forecastle head. From the well deck aft, the upper deck was surrounded by a turned stanchion rail, while the deck itself was confined behind solid bulwarks as typical in many of the five-masters.

She was framed with white oak and her planking and ceiling was hard pine, with garboards eight inches thick, planking six inches thick and her fastenings were of 1⅜ and 1¼ inch iron. Her cabins and staterooms were handsomely finished in cherry, sycamore and ash and were supplied with baths, hot and cold water, steam heat, electricity and a telephone that ran to the galley and the engine house. Such modern gadgets would have made old timers click their tongues and shake their beards in amazement.

Her six lower masts were named, the fore, main, mizzen, jigger, driver and spanker, going from forward, aft, and were huge single sticks of Oregon Pine. These lower masts were 119 feet in length and her topmasts were 58 feet long. As was the case in all schooners, the fore-topmast was slightly larger in diameter than the rest of the topmasts. Her jibboom was 75 feet long and her spankerboom was 72 feet long and the distance between the outboard end of each was 425 feet. When all of her 22 sails were set, she carried approximately 12,000 square yards of canvas.

The "Wells" had five houses, or cabins on deck; one at the foremast, one at the mizzen, a small donkey and pump house at the drivermast, her main cabin at the spanker and she also carried a wheelhouse aft of the main cabin. The wheelhouse was a feature found on many of the vessels owned or managed by Captain John G. Crowley. The ground tackle on the "Wells" was very heavy, one anchor weighing 8,250 lbs. and the other weighing 7,500 lbs. and to each of these was attached 800 fathoms of 2½ inch chain.

At the time of her launching, the "Wells" was painted black with white trim and white rails and with her pronounced sheer, she made for a most graceful looking schooner, in spite of her great size. The job of rigging was finished after her launching and the "George W. Wells" was then placed in command of Captain Arthur L. Crowley, of Taunton, Massachusetts, former Captain of the "John B. Prescott".

The "Wells" proved to be a fast vessel, making the shortest run of any of the coal fleet between Portland, Maine and the Virginia Capes. This was accomplished from December 12th to the 14th, in 1907, when running light, she covered the 518 mile distance in 51 hours. Her designer, J. J. Wardwell, said that he believed his creation would be capable of 12 knots under favorable circumstances, but it was later claimed that she was able to do 15. However,

Wardwell later stated that he thought the huge wooden six-masters were impractical. Due to their great length, they were even more susceptible to strain and to hogging; faults which had already shown themselves in the large five-masters.

The second six-master was also launched in 1900 and was set afloat only two months after the "Wells" went in the water. This was the huge "Eleanor A. Percy", built by Percy and Small at Bath, Maine. The "Percy" measured 3,401 gross tons and was the third largest of all the wooden six-masters. In the summer of 1901, the "Wells" and the "Percy" were in collision with one another on the back side of Cape Cod. If the "Wells" had not been light at the time she probably would have gone down, as there was a large hole rammed into her port side. Both vessels reached port safely with the smaller "Wells" being severely damaged.

The "George W. Wells" continued to sail the coast until 1913, when she earned for herself the dubious distinction of being the largest sailing vessel ever to be lost on the coast of North Carolina. This took place under the command of Captain Joseph H. York, while she was bound on a trip from Boston to Fernandina, Florida. In addition to her crew, she was carrying on board as passengers; one man, two women and three children. On the morning of September 3, the "Wells" ran into winds of near hurricane force, became unmanagable and began to take in water at a rapid rate. During the following afternoon, in sinking condition, she drifted in among the breakers about 6 miles southwest of the Hatteras Inlet Lifesaving Station and struck bottom several hundred yards from the beach. Fortunately for those on the schooner, she had been sighted by two lifesaving stations that were 14 miles apart, so when she finally struck, the lifesavers had all their gear waiting on the beach.

It was decided to attempt to rescue the people on the "Wells" by breeches buoy, but the first three shots that were fired failed to reach the stricken schooner because of the terrifically high winds. The crew of the "Wells", seeing the failure of those on shore to reach them, then attached a line to a spar and tossed it overboard in hopes it would drift ashore to their intended rescuers. Twenty minutes later their prayers were answered when the lifesavers picked up the line on the beach.

A whipline was fastened to the one from the schooner and the crew of the "Wells" started to haul it off. Unhappily the "Wells" was lurching and rolling in the heavy surf all this time and the violent motion of the vessel parted the whipline before it could be secured. Another was attached to the original line which was again hauled off and finally the breeches buoy was set up. Before it could be used however, the tackle on shore parted and it took another half hour before it could be repaired and made ready for the first passenger. All the passengers were landed first, then the crew. Captain York, following the tradition of the sea, was the last to leave his doomed vessel. The survivors were then taken to the Hatteras Inlet Station, where they remained several days.

The "George W. Wells", reputed at the time to be valued at $80,000, was smashed beyond repair and all hope of refloating. Her hull was later set on fire resulting, so some said, from a dispute as to who was to have the right to pick over the bones of this once stately sailing vessel.

In all there were eleven six-masted schooners that originated on the east coast. Following the "Wells" and the "Percy", there were eight more built between 1902 and including 1909. These became known as "The Big Ten". Following this, in 1917, a former wooden sound steamer, which was doing service as a barge, was rebuilt at New York and was rigged as a regular six-masted schooner.

The number of schooners with six masts that were launched in the years between 1902 and 1909, are listed as follows: one in 1902, one of steel construction in 1903, one in 1904, none in 1905, one in 1906, one in 1907, two in 1908 and one in 1909.

The ten vessels that were laid down and launched as six-masters were truly tremendous in size, seven of them measuring over 3,000 gross tons, with only two of the ten being under 300 feet in length. The smallest of these in terms of both gross tonnage and length, was the "Addie M. Lawrence", built by Percy and Small at Bath, Maine, in 1902. This vessel measured 2,807 gross tons and was 292.4 feet in length.

The largest of the six-masters, in terms of gross tonnage, was the "Wyoming", which was also built by Percy and Small and launched in 1909. Not only was she the largest, but she was also the last six-master to be designed and built as such on the east coast. Her dimensions are absolutely astounding for a wooden schooner, measuring 3,730 gross tons, 3,036 net tons, 329.5 feet in length, 50.1 feet beam and 30.4 feet in depth. This great size gave her the distinction of being the largest wooden sailing vessel ever to carry a cargo. On one occasion this colossal schooner carried away from Newport News, Virginia, the staggering amount of 6,004 tons of coal.

The loss of the "Wyoming" is still an unsolved tragedy and is best described in "Wrecks Around Nantucket", by Arthur H. Gardner, in the list for the year 1924.

"March 11th, the six-masted schooner "Wyoming", bound up the coast from Norfolk with coal, was caught in the blizzard in Nantucket Sound and lost with all on board. The vessel was last seen at anchor near Pollock Rip lightship. The first knowledge of the disaster was when wreckage bearing the name "Wyoming" was washed ashore on the north side of the island, including her quarterboard. It is thought the big vessel pounded to pieces on the shoals north of this island during the storm and that the crew had no chance to save their lives."

The loss of the "Wyoming" occurred during the night and whatever happened to her and her crew of thirteen men will never be known. There have been many theories as to why she went to pieces. Some thought she struck bottom during the storm when the tide went out. Some thought she pulled her bow out. She was at anchor and fully loaded at the time and others said her hatches or cabins might have been stove in when the tide turned her broadside to the seas. Whatever the reason, her wreckage, which thoroughly covered the north shore of

Nantucket and Tuckernuck Islands, was chewed into small pieces, attesting to a very violent end.

The second largest six-master was the steel schooner, "William L. Douglas", designed by B. B. Crowninshield and built by the Fore River Ship and Engine Co., at Quincy, Massachusetts, in 1903. She grossed 3,708 tons and was built for Captain John G. Crowley at a contract price of $212,000. She was the only steel six-master built on the east coast and differed from most of the wooden vessels by having a large well deck with a short poop and forecastle.

The third largest six-master was the 3,424 gross ton, "Edward B. Winslow", built in 1908 and the fourth largest was the "Eleanor A. Percy". Both of the latter vessels were built by Percy and Small, who held the record for building the majority of these gigantic schooners, having seven in all to their credit. These were: the "Eleanor A. Percy", the "Addie M. Lawrence", the "Ruth E. Merrill", the "Edward J. Lawrence", and the "Edward B. Winslow", all built for the J. S. Winslow Co., of Portland, Maine, plus the "Alice M. Lawrence" and the "Wyoming" which were built for the account of Percy and Small.

The only other six-master which was a member of the so called "Big Ten" and so far unmentioned, was the "Mertie B. Crowley", whose construction was begun at the yard of Holly M. Bean of Camden, Maine. Because of financial difficulties, the frames and keel were taken down and moved to the yard of Cobb, Butler, Co., in Rockland, Maine, where they were again set up and the vessel finished in 1907. The "Crowley" was built for the Coastwise Transportation Co., under the management of Captain John G. Crowley. She had one of the shortest careers of all the six-masters, being wrecked a little over two years later on Jan. 10, 1910, on Wasque Shoal, between Martha's Vineyard and Nantucket, while bound north with coal.

The "Ruth E. Merrill" and the "Eleanor A. Percy" share honors for having the longest careers for vessels of this rig, both of them lasting almost twenty years. The "Edward J. Lawrence" had the distinction of being the last of the huge schooners to remain afloat. She finally came to a fiery end at Portland, Maine, on December 27, 1925, where the burning fortunately was attended with no loss of life.

The six-master with the shortest life span of all, is one very seldom mentioned by marine historians. This was the "Dovrefjeld", owned in New York City. The "Dovrefjeld" deserves more recognition than she gets, for she can lay claim to being the longest of all the six-masters, measuring 332.2 feet. She was however, the smallest in terms of gross tonnage, measuring only a meager 1,858 gross tons.

The "Dovrefjeld" was originally built as the magnificent paddle steamer "Rhode Island". She was intended to carry passengers on Long Island Sound and was launched in 1882 from the famous Palmer yard at Noank, Connecticut. This yard, incidentally, had in no way any connection with the famous Palmer Fleet of schooners in Boston. The "Rhode Island" measured 2,888 gross tons, was 332.2 feet long and was regarded as one of the finest inland steamers afloat. She continued to operate as such until a few years before World War One, when she was cut down to a 1,706 ton barge which was owned at Greenpoint, New York.

In 1917, due to the demand for hulls that was created by the war, she was built up, rigged as a six-master schooner and renamed "Dovrefjeld". She certainly was no beauty, having a rather ugly bow with a long spike bowsprit and a forecastle-head-deck that ran almost to the main mast. She had a long well deck, followed by a short poopdeck about which was constructed a turned stanchion rail. She carried four headsails and was completely rigged as a schooner, having usually high topmasts.

Shortly after she was rigged as a schooner in 1917, the "Dovrefjeld" sank in shallow water near Stapleton, Staten Island, New York, while loaded with coal. She was subsequently raised, however her career was not destined to last long as a windjammer. Less than two years later, on Feb. 28, 1919, she foundered about 32 miles east of Cape Hatteras, North Carolina, while on a voyage to the River Plate with lumber.

Although the life spans of the "Dovrefjeld" and the "Mertie B. Crowley" were indeed short, a study of the eleven six-masters with regard their length of service, gives 12.3 years as the average time these tremendous vessels lasted. This is not bad when one considers that 2 of them had the misfortune to be lost while in or near their second year.

Of the eleven east coast six-masters, two had large well decks, with short poop and forecastle, four had short well decks such as found on the "George W. Wells" and five were completely flush decked with turned stanchion rails running the length of the vessel. The "George W. Wells", the "William L. Douglas" and the "Mertie B. Crowley" had wheel houses and all three of these were under the management of Captain John G. Crowley of Boston.

All of the six-masted schooners were designed to be coal carriers, however as the barges began to cut into the trade, some of them were put to work carrying other cargos. None of them were degraded to the point of being laid up in some forgotten creek where they could end their days as slowly rotting piles of lumber. This was the fate allotted to some of the four and five-masters, but all of the six-masted schooners met violent ends, practically all of them coming while they were still in harness. Only four of them died, however, while actively working at the coal trade for which they were intended. The rest were carrying such cargos as they could find and of these, four went down far away from home and the routes that they were meant to travel.

Considering that these huge sailing vessels were manned only by 12 to 14 men, plus their captain, and that they were able to make trip after trip, year in and year out, carrying from 5,000 to 6,000 tons of coal per trip, they cannot be called failures. They did their jobs and did them well. They were something unique in the history of seafaring and most definitely were something American in adaption if not in creation.

While many Americans were proud of these great schooners, not everyone thought of them in a favorable light. The English frequently termed them as man-killers and often referred to them in an uncomplimentary manner. An article that appeared in the September, 1927 issue of Sea Breezes magazine, a publication eminating from Liverpool, England, gives some idea as to how the big American schooners were viewed by at least one Englishman. The article was written by W. L. Leclercq and is entitled, "Big Schooners, Were They Over-rated?"

"The picture of the five-masted "Rose Mahoney," in the March issue, re-minded me of a question much discussed by sailors a few years ago, whether these up-wards-of-thousand-ton schooners were to be considered ships or merely as barges, although enjoying a very limited sailing ability. The pros, who, I must say were not many, held they were cheap and handy, and told fabulous tales of their speed on a wind. The contras pointed out that their only virtues were they carried a lot of cargo and could be handled by a handful of men, but for the rest they were clumsy tubs, and to call them ships at all was rank blasphemy. A Schooner of upwards of 300 tons they considered an eyesore and a disgrace for a sailorman to set foot of.

"Personally, I thing the contras were right. With very few exceptions, such as the "Thomas W. Lawson", they were ugly brutes to look at, and the tales of their speed I have never been able to verify, although from time to time they made a smart passage. Their sail area was a joke as compared with their ton-nage, and this could not possibly be otherwise; their lowers would be too large to stand the wind-pressure properly. Besides, they were rather clumsy to handle, and, if I am not mistaken, this was the cause of the loss of the "Thomas W. Lawson", most famous and biggest of them all, being a seven-masted fore-and-aft schooner of 10,000 tons displacement, built of steel at Quincy, Massachusetts, in 1902, when she went to pieces on the Scillies in December, 1907.

"Other giants of the fore-and-aft rig were the "Helen W. Martin", a wooden five-master of 2,265 tons gross, measuring 283 feet in length, and the 'Eleanor A. Percy', a six-master of 3,700 tons gross, with a length 323 feet, both built in 1900 by Percy & Small, at Bath, and both a living, or, rather a sailing argu-ment for the contras. Time, however, has vindicated the latter, for these big schooners are growing very rare, while three and four-masted schooners from 200 to 600 tons still flourish".

Leclercq then devoted some space in his article to the speed of various schooners while engaged upon ocean passages and closed his discussion of the schooners with this remark.

"But on the whole I am afraid the disappearing of these monster fore-and-afters- is not a matter to be deeply regretted".

Besides raising the blood pressure of a few tarry old schooner men who would have probably invited Mr. Leclercq out back to settle a point or two, the article demonstrates a misunderstanding that was common with regard to these vessels. Many of their critics did not understand the purpose for which they were designed. The big schooners, in the main, were never intended as deep-water voyagers, but rather, they were evolved to compete with the ever en-croaching barge lines and were intended to carry very large quantities of coal along a coastline that was difficult to navigate, especially in a square rigged vessel. In addition to this, they had to sail with comparatively small crews in order to show a profit for their owners. Also, Mr. Leclercq's selection of the "Thomas W. Lawson" as an exception to ugliness, probably lifted more than one eyebrow.

*Building The "Thomas W. Lawson"*

## Chapter IX

## THE MIGHTY THOMAS W. LAWSON

Sooner or later, when discussing coasting schooners, someone brings up the name of the "Thomas W. Lawson". To many people this vessel represented a pinnacle of success in the evolution of sailing craft, while to others she was a monumental flop. Regardless of how one feels about the "Lawson", no history of the coasters would be complete without a good look at this tremendous steel windjammer.

The history of metal sailing hulls in America is not nearly as impressive as it is in Europe. While the English, German and French were busy building sailing ships of iron and steel, the Americans and Canadians stuck to the building of soft-wood vessels until, with few exceptions, the very end of the sailing ship era. The few exceptions were mostly with square rigged vessels, such as Sewall's ships of steel, built in Maine and earlier a few iron sailing ships which were built in the region of Philadelphia.

There were very few fore-and-aft rigged vessels possessing metal hulls that were originally built as sailing ships in the United States. The earliest metal hulled schooner that has come to light, so far, was the "Josephine", an iron hulled three-master, measuring 365 gross tons, 347 net tons, 129.3 feet in length, 34.0 feet beam and 10.5 feet in depth. The "Josephine" was launched in 1880 at Philadelphia, Pennsylvania, and for considerable time was owned in that city. The "Red Wing", a slightly larger three-master built in 1884, measured 437 gross tons, 415 net tons, 136.4 feet in length, 33.2 feet beam and 11.7 feet in depth, and was also launched and owned in Philadelphia. Of the two, the "Josephine" lasted the longest, continuing until well into the 1900's, although her ownership was changed from Philadelphia to Mobile, Alabama, shortly after the turn of the century. In 1888 the little 96 foot iron schooner "Sea Fox" was launched at Wilmington, Delaware.

Two small iron sloops, the "Pioneer", launched in 1885 and the "Climax", launched in 1888, were both built as coasting craft. These two little vessels were launched at Marcus Hook, Pennsylvania, and for a long time were owned at Philadelphia. The "Pioneer" measured 43 gross tons, 41 net tons, was 57.0 feet long, 21.0 feet beam and 4.6 feet in depth. The "Climax" was slightly larger, measuring 46 gross tons, 44 net tons, 58.4 feet in length, 22.2 feet beam and 4.6 feet in depth. The "Climax" remained sloop rigged until around 1910 and shortly thereafter went out of the register. The "Pioneer" had a somewhat different career, being rerigged as a two-masted schooner between 1896-98, and then between 1901 and 1905, being stripped of masts and sails, she was converted to power. In 1968 she again made her appearance as a two-masted schooner after extensive rebuilding, attesting to the durability of iron hulls.

Other iron schooners and sloops were in operation in the eastern United States; however, even though they were being used for commercial purposes, they had either not been built for such purposes, or were vessels rerigged, as in the case of some iron schooners built originally as steamers. The vessels falling into this category are not, of course, listed among metal hulled vessels originally built as sailing craft.

It is my belief that the first steel hulled schooner so constructed on the east coast of the United States, was the mighty "Thomas W. Lawson", launched in 1902. She was followed by two more steel fore-and-afters in the United States and one in Canada, but according to available records, there was none built earlier. The two American steel schooners that followed the "Lawson", were the "William L. Douglas" and the "Kineo", which have already been discussed. The Canadian vessel was the steel three-masted schooner, "James William", launched at New Glasgow, Nova Scotia, in 1908. She measured 440 net tons, 146.4 feet in length, 33.5 feet beam and 12.7 in depth.

The "James William" was in operation as late as 1934. Unhappily, she went aground near Clarke City, Quebec, and became a total loss. At the time she was owned by John C. Campbell of Summerside, Prince Edward Island and was loaded with pulpwood. She was a good sailor, making some fast passages, however, her building cost was so high that, following her launching, no other attempts were made in Canada to build steel sailing ships.

52

When comparing the other metal schooners to the "Lawson", one begins to realize how truly gigantic was this unique sailing vessel. She was 1,510 gross tons larger and almost 60 feet longer than the "William L. Douglas". She was the first and only windjammer to carry seven masts, and whether successful or not, she would rate a first place in maritime history just on size alone.

The "Thomas W. Lawson" was designed by B. B. Crowninshield and was built by the Fore River Ship & Engine Co., of Quincy, Massachusetts. This vessel was largely the brainchild of Captain John G. Crowley and was named after Thomas W. Lawson, famous financier and one of the principle backers of the vessel. The keel for this huge schooner was laid in 1901 and she was launched during the following year with her tremendous steel lower masts already in place. The "Lawson" measured 5,218 gross tons, 4,914 net tons, was 375.6 feet in length, 50,0 feet beam and 32.9 feet in depth.

She had two complete decks, including a large main, or well deck, with a raised poop and forecastle head. In addition to the full decks, there was in the hold, a tier of widely spaced beams. She had a wheel house, as in other Crowley vessels, but the houses on her main deck were arranged in a different manner than was common on other large schooners. Her foreward house was tied into the forecastle head, the deck of which ran aft of the foremast. Further aft, at the base of the fifth mast, was another house and immediately aft of this was another, smaller house at the base of the sixth mast. The seventh mast, called the Spanker by schoonermen, was at the forward end of the main cabin and following this was the wheel house. Over the stern, hung on heavy metal davits, was the motorized yawl boat. There were no turned stanchion rails on the "Lawson", the main deck being confined behind solid bulwarks and both the forecastle and the poop were bordered by a pipe stanchion and rail arrangement.

With the exception of her topmasts, spars and decks, which were hard pine over steel, the "Lawson" was steel throughout. She had a double bottom, 4 feet deep, which was capable of holding 1,069 tons of water ballast. She had all the latest in up to date machinery for working the vessel, handling cargo and operating the pumps. Even her steering gear was operated by steam. She not only had electricity and a telephone hook-up, but in addition, had steam heat for the crews quarters.

Her ground tackle was of the heaviest, each stockless anchor weighing 10,000 lbs. and being attached to 2¾ inch chain. Her steel lower masts, weighing almost 20 tons apiece, were 135 feet long and 30 inches in diameter, with the exception of the foremast, which was 33 inches in diameter. Her topmasts were 58 feet long, which meant that the heads of these masts were almost 150 feet above the deck. She had an 85 foot steel, bowsprit which carried a dolphin striker and when she set her full suit of sails, she had an area in excess of 44,000 square feet of canvas exposed to the wind.

The names of the seven masts carried by the "Lawson" have caused considerable debate in seafaring circles and this is one debate that has never been settled and probably never will be. Every authority that comes along has a different way of naming the masts. From time to time, various members of the officers and crew who had served aboard the "Lawson", were qucried as to the correct names of her masts and even they could not agree. Let it suffice to say, that in all probability they were not named after the days in the week and more than likely, in as much as new hands were continually coming aboard, the masts were probably referred to by number more often than by name.

The "Lawson" took three months to fit out and finally, on September 8, 1902, she was towed to an anchorage at South Boston, her home port. From waterline down, she was painted red, her topsides were light steel gray, inside of the rails and bulwarks were white, and the houses were white with green tops. With her varnished decks, yellow masts and her topmasts scraped and slushed and her spars scraped and oiled, she must have made a most colorful picture. She was built at a cost of upwards of $250,000 and after arriving at Boston from Quincy, went immediately into the coal trade in command of Captain Arthur Crowley, brother of Captain John G. Crowley. Captain Arthur Crowley did not stay with the "Lawson" very long however, and was soon followed by Captain Emmons Babbitt.

When in ballast, the "Lawson" drew 12 feet of water. Fully loaded with 9,000 tons or more, of coal, she drew in excess of 29.5 feet of water and this fact alone kept her away from many of the coastal loading ports. Newport News, Virginia, was about the only place where she could take on a full cargo and still stay afloat. She had the misfortune of going aground several times in various places along the coast, which did much to hurt her reputation as a competent coaster.

The "Lawson", in fact, was anything but a typical coasting vessel and should not be compared with the other schooners in the trade. Her sailing qualities will always be subject to question. Her designer B. B. Crowninshield, claimed she could sail well when loaded, but was rather crank when light. In light winds she very often refused to come about and in order to change tacks, she had to wear around by going down wind and jibing over, or she would have to be "club hauled", a term used for changing tacks through the use of her anchor. Neither of these methods were prone to endear her with her officers and crew.

Certainly when light, her massive freeboard must have made her something to cope with on a wind. Her high, unattractive bow, besides hindering her sailing qualities, did little to enhance her already bulky looks and how anyone could call the "Lawson" a pretty, or even a handsome vessel is beyond comprehension.

The "Thomas W. Lawson" stayed in the coal trade until 1906, when she was converted to an oil tanker by the Newport News Shipbuilding Co. She was then leased to the Sun Oil Co., the lease being for a period of five years. She had been shorn of her topmasts and sailed, or rather, was towed most of the time, between Port Arthur, Texas and Marcus Hook, Pennsylvania. During this period she was under the command of Captain Elliot Gardner. At one time while loading oil at Sabine Pass, Texas, she suddenly rolled over and was righted only with great difficulty; improper ballasting being blamed for the accident.

Finally in the fall or 1907, fate caught up with the big schooner. She was chartered to the Standard Oil Co., for a trans-Atlantic trip in an attempt to compete with the steam tankers, which at the time were trying to force higher freight rates. Also the "Lawson" acquired a new captain named George W. Dow, who was a native of Hancock, Maine, and an experienced deep-water seaman.

A rather interesting, but tragic story is told concerning the mate of the "Lawson", which proves the fact that it's bad business to be in debt, or to owe a favor to someone else.

Before Captain Dow took over the "Lawson" in 1907, he had for many years been in command of the bark "Auburndale". At one time, while on this vessel, Captain Dow signed on a young man named James Libby, to whom in time he took a liking. With Captain Dow's help, Libby did well and he eventually rose to the position of mate.

Libby later quit the sea, was married and acquired a good job ashore with Armour & Co., of Boston. He was very much the picture of the sailor who had swallowed the anchor and had turned his back upon the sea. However, when Captain Dow took command of the "Lawson", he was in need of a responsible man for chief mate and he wasted no time in contacting Libby in Boston and asking him to fill the job. Libby was extremely reluctant to go, but feeling he owed the Captain a debt for his previous help and encouragement, he finally accepted, reporting on board the "Lawson" with second mate Crocker, on November 4th, at Philadelphia. In this way Libby paid his debt to Captain Dow. It was destined to be a debt paid at a high price, for Libby's decision was to cost him his life.

In the 10 days following, the "Lawson" took on board a cargo of 2,003,063 gallons of oil which was valued at $71,000. Having had her topmasts replaced, she was now ready for her voyage. With her crew of 18 men of mixed nationalities, six of whom were picked up at the last minute, she towed to sea on November 19, 1907, in charge of the tug "Paraquay".

Off the Delaware Capes she cast off her tow line and set sail on the wintery Atlantic. Heading for England, she ran into winds of hurricane force off Newfoundland and her troubles started. With icy blasts tearing at her with velocities in the neighborhood of 80 and 90 mile an hour, the "Lawson" began to lose her sails and was forced to run before the storm. In a few days she was down to bare poles and her lifeboats were gone.

With the storm showing no sign of letting up, the "Lawson" continued at its mercy with no one being sure of their position due to the impossibility of taking a sight. They kept the laboring seven master headed to the east as best they could and awaited the pleasure of the weather. Finally, after many days, the storm began to show signs of losing some of its steam, although the sky continued dull and overcast. On December 12th, they made soundings and the next day land was sighted. Both anchors were then let go and were paid out to 75 fathoms of chain cable.

Captain Dow had hoped to make his landfall 10 miles south of Bishop Rock, near the approach to the English Channel. Due to the fog and drizzle, however, he had been prevented from obtaining an accurate fix for 48 hours and he found himself anchored in Broad Sound, to the northward of the light with the wind blowing light northwesterly. This area is near Lands End and a rocky group known as the Scilly Islands. When the "Lawson" brought up to her anchors, she was riding precariously close to one of these stoney clumps, known as Annet Island.

With the surf booming on the rocks, the situation was not good and those watching from the shore were fully aware of Captain Dow's predicament. If the wind picked up, the waiting rocks might be fed another vessel. They had seen such happenings before.

The St. Agnes lifeboat was soon launched and arrived alongside the "Lawson" about 4 p.m. The coxswain inquired as to whether Captain Dow wanted any assistance and the Captain replied that he did not think so at the moment, feeling his anchors were adequate for the job at hand. There was a Trinity House pilot aboard the lifeboat named W. Cook Hicks and he, with some difficulty, was put on board the rolling schooner.

In a very short time it was apparent that the wind was increasing and within an hour or so, was blowing strong. The anchors were paid out to 90 fathoms of cable. The St. Mary's lifeboat arrived and made an attempt to get alongside of the plunging schooner. The main mast on the lifeboat was snapped off against the "Lawson" before anyone could prevent it and the lifeboat had to pull clear. Captain Dow requested them to return to shore and telephone for a tug as the situation was becoming more serious by the minute.

The St. Agnes lifeboat, which had been standing by, also had to leave because of a sick crew member aboard, but before departing told those on the schooner to send up a rocket if help was needed.

By midnight a real snorter of a gale was tearing through the rigging of the struggling "Lawson", sending big seas rolling past to crash with a roar on the rocks, barely a half mile astern. The crew, realizing that things of dire consequences were in the making, put on their lifejackets.

At 1:15 the port anchor cable parted with a snap and when Captain Dow ordered the rockets fired, Mate Libby found to his dismay, that they were wet and would not work.

The storm continued to increase to hurricane intensity with tremendous bursts of wind. At 2:30 a.m., in the midst of one of those screaming gusts, the starboard cable let go and thousands of tons of heaving metal swung off to the wind and sea.

Captain Dow immediately ordered all hands into the rigging, most of them lashing themselves forward. Engineer Rowe, Mate James Libby, Pilot Hicks and the Captain secured themselves further aft. Within 10 minutes the mighty "Thomas W. Lawson" was hurled on the rocks of Hellwether Reef, split in two between the 6th and 7th masts and rolled over and sank in deep water.

Hellwether Reef is an outlying ledge of rocks near Annet Island and one man, an English sailor named George Allen, was swept clear across the reef and slammed ashore on Annet Island, splitting his side open in the process. Although he was later discovered alive, he died in agony a short while after his rescue due to the terrible battering he had received.

Two other survivors, Captain Dow and Engineer Rowe, found themselves clinging to a wave washed rock, both badly injured, but alive. How they managed to get free from their lashings when the schooner rolled over, not even they could tell. Captain Dow had a broken arm and smashed ribs and Rowe was suffering the pangs of a broken knee cap. In spite of his pain, Rowe helped drag Captain Dow clear of the crushing seas, to a more secure position on the rock where they waited for daylight and possible rescue.

When the inhabitants of this rocky coast awoke next morning, they beheld the broken, upturned hull of the "Lawson" sticking above the water like the bloated belly of a dead whale and they knew it was all over for those on the big schooner.

Boats were soon launched to search for possible survivors. The son of the drowned Pilot Hicks was in the boat that found and rescued Captain Dow and Engineer Rowe.

Seventeen people died as a result of the wreck of the "Thomas W. Lawson" and fourteen bodies were recovered, all of which lie buried at St. Ives. Although the cargo was insured, the schooner was not and the loss to Lawson and his family was estimated at $150,000. Engineer Rowe outlived Captain Dow, dying on Cape Cod in the early 1960's, thereby cheating for over 50 years a fate that was shared by all but one of his comrades on that wild, winter night off Annet Island.

*Two Masted Schooners*

## Chapter X

## THE LAST TO BE BUILT

With the launching of the "Lawson", it might be said that the large schooner had finally reached its last stage of development. Even though the "William L. Douglas" was launched a year later and the greatest of all wooden vessels, the "Wyoming", was launched seven years following the "Lawson", it cannot be said that these two vessels really offered anything new as far as rig or hull was concerned.

Barges were steadily cutting into the trade for which the large schooners were built and barges could be operated cheaper than could the big sailing vessels. Where a large schooner might require a crew of 10 or 12 men, the same size barge could be efficiently manned with a crew of only four.

If the First World War had not come along, one wonders how many large schooners might have gone down the ways after 1914, for their production had already greatly decreased after 1909. There is little doubt but that the war's heavy demand for anything that would float, sparked the last major effort in the building of wooden sailing vessels.

However, by the time the demand for vessels was felt, there were not many men left who could build them. Many of the old timers had either passed away or had moved into other fields, away from coastal areas. The younger generation, seeing the handwriting on the wall early in the twentieth century, had turned their backs upon the sea and shipbuilding and went seeking jobs with a better future. Many of the Down East yards that had turned out handsome fore-and-aft craft, by the time war was declared, were little more than weed patches with a few rotting pilings sticking out of the mud to mark what was left of wharves and ways. A few of the yards had managed to hold on, building an occasional small vessel and hoping for better times and when the call for shipping finally came, they were not only flooded with work, but they had to help other yards by passing on the know-how of wooden sailing ship construction.

During and shortly after the war, and in addition to those built in the old yards, some fairly large schooners were constructed in places that had never built large coasting vessels before. Wilmington, North Carolina, Brunswick and Savannah, Georgia, Jacksonville, Florida, Handsboro and Gulfport, Mississippi, and Beaumont, Texas, just to mention a few, can all lay claim to building four-masted schooners as a result of the World War I shipping boom.

By 1920 however, time was rapidly over-hauling the builders of sailing vessels. The last five-master was launched in that year and in 1921 the last four-master went overboard. Not only was the building of large schooners coming to a halt, but so was the building of commercial sailing craft of practically all types. Only a few sailing fishermen were exceptions to this, they being one of the last types to be built.

Arthur D. Story in Essex, Massachusetts, was a well known builder of Gloucester fishermen and from his small yard came some of the most famous of these sleek vessels, the celebrated "Columbia" being one of his creations. However, although famous for fishermen, not many people realize that Story built a few coasters as well and it was Arthur D. Story who built and launched the last American three-masted schooner on the east coast.

This proved to be the "Adams" launched from the Story yard in 1929. The "Adams" measured 370 gross tons, 325 net tons, was 147.6 feet long, 30.8 feet beam and 13.3 feet in depth. She had a raised forecastle head and a short quarterdeck with a turned stanchion rail and carried a spike bowsprit.

In an interesting letter written to Mr. Charles F. Sayle of Nantucket, Mr. Dana Story, the son of Arthur D. Story, tells of the building of the "Adams".

"Father named the vessel for my mother's family. He built her to his own account, beginning as nearly as I can tell, in the late fall of 1920. Because there was no particular rush for it, they worked on the vessel as time allowed. By April, 1922, she had her forward deck laid and the raised deck aft was framed in. As 1922 was a rather slow year in the yards here, it appears that in the fall of that year, she was finished up, except for the joiner and finish work below. Then as there was no sale for the ship and since Father did not wish to operate her himself, she just sat there until the fall of 1928, I believe. At that time his other three-master, the "Lincoln", launched April, 1919, was rammed and rendered unfit for service, (the "Lincoln", according to the U. S. List of Merchant Vessels, was slightly larger than the "Adams", measuring 405 gross tons, 352 net tons, 143.9 feet in length, 31.2 feet beam and 13.2 feet beam and 13.2 feet in depth) so

Father finished off the "Adams" and launched her on April 13, 1929 in a North East snow storm. As I remember, the spars and rigging of the "Lincoln" were used in the "Adams".

"Father operated the "Adams" in the coastal trade until his death in March, 1932, at which time his estate sold the ship to Captain Louis Kenedy. An interesting account of his experience with her appeared in the Saturday Evening Post in 1953. I do not have her registered dimensions except that her gross tonnage was 370 and her net 325. I believe she was built to the same model as the "Lincoln" except that she was given a clipper bow."

According to the article in the Post, Kenedy was not at all happy with the "Adams". He purchased the vessel from the estate for only $2,000 and operated her in the salt trade from Turks Island. On one occasion he nearly lost the "Adams" on Turks Island when caught there in a hurricane, narrowly escaping to open water, where he succeeded in riding out the storm. Kenedy claimed that the "Adams" had been built of odds and ends and was structurally weak, which was one of the causes of her eventual loss. Certainly laying around in the yard for eight years, collecting rain water, was no help to her timbers, regardless of their original quality. Her structural character, notwithstanding, it came to pass in 1933 that the "Adams" was again caught in another severe Atlantic storm while loaded with salt. Her pumps were going continuously, but as the storm persisted, the leaks in the vessel kept getting worse. Finally, as the pumps were giving trouble and although she had received assistance from a passing steamer, it became apparent that her time afloat was numbered only in hours. Her crew of six decided to abandon her on December 11, 1933, near the Bermudas and all but one managed to transfer to a Scottish steamer, the "Blairest", of Glasgow, that was standing by. Unfortunately the mate of the "Adams" failed to survive, being swept away and drowned while attempting to get to the steamer. The "Adams" foundered only a few hours after she was abandoned.

The last Canadian three-masted coasting schooner was the "Mary B. Brooks" launched in 1926 at Plympton, Nova Scotia. The "Brooks" was a 214 net ton vessel and after some years of carrying lumber and pulp between New England and provincial ports, was diverted to the West Indian trades in 1938. She operated for several years in these island trades and was finally abandoned on the beach at Turks Island.

The Canadians launched one more three-masted schooner following the "Brooks" but this latter vessel wasn't built for the coasting trade. Her name was the "Venture" and she was launched in Nova Scotia in 1937 and was intended as a Canadian training ship. She looked more like the fisherman, "Bluenose", with an added mast, than she did a regular coaster. World War II halted her career as a training vessel and she was laid up. She subsequently made a couple of freighting trips to the West Indies, had her registry changed to Barbados and had her name changed to "Alfred and Emily". In 1948 she fitted out as a sealer. Her end came one night in October, 1951 while off the Strait of Belle Isle when her auxilary engine caught fire and her crew was forced to abandon ship.

While the "Adams" and the "Brooks" were the last three-masted coasters built in their respective countries, they were by no means the last to be in opera-

60

tion. The sailing coasters continued in service all through and after the Second World War, although the number to survive the war years was pitifully small.

As mentioned before, the last sailing coaster to be built in the United States was the little two-master "Endeavor", built in Stonington, Maine in 1938. As the history of the schooner began in colonial times with a two-masted craft which gradually evolved to a Goliath with seven masts, it then reversed itself and ended as it began, with the launching of a two-masted schooner.

*A Typical Launching*

## Chapter XI

## LET'S BUILD A SCHOONER

As America's seaboard towns grew in size, each was soon found to possess a shipyard of some sort. In this yard were repaired and built many of the vessels which were used for transporting goods necessary to the economy of the town and the surrounding countryside.

Fortunately for the early shipbuilders on the Atlantic coast, they did not have to go far afield for the raw materials necessary for ship construction. Untapped sources of lumber lay at their very doorstep, and although attacked mercilessly and often used wastefully, this great supply of timber was destined to last for many years of shipbuilding.

The process involved in the building of a sailing vessel became fairly standardized at an early date and were to remain virtually unchanged for most of the period of wooden shipbuilding in America. Whether a ship was built in the 1700's, the 1800's, or early 1900's, the basic approaches were much the same. No great amount of equipment was required in early shipyards, nor was much added as time passed. In most yards a power circular saw, a steambox, a blacksmith's forge and a couple of teams of horses or oxen for heavy hauling, were about all the heavy equipment necessary to the building of a sailing ship. Boring, planing and sawing were done by hand. It wasn't until the very end of the era, in the twentieth century, that the latter processes were done with power.

From colonial times, up until the Civil War, and even later in many yards, the sawing of the heaviest timbers was done by hand in a sawpit. Huge trees that had been squared with a broad ax, were carted or dragged by a team of horses, or oxen, to a sawpit where two men, one on top of the timber and the other underneath in the pit, worked a two handled saw up and down, slowly reducing the large bulk to sawn planks.

For many generations, while the supply lasted, New England builders had in their immediate neighborhoods all the oak, hackmatack (juniper), white pine, birch, fir and spruce they needed for shipbuilding and yard crews were frequently kept busy cutting timber for vessel construction during the winter months. The builders further south, in the region of the Chesapeake, made indiscriminate use of white oak, mulberry, pine, sassafras, chestnut and cedar.

After the War of 1812, southern builders were more inclined to the use of oak and cedar, with oak, hachmatack, pine and spruce still much favored in the north. Yellow pine and southern live oak were brought north as early as 1840, and soon proved very popular with the northern shipbuilders. The first northern vessels in which southern hard pine was actually used were built in 1838 by George Patten and William D. Sewall, at Bath. The pine considered best was the "long leaf" variety which was found in abundance in Georgia and Florida. By 1890, due to the great demand for this pine, its principal source had moved to the Florida Gulf Coast. Southern oak came from the Chesapeake Bay area and was shipped north for use as framing material. Lumber was not only shipped north from southern states, but was also shipped in from Canada and this trade in lumber, of itself began to make up a very important part of the coasting business.

Unfortunate as it is for today's model makers and marine historians, the sailing vessels built in the old days were not constructed from a carefully worked out set of plans. They were instead built from measurements taken from a half-model that was carved to represent in miniature, an exact formation of one side of the hull. The model was made of a series of laminated layers of wood called lifts which were parallel to the water planes and constructed so that it could be taken apart at the various laminations. It was carved by hand by an expert, and was the result of many, many previous models, and much trial and error over a period of many years. Models that had proven successful were remembered and successful characteristics were copied, while others, less successful, were changed. Certain characteristics were found to work best on vessels in particular trades and not so well in others.

Of course each model maker could not help but put a bit of his own personal artistry into his work and soon certain men gained preference as the designers of especially efficient types of coasters. Often these men had started their careers as shipwrights and took to modeling vessels as a side line, or part of their spare time work.

One of the famous model makers of the 1870's was Albert Winslow, who lived in Taunton, Massachusetts, and who was responsible for modeling most of the coal schooners hailing from that port between the 1870's and the 90's. These "Taunton Flyers" were distinctive vessels and were much admired and copied all along the Atlantic coast. Connecticut vessels copied the Taunton styles, discarding the old fashioned high freeboard and heavy square stern for the more sweeping sheer, lofty rig and generally improved looks of the newer vessels.

Later designers, such as John J. Wardwell, B. B. Crowninshield and John J. Alden, laid out fairly complete plans on paper, however the "half-model" was still used until the very end of wooden shipbuilding. Sail and other plans were also drawn and often the drawings and model were used together.

Although both Crowninshield and Alden designed coasters of various sizes, they were perhaps just as equally well known as yacht designers, many of Alden's designs proving so popular they are still going strong today.

The models usually were made of pine and indicated only one half of the vessels hull, depicting either the port or starboard side, hence the name "half model". They were usually carved to a ⅜ of an inch to 1 foot proportion, although occasionally ¼ of an inch to 1 foot was used.

Upon completion of the model, it was shown to the prospective owner or owners and of course, much discussion usually followed as to the merits of the proposed vessel. Often, alterations resulted from these discussions and finally when everyone was satisfied, the model was taken to the mold loft where measurements were taken from the model and laid out full sized on the mold loft floor. Wooden molds were then made and from these the wooden frames or "ribs" were fashioned, using the molds as patterns. The frames used in large vessels were not bent as were those used for small boat building. They were instead, cut pieces put together in overlapping sections, side by side, with the natural growth curve of root or limb being used wherever possible. These sections were pinned or bolted together and then awaited their erection upon the keel.

The keel was laid upon the building ways and the stem and sternpost then were hoisted into position by sheer-legs and bolted fast to the keel. The sternpost was usually nearest the water as it was common practice for most vessels to be launched stern first. The frames were then bolted to the keel and the whole skeleton of the vessel was tied together with battens, or stringers.

Copper bolts were used in many of the colonial vessels and iron bolts were usually used in the later vessels; however, the most common fastening found on all wooden sailing ships were wooden bolts called "trunnels", short for tree nails. When these wooden fastenings were driven home and wedged in frame or plank they stayed put. Not having the corrosive faults of metal fastenings and having the facility of swelling when becoming wet, they thereby maintained even a stronger grip than when first set in place.

There were literally hundreds of shipyards along our coastline. Some of these yards were small and often temporary operations, where a company gathered along some creek bank to build a vessel or two and then dispersed. Others however, were of a much more permanent nature, lasting for several generations and were often owned and operated by the same family. While practically all large yards built both square rigged and fore-and-aft rigged vessels, some yards seemed to show a skill or preference toward one particular type. The Bowkers of Phippsburg, Maine, for example, became well known for building three and small four-masted schooners, while Percy & Small of Bath,

64

Maine, were famous for their building of large schooners with four, five and six masts.

It was customary in many yards to build only in summer months and often large vessels took two summers to complete. The winter months were spent in cutting wood and getting materials ready for summer. The ships carpenters lived on credit and as was typical in Phippsburg, bought at a store owned by one of the shipyards. A work week was 55 hours long and the men were paid each Saturday noon for their time up to Friday night. Wages paid before World War I were from $1.25 to $1.75 per day for a ten hour days work. One can't help but remark, "how times have changed".

The cost of building a vessel around the year 1830, was upwards of $23 a ton. After 1861 the price rose to around $70 per ton and then finally settled back to about $55 per ton in 1880.

The work on the vessel in a yard progressed at a steady pace. Various work gangs performed highly specialized jobs. There were the carpenters who were expert workers with wood and who could join wood to the total exclusion of water. There were caulkers and riggers and the blacksmiths who turned out not only metal bolts and fastenings, but the metal work required in the rigging, such as bands, straps, rings and hooks and countless other parts too numerous to mention. The adze was an instrument that was much in demand and an experienced hand with the adze could stand a-top a spar, while rounding it, or smooth off a hull timber so perfectly, that no bump or mar could be seen or felt. The sour smell of oak, rigging tar and wood smoke permeated the air and the ground in the yard was hidden beneath a soft layer of pungent wood chips and sawdust. With the clang of the smithy's hammer, the thump of the adze, the ringing clatter of many caulking mallets and the general humming chorus of sawing and cutting, the yard was a bustling scene of industry from sun up 'til dark.

Gradually the frames of the vessel would disappear as she was planked in. Decks were laid and deck houses constructed. The larger schooners in late years had to be reinforced on the inside and huge keelsons, six or seven feet in height were set in the bottom of the hull over the keel. Sister keelsons were often placed on either side as an added stiffening agent. Diagonal iron strapping running obliquely over the frames was also used in an effort to overcome the bothersome hogging.

As the decks were closed in and cabins were finished, the necessary equipment needed for the operation of the vessel was brought aboard. The mighty windlass and heavy chain and anchors were made ready. In the forward house was located the forecastle, or crews quarters, and also there was a room for the donkey engine and engineer. The donkey was installed as soon as possible as it was used in the finishing and rigging of the vessel. If there was a midship house, this would contain the galley and carpenter shop and these were made ready to function before the launch. The main cabin, or afterhouse, was arranged in much the same way on most coasting vessels. It was half sunk into the deck abaft the spanker mast and foreward of the wheel and was usually the largest cabin on the vessel. It was decorated according to the tastes of the times, often with inlaid paneling of mahogany, oak, cherry, maple or other choice wood.

The captain's room was on the starboard side at the foot of the after companionway. It was large and well lighted and had a real bed, easy chairs, desk, dressers, closets, and all the comforts of home. Directly across the companionway, to port, was a bathroom with a tub and not infrequently there was both hot and cold water, thanks to the donkey boiler. The main cabin was forward of the captain's cabin and was fitted out like a parlor with upholstered furniture and plush carpets.

A large owner's room and two or three spare guest, or passenger, staterooms opened off the main cabin. The forward part of the after house contained the dining room, with the mate's room to port and the pantry and forward companionway to starboard. All the living quarters in the later schooners were heated by steam from the donkey boiler.

A short way from the spot where the schooner was being built, the masts and spars were in preparation. Usually these were made from single trees, although made up masts, that is, lower masts that were made in sections, were not unknown to the schooners. Usually, however, a single tree was squared off with a broad ax, then shaped octagonally, and finally rounded to the desired dimensions, except at the doublings, where the masts were finished square. Oregon Pine was much in favor for masts in the schooner afloat during the later years.

The "Lavinia Campbell", a pretty three-master built for the coal trade in 1883 by David Clark, at Kennebunkport, Maine, had lower masts of Oregon Pine which were 94 feet long and 28 inches in diameter. The mighty "Wyoming", by comparison, had lower masts that were 126 feet long and 30 inches in diameter, except for the foremast which was 32 inches in diameter. Her topmasts were 56 feet long and 16 inches in diameter, except for the fore topmast which was 21 inches in diameter. Her jibboom was 75 feet long by 20 inches in diameter, her bowsprit, outboard, 30 feet long by 30 inches across and her spanker boom was 78 feet long and 16 inches in diameter. The cost of the 3,730 gross ton "Wyoming" launched in 1909 was $190,000, against the 733 gross ton "Lavinia Campbell's" cost of $45,000 in 1883.

Although very few schooners carried figureheads, practically all had some decoration at the stem-head and stern, so it can be said that the ship carvers art was not lost with the increasing use of vessels of this rig. A schooner was painted and in the majority of cases, was rigged, prior to launching. There would be from two to four shrouds on each side of a mast, depending on the size of the schooners, and a topmast backstay and two topmast shrouds on each side of the various topmasts. The foremast on a typical four-master would carry four shrouds on each side of the lower mast and two topmast backstays, plus topmast shrouds. There would be ratlines rigged for each mast enabling the crew to go aloft when necessary. If a schooner carried five jibs, she would have that many jibstays or headstays, plus one, and from the top of doublings aft to the next mast was run a spring stay, cap to cap and a topmast and a preventer stay ran up to the topmast astern. Many of the later, larger schooners had what was called jumper stays, or sometimes cathead stays, which ran from the doublings on the foremast to a position corresponding to the position of the catheads, or where the catheads would have been on vessels not equipped with them. Each boom had a topping lift which prevented the boom from falling on the deck when the sails were not set. The swing of the boom to starboard or port was controlled by its sheet and boom tackle. Each jib had a sheet, port and starboard and very often the fore staysail and sometimes the main jib, had a club or boom attached to its foot. The rigging on the bowsprit had the usual bobstays, guys, footropes, etc., found typical on most wooden sailing ships. The gaff headed lowers were raised with two halyards, namely the peak and the throat and there were halyards and downhauls for all of the topsails, staysails, and jibs. Most of the heavy hauling on the big schooners was handled with the help of the donkey, however there were plenty of times and places on all of them where the old fashioned "pulley haul" came into play. Very often on a new vessel the sails were bent and she was in every way ready to put to sea immediately upon her entry into the water.

During her building, the schooner's owners and often her future captain, who was usually required to own a share or half share in his new command, would frequently be on hand to see the progress being made and to make sure that all was going according to specifications. Often the captain stayed with the new vessel until she was finished. In later days, a surveyor from the American Bureau of Shipping might periodically inspect the schooner as it was being built and would also check the quality of the materials going into her. This was done for insurance purposes and wooden vessels which complied with the highest standards set forth by this bureau were listed A-1 for 14 years. Vessels so listed were automatically insurable, while vessels that were not so listed had to be inspected and assessed for each voyage when insurance was required. The rules for construction set up by the American Bureau of Shipping, the Bureau Veritas, and Lloyds, were evolved over a long period of time and did much to improve the quality of vessel construction as well as standardizing the various parts.

As launching day drew nearer, the work in the yard increased to a feverish pitch. The day chosen was one in which the tide would be at its highest and conditions judged most opportune. The launching ways were made ready to be greased and again checked to make sure they would not sag or spread, causing the vessel to stick or fall over before she became water-borne.

Honored guests were invited to launch aboard and the person after whom the schooner was named was expected to supply the great pennant with the vessel's name on it, plus other necessary flags, all of which would be hoisted while the schooner was still on the ways. Sparkling in her new paint and bedecked with flags, the new craft waited for the big moment and the whole town turned out to witness the great event. Businesses were closed for the day and school was let out. It might as well have been, for the boys would have been there whether school kept or not. People came in wagons, buggies and on horseback from miles around and most all were decked out in their "Sunday best", for there was a gay holiday spirit in the air. Many would expect to see friends they hadn't seen in months.

As the time approached and all were aboard who were supposed to be and those on the christening platform at the bow made ready with rum or roses, depending upon the dryness of the state, a hush fell on the crowd. The "lanchin" was about to begin.

After a searching glance to see that all were ready, a command from the yard foreman issued forth, the shores were knocked out and a sweating gang on each side of the keel began steadily striking wedges with heavy mauls endeavoring to raise the vessel. When this was done the dog shores were knocked out and with a tremble, the vessel started to move down the ways. At this moment she was hurriedly christened.

Prior to this, a poem of sweet sentiment might have been read with regard to the schooner's future life, "on the billowing wave with her gallant crew", by the young lady who was to do the christening. In Maine, which was dry during the period of the launching of the big schooners, a bouquet of roses was generally an acceptable replacement for the time honored bottle of rum. The young lady was usually the daughter, wife, or niece of the owner, builder, or person after whom the vessel was named.

If all went well, the bouquet of roses was dashed against the ever faster receding bow of the schooner as the words, "I christen thee --" were called out. Nobody heard the naming, for amid the roar of the crowd, the blasts from the yard whistles, the waiting tug and other craft, the din was terrific. The new schooner gathered speed and on smoking ways plunged stern first into the water, sending forth a huge spray and wash that frequently inundated those who were careless enough to get too close.

Unfortunately, in spite of the care taken to check everything prior to a launching, sometimes things did not go as planned and the cheers of the crowd struck in their throats as the new vessel, instead of going into the water, came to a shuddering halt on broken or spreading ways.

Smiles turned to frowns and cheers to curses, as efforts were made to get the unlucky vessel moving again toward the waiting water. This was not always easy.

When Green Brothers Shipyard in Bridgeport, Connecticut, launched the four-masted schooner "Perry Setzer", on July 22, 1902, she was hailed as the biggest vessel built in that city up to that time.

With flags flying and the crowd cheering, the "Setzer" started on her slide to the water, when with a crash, the ways collapsed beneath her and she came to a sickening halt in the mud. Neither afloat nor ashore, she presented quite a problem. Sadly the crowd of spectators went home and the yard had to bring in salvage experts to help get her off. It took a hydraulic jack, a fleet of tugs, 175 empty oil drums and five days of frustrating hard work before she came free and then she grounded again while being turned around in the channel.

In spite of her hard luck start in life and the many superstitious views held toward her future, because of the bad launch, the "Perry Setzer" had a prosperous career, lasting well into the 1920's when she was sold to British interests.

When a vessel was launched there were always restraining lines placed on her to keep her from driving across the river or harbor and into the opposite bank. However, these occasionally failed and in at least one case, another vessel, an innocent bystander, was rammed by a frisky new schooner.

This happened when B. W. & H. F. Morse Shipyard at Bath, Maine, launched the four-masted "T. A. Lambert", on March 22, 1887. When the "Lambert" hit the Kennebec River, she kept right on going and went out and walloped the timber schooner "Lizzie B. Willey", which was peacefully minding her own business at anchor. Fortunately, not too much damage was done, however the Morse's had to repair the "Willey" at their own expense.

The Morse's put the "Lambert" into the coal trade, but she wasn't destined to last long. In 1888, the same storm that dismasted the "Gov. Ames" caught the unlucky "T. A. Lambert" and also took the masts out of her. For three days and nights her crew stayed with the derelict schooner, until they were finally taken off by the British Steamer "Glendonia", which landed them at Gibralter.

The big five-master, "Jennie R. Dubois", launched at Mystic, Connecticut, in 1902, had her launching get a bit out of hand as far as many of the spectators were concerned. The "Jennie R. Dubois" was christened by her namesake, who was the wife of a Providence, Rhode Island judge. She was christened with nothing less than champagne, which seemed to have a "heady" effect on the new schooner, for she hit the water with quite a splash.

To quote from a contemporary newspaper account:

"The plunge into the water broke all the ice along shore and fairly inundated the people close to the shore. A Providence drummer got buried up to his waist and a Stonington bank cashier was almost lost to sight when the tidal wave struck the wharf. Many women along shore could not escape the rushing water and were badly drenched".

The "Dubois" was a three-decked vessel designed to carry over 3,500 tons of coal or 2,000,000 feet of lumber. Unfortunately she also carried a jinx upon her back, for less than two years later, in September, 1903, she was rammed and sunk by the steamer "S. S. Schoenfels", off Block Island.

As a rule, however, in spite of all the worries at launching time, everything usually went as planned and the vessel made a spectacular splash into the water, her sternway was stopped in time to prevent grounding or damage, and everyone was happy.

While the new craft was in the stream, a splendid luncheon was served aboard for the benefit of the specially invited guests. Those guests usually included backers of the new vessel and their families, important members of the shipping fraternity, socially prominent people and local officials, and with some shrewd Yankee speculation, some potential backers of sailing craft might be there to see how impressive it was to be in on a new vessel. Usually the vessel's steward officiated at this function, or if a caterer was obtainable from some place nearby, the added impressiveness of this gentleman was acquired.

Frequently during the course of one of these luncheons, a few very special guests were invited into the sanctity of the captain's cabin to drink to the success of the new vessel and whether the state was dry or not, one can wager that they used something stronger than lemonade.

When the "Mertie B. Crowley" was launched at Rockland, in 1907, the Rockland Courier-Gazette, reported the following:

"It was a splendid launching, the most notable in Rockland's shipbuilding history. It was witnessed by the largest crowd that ever came to this city for that purpose. Estimates vary all the way from 6,000 to 10,000, but it was certainly somewhere between the two. . ., vehicles of every description brought in the sightseers. On board the six-master the Rockland Military Band was discoursing inspiring music. About an hour before the launching the crowd was reinforced by Boston Grand Army men and the Woburn Band, which also gave a concert."

Usually after a particular eventful launching, there was a grand ball held in the evening at the local hotel, opera house, or some equally suitable place. The entire town geared for this event as it was one of the big social affairs of the year. The local merchants, hotel keepers and other business establishments were also rubbing their hands in happy anticipation when such plans went into effect, for it meant a great deal to the town's economy.

After the launching of the history-making "George W. Wells", the ceremonies were completed with a dance at the opera house in the evening, which was given by the society women of Camden. The officers of the battleships "Kearsarge" and "Indiana", which were in the harbor, were among the guests and a grand time was had by all.

When the big five-masted "Singleton Palmer" was launched by George L. Welt at Waldoboro, Maine, on April 16, 1904, great plans had been made for a tremendous celebration in town. However, along with the launching...they had a blizzard!

The Lincoln County News in nearby Damariscotta, sadly reported the bad news. Although the launching itself went off in fine style; "The storm made a great difference to the town financially, for had it been a nice pleasant day there would have been quite a business at our stores, while as it was there was nothing. They were not the only ones to suffer. The ladies of the Baptist and Methodist societies had made preparations to feed large numbers at dinner and as it was they were obliged to abandon it entirely. Then the Hotel Savoy and the Bakery had also made great preparations for large numbers at dinner and they, too, were doomed to disappointment and loss. But that night at least, there was a proper dance in honor of the launching; it was well attended despite the inclement weather, about 60 couples participating, and a very pleasant evening was passed".

As mentioned before, many of the New England schooners were practically ready to sail when launched and once in the water their stay at their place of birth was a short one. Within a very few days, with a full crew aboard, the new vessel was towed to deep water by a puffing tug; the tow line was cast off and spreading white wings, she started on her maiden voyage.

*A Ram*

## Chapter XII

## SOME BUILDERS AND THEIR VESSELS

The building of coasting craft by builders both large and small, occurred all along the Atlantic coast and from early times, vessels for differing purposes were built both on order and on speculation. After the turn of the Twentieth Century, the rising cost of construction, due to the increasing cost of materials, gradually turned most builders away from building on "Spec". However, regardless of size or purpose, method in building or in financing, the numbers of shipyards in the east were very large.

To attempt the story of even the most prominent builders of coasters would in itself, entale a thick volume. There were just too many. However, a general look at various builders, large and small, who were located in different areas of our coast, would be of interest and will help in an overall understanding of coaster construction on our Atlantic seaboard.

Bethel, Delaware, or Lewesville as it was called before 1880, became well known as a southern shipbuilding center in the 1860's. This little town is located on the Nanticoke River and is miles from Chesapeake Bay, into which the Nanticoke flows. In order to reach the bay, a traveler from Bethel had to journey downriver and would have to pass through the state of Maryland before arriving on the bay itself.

A great many two, three and a few four-masted schooners came from the Nanticoke area. J. M. C. Moore, who, in company with two partners, operated a marine railway and shipyard at Lewesville, built many of these smaller vessels. He is also credited with designing the ram, a type of schooner peculiar to this region. No one knows for sure just how the "ram" came by its name, but it certainly was a distinct type as far as coasting vessels were concerned. They were rigged as three-masted schooners, with the exception of two large ones which were rigged with four masts. The original purpose for their strange construction was to enable them to transport loads of lumber through the 24 foot wide locks of the Chesapeake and Delaware Canal. As a result, all the early rams, regardless of their length, never exceeded 24 feet in beam. They were absolutely flat bottomed, wall sided, had a centerboard, and in most cases carried no topmasts or jibboom, thus enabling them to operate with two less in the crew. They were surely not the most beautiful of sailing craft and were intended to operate on the coastal waters in and near the bay. A few of the later rams did make some notably long passages "outside", but these were larger, beamier vessels, which in some cases carried topmasts and jibboom.

The first ram was the "J. Dallas Marvil" built by J. M. C. Moore at Bethel in 1889. This vessel measured 160 gross tons, 152 net tons, 112.8 feet in length, 23.6 feet beam, 7.4 feet in depth and was owned at Seaford, Delaware. On June 15, 1910 she collided with the steamship "S. Everett" off Sandy Point, Maryland, and sank.

Moore built many rams at both Bethel, Delaware and at Sharptown, Maryland, which was located further down the Nanticoke River. Sharptown, in addition to the rams and many two and three-masted schooners built there, was the birthplace of the majority of the eight four-masted schooners built in Maryland.

It is interesting to note that the Lewesville Marine Railway Yard, in the 1880's, converted four canal boats to three-masted schooners. These canal boats were all built in Hamburg, Pennsylvania, on the Raritan Canal, and might possibly have been the inspiration for the rams.

A ram was built, on the average, in 90 days time. When compared to the six or eight months required for vessels further to the north, (for example the 114 foot, "Peaceland", a three-master launched in 1919 at Annapolis Royal, Canada, took 146 days in building) it can be seen that the rams were a much less complicated sailing vessel.

A typical ram usually possessed a short foc'sle-head-deck, followed by a deck house at, or just abaft the foremast. The main deck was large and the hatches surprisingly small. The main cabin was aft on a short, raised quarter deck and some of the rams had a turned stanchion rail around their quarter deck. For sail, they carried only two or three jibs and the three lowers. In all there were about 27 of these rams built in the Nanticoke River area.

The last ram to be built was the "Granville R. Bacon", which was launched in 1911, at Bethel. The "Bacon" measured 385 gross tons, 339 net tons, 133.0 feet in length, 31.6 feet beam, 11.8 feet depth and was owned at Seaford, Delaware. She was the last sailing vessel built by J. M. C. Moore and was wrecked on December 20, 1933 at Weekapaug Point, Rhode Island.

Before the launching of the "Granville R. Bacon", the yard had been sold and the only vessels which were to follow were some barges, the last two of which were launched during World War I. J. M. C. Moore, who supervised construction on every vessel built at the yard, died in 1928.

Unlike many New England launchings, the vessels built on the Nanticoke were launched unrigged and in some cases went over sideways, due to the confines of the river. Most of the old time record books show about 15 men were employed in the building of a ram, with wages being 20 cents an hour for a ship's carpenter. These men were expected to work a 10 hour day, five days a week, plus 5 or 6 hours on Saturday.

It is interesting to discover that of the several thousand three-masted schooners built here and in Canada, the only one afloat today is a ram named the "Victory Chimes". The "Victory Chimes" was originally named the "Edwin and Maud" and was built by Moore and launched in Bethel in April, 1900. She measures: 208 gross tons, 178 net tons, 126.5 feet in length, 23.8 feet beam and 8.6 feet in depth; measurements typical of the earlier rams. Like many of her sisters she eventually wound up in the "dude" windjammer fleet. In 1954 she was sold to Captain F. B. Guild, of Castine, Maine, who changed her name and is using her today as a party cruise ship for summer trips along the Maine coast.

Throughout the Chesapeake Bay region, wherever there was a suitable site, there is usually a record of a schooner or schooners, being built. Two, three and four masted schooners were constructed, with two-masted vessels far outnumbering the other types. However, the number of three-masted schooners launched was not small, with six vessels of this rig and one four-master being built as far inland as Alexandria, Virginia. Alexandria is located on the Potomac River and is not too far below the site of our nation's capital, Washington, D. C.

Several of these Virginia schooners were built by Maine men who had come south following the slump at the end of the 1870's. As mentioned before, much of the white oak that had become popular with New England shipbuilders was to be found in the Chesapeake area. The men from Maine came to Alexandria to try and experiment with the building of schooners near the source of the timber supply and also to cut material for use in northern yards.

The first coaster built at Alexandria was the "Robert Portner", a 631 ton, three-master, built in 1876 by the Alexandria Marine Railway and Shipbuilding Co., and owned by the vessel's namesake, Mr. Robert Portner. The "Robert Portner" was considered a large vessel at the time of her building. Unfortunately she did not last long. The year following her launching, under the command of Captain David Strange, of Marshfield, Massachusetts, the "Portner" was lost in the Indian Ocean with a cargo of rice from India to England. This may seem a bit far from home to those who are inclined to think of our coasters as they were operated on the Atlantic seaboard after the turn of the century. However it wasn't at all uncommon for three-masted schooners to make long deepwater voyages during the 1870's, '80's and '90's. Captain Strange and his crew had a most difficult and trying time getting back home after the loss of their vessel.

"Strange" to relate, but Captain David Strange had a brother named Charles Strange who was captain of the three-masted schooner "Henry A. Paul", a vessel very similar in size to the "Portner". As fate would have it, the "Paul" was wrecked at Tristan d'Acunha while bound for Capetown and both of the Strange boys arrived home about the same time; both without a ship and both telling much the same "strange" story.

The prime concern of the Alexandria Marine Railway and Shipbuilding Co., was the maintenance and repair of the many coal schooners which were working out of Alexandria and Georgetown during the 1870's. Shipbuilding was really a secondary function and it wasn't until 1880 that a second vessel was built. This was the three-masted, 678 ton, "James B. Ogden", which, as had been the "Portner", was owned in New York.

On July 1, 1882, Mr. William H. Crawford, recently of Kennebunkport, Maine, and the partnership of Crawford & Ward, launched the wopping big 835 gross ton, "Ellwood Harlow" from the Alexandria Marine Railway and Shipbuilding yard, which he had leased from its new owners, John P. Agnew & Co., coal dealers. The "Ellwood Harlow" was completed in slightly over four months time, was three-masted, had a centerboard and cost $38,000.

Mr. Charles Ward, also of Kennebunkport, and the other half of the Maine partnership, also went to Virginia and started building at the Potomac Yard, also located in Alexandria. On December 4, 1882, he launched the three-masted schooner, "James Boyce, Jr.", a 729 gross ton vessel and one of the few schooners fitted with a figurehead. On July 9, 1883, Ward launched the three-masted "Wilson & Hunting", a 418 ton vessel intended for the Jacksonville lumber trade and already mentioned as the first schooner to carry a wheelhouse.

The Agnew yard, with Crawford as foreman, then launched the "William T. Hart", one of the early four-masters and the only one to come from Alexandria. The "Hart" was launched on July 21, 1883 and measured 943 gross tons, 896 net tons, was 198 feet long, 38 feet beam and 19.6 feet in depth. She had a centerboard and cost $45,000. The "Hart" had only one owner, this being Captain Jos. F. Davis, of Somerset, Massachusetts.

There was only one more large sailing vessel launched at Alexandria and that was the three-masted "Henry S. Culvert". She was started by Crawford, but was finished by Ward because of an illness suffered by Crawford during her building. She went into the water of the Potomac on October 27, 1883 and grossed 753 tons. Most of her shares were owned in Taunton, Massachusetts, and she was under the command of a young man eventually to carve quite a name for himself in the coasting business. This was Captain John G. Crowley, who also held 1/16 share in the vessel.

The experiment of bringing the know how to the timber source didn't work. Too many articles, such as anchors, hoisting engines, windlasses, sails and other expensive materials had to be shipped in. After the launching of the "Culver", no other sailing vessels of any consequence came from the Alexandria area.

Charles Ward eventually returned to Kennebunkport and leased a shipyard where he continued building wooden vessels until 1918. His first contract upon his return from Virginia was for the four-masted schooner "Sagamore", which he launched in 1891. The "Sagamore" was the largest of the schooners built on the Kennebunk River, measuring 1,415 gross tons and 219.5 feet in length. In 1917 he built the 299 net ton, three-masted auxilary schooner, "Charles B. Wiggin", and in 1918 he launched the 719 net ton, four-masted "Kennebunk", which was the last schooner to come from this famous shipbuilding port.

74

The last four-masted schooner built in the Chesapeake Bay area was the "Anandale", launched at Sharptown, Maryland in 1919. During the next year the last large sailing vessel to be launched in this region went in the water. This was the "Lillian E. Kerr", which was launched as a three-master at Pocomoke City, Maryland in 1920. She was built by E. James Tull, and measured 548 gross tons, 475 net tons, was 160.2 feet in length, 35.5 feet beam and 12.7 feet in depth.

Tull built the "Kerr" exceptionally strong, however she was rather large for a three-master and often proved difficult to handle. She was generally considered to be a slow sailer, in one instance taking 41 days to go from Georgetown, South Carolina to New York. However she could stand driving and was reputed to be fairly stiff, when required to stand up to a hard breeze. She demonstrated this ability by sailing through the hurricane of September 21, 1938, off Cape Hatteras, arriving at La Have, Nova Scotia with only minor damage and loss of a few sails.

During the late 1920's and the early '30's, the "Lillian E. Kerr" was engaged in the general coastwise trade under the management of C. A. and B. F. Small Corporation of New York. Late in 1937 she was sold to Captain James L. Publicover of Dublin Shores, Nova Scotia, who planned to operate her in the West Indies trade with his son William as captain.

On April 17, 1938, the "Kerr" arrived at Robar's Shipyard at Dayspring, Nova Scotia, where she was rigged as a four-masted schooner. Captain Publicover felt this would make a better sailer of the "Kerr" and also make her easier to handle. While this experiment did not do much to increase her speed, it was found helpful in making the schooner easier to handle, so the expense was felt justified.

Unfortunately, before Captain Publicover could do much with his plan for working the "Kerr" in the West Indies, he lost his other four-master, the "Laura Annie Barnes", when the "Barnes" misstayed and struck on Tuckernuck Shoal, northwest of Nantucket Island, on January 17, 1939. Captain Publicover then decided to put the "Kerr" into the Nova Scotia to New Haven, Connecticut, run in which the "Barnes" had been engaged. This involved carrying lumber or baled pulp wood west and returning light or with coal that was loaded at New York. The "Kerr" entered this trade and continued to operate successfully for the next four years.

On November 13, 1942 while sailing from New York to Halifax with a cargo of coal, she was run down and sunk during the night by the steamer "Alcoa Pilot", which was part of a westbound convoy in the Gulf of Maine. Due to war time regulations, none of the vessels in the convoy were allowed to stop or render any assistance.

The "Alcoa Pilot" crashed into the "Kerr" at 12:15 a.m., in spite of the fact that the "Kerr's" running lights were lighted and the visibility was good enough for those in the convoy to see that she had, in addition to her lowers and jibs, three of her topsails set. The "Kerr" sank in two minutes and the cries of her doomed crew were plainly audible to those on the departing convoy.

After the convoy had passed about three miles from the scene, one of its members, the steamer "Cyrus Field" was sent back to search for possible sur-vivors. About one half mile from where the sinking had occurred, the "Field" lowered a boat and picked up one man who blurted out that he was the only one saved out of seven and then lapsed into unconsciousness. Although he was taken aboard the steamer as quickly as possible and given all the medical aid available, he died at 2:15 a.m. without ever regaining consciousness. He had been floating in those wintery seas about 55 minutes before being picked up. Although wreckage was sighted, no other members of the crew of the "Lillian E. Kerr" were found. The body of the only one picked up was later put ashore at Cape Cod.

Vessels such as the "Lillian E. Kerr" speak well for the builders of Chesa-peake Bay. Commencing with their famous, sleek pilot schooners and Baltimore Clippers, the schooner builders in this area continued to turn out fore and aft rigged craft until the cessation of sailing ship building in the 1920's. As they built two-masted schooners in the beginning, so they finished by building two-masters in the end.

The Chesapeake two-masters were usually smaller than their northern counterparts and were most distinctive in style, their builders giving them the long, deep clipper bows with carved fiddleheads and trailboards still to be seen on small Chesapeake oyster craft today.

There were in fact, two types of two-masted schooners in this area. The pungy, was a direct descendant of the pilot boat model of earlier days, having the low freeboard, raking masts and deep draft aft, while the other type was the shallow draft, centerboard schooner.

Pungies were used in the local fisheries for a while, but were found too deep to compete successfully with the shallower vessels and most ended their days carrying freight. Most of the centerboard schooners had the typically long south-ern bow and straight masts and were used both for fishing and for freighting. These two-masters were built all over Chesapeake Bay, coming from such ports as Cambridge, Baltimore, Madison and the Solomon Islands, just to mention a few. They were turned out steadily until the turn of the twentieth century, after which time their output slowly dwindled.

A typical two-masted schooner of the Chesapeake Bay area was the "Bo-hemia", built by T. Kirby, at St. Michaels, Maryland in 1884. The "Bohemia" was reported to have cost $7,700 and measured 71 gross tons, 61 net tons, was 81.3 feet in length, 23.8 feet beam and 6.0 feet in depth. She was built for J. H. Steele of Chesapeake city and John Chelton, who was her captain during the early part of her career. Under the command of Captain Chelton, she freighted wheat, corn and fertilizer, continuing in this trade until the death of Captain Chelton. She changed hands several times thereafter and was rebuilt in 1914 at Beacham's Shipyard in Baltimore. In 1915 she was bought by Captain Edgar B. Riggin, who used her in part for freighting and for dredging oysters. In the middle 1920's, Captain Riggin discontinued dredging for oysters and stayed in the business of carrying freight throughout the region of Chesapeake Bay. In September, 1947, Captain Riggin sold the "Bohemia" and her condition rapidly started to go down hill. She eventually wound up on a mud flat in Sarah Creek,

Gloucester County, in the early 1950's. There abandoned and forgotten, she slowly went to pieces.

From the Chesapeake, northward, one can find traces of a great number of shipyards that were engaged in the building of coasting craft; from small two-masters to the big six-masted goliaths of Maine. Abbott's shipyard for example, at Milford, Delaware was 15 miles up the narrow and winding Mispillion River, but turned out schooners such as the four-masted "George May", a 654 gross ton vessel launched in 1900. The four-masted "Albert F. Paul", launched in 1917 and grossing 735 tons was also a product of the Abbott yard. She had a long career, outlasting most of her sister coasters until she finally set sail from Turks Island on February 22, 1942 and was never heard from again.

Jackson and Sharp, in Wilmington, Delaware, turned out many fine coasters as did Morris and Mathis of Camden, New Jersey. Coasters were built in New York, Staten Island and Long Island. The little "Wm. P. Boggs", a two-masted schooner of 35 gross tons and 56 feet in length, was built in 1864 at Staten Island. She was typical of many of the vessels built in the area that were intended for the brick trade. She eventually wound up as a single hander, carrying freight to Nantucket.

J. M. Bayles & Son, builders at Port Jefferson, Long Island, from 1863 to 1891, launched the following commercial sailing vessels: two sloops, two brigs, three barks, one ship and 41 schooners. The schooners ranged in size from 129 to over 500 tons, with an average being somewhere near 350 tons per vessel. Setauket, Port Washington, and other places on Long Island, all contributed to the number of vessels intended as coastal carriers.

All along the Connecticut shore there was much construction going on, with towns such as New London, West Haven, Mystic and Noank leading the way. Mystic in particular earned a fine reputation as a shipbuilding center in Connecticut. In nearby Noank, the Palmer Yard was the largest yard between New York and Boston during the last quarter of the 19th century. The Mystic Ship-yard and the Gilbert Transportation Co., were building large coasters after the turn of the century and it should be noted that most of the five-masted schooners not originating in Maine, came from this area. Ports on Narragansett Bay, Boston, Newburyport, Portsmouth, New Hampshire, and many more all added greatly to the coasting fleets and to try and mention all of them, or name all the builders would be much too big a task; suffice it to say there were many hundred.

There isn't much doubt however, that if a choice had to be made giving top honors to a state for building the biggest coasters and the most in terms of numbers, Maine would lead the field in both catagories, beating any other single state. From the pinnace "Virginia", built in the early colonial period, right down to the little "Endeavor", the last of the sailing coasters to be launched, Maine built many, many hundreds of coasting vessels of all types and sizes.

The Crosbys of Bangor, the Bowkers of Phippsburg, the Minotts of Phippsburg, H. M. Bean of Camden, Dunn and Elliott of Thomaston, Cobb and Butler of Rockland, David Clark of Kennebunkport, these are just a few of the many great builders of schooners to be found along the shores of Maine. However, if one port in particular had to be chosen as the leading light of wooden sailing ship building; Bath, Maine is the one most likely to be selected. Bath was the home of the giant schooner builders.

Percy & Small, from 1894 to 1920, sent 41 schooners into the waters of the Kennebec River. Of these, 19 were four-masters, fifteen were five-masters and seven were six-masters. Goss, Sawyer & Packard, besides building square riggers, built somewhere in the neighborhood of 96 schooners---mostly three-masters. The New England Shipbuilding Co., which succeeded them, launched 22 schooners and the New England Co., which succeeded the previous company, launched 44 schooners carrying from three to five masts, making a total of 162 schooners from 1866 to 1908. Kelley, Spear & Co., launched 51 schooners, most of which were four-masters, from 1887 to 1912, when they concluded with the launching of the "William C. May". Although they continued in business until 1923, they built only schooner barges for the remainder of the company's existance. The grand total constructed by these 3 groups is 254 coasting schooners. This by no means includes all of the builders located in Bath, nor does it include the brigs, brigantines, barkentines and other square rigged vessels intended for any coastal work. It's small wonder that Bath earned for herself the title of, "The City of Ships".

Aside from the building of the big schooners, Maine turned out many hundreds of small coasters. Lubec, for example, built about 50 schooners for the coasting trade and of these, only two were three-masters; the rest being two-masters. Boothbay and many ports on Penobscot Bay turned out small coasters and as was the case on the Chesapeake, it is very difficult to find a level section of land on the Maine coast that does not have a history of shipbuilding. The Maine built two-masters however, were usually more burdensome craft than their southern counterparts and generally had more freeboard.

*House Flags*

PCM

## Chapter XIII

## THE SHIPOWNERS

Since the earliest days of shipbuilding in the United States, vessel property was usually owned in shares, commonly held by people in the vicinity of where the vessel was built. A share was 1/64 of the cost of the vessel and often various fractions of this amount, or a "part of a share", were sold. It was customary for the builder to hold several shares and often many of the tradesmen in town would also hold a share or two. Holding a share of a coasting vessel during the hey-day of the trade was considered one of the best investments available, however, very few vessels were owned outright by one person. Investors felt there was safety in numbers and preferred to spread their money around in a large group of vessels, lessening the chance of financial disaster in case any one craft should be lost.

As stated earlier, a captain usually had to own a share in the vessel over which he was in command. He was paid a monthly salary and also received a small percentage of the gross freight. Although one can find throughout the history of the trade, cases of ownership being held entirely by the captain of the vessel, this was usually true only with smaller vessels. As cost increased and vessels became necessarily larger, 100% ownership became increasingly difficult and vessels with more than three masts were commonly owned in shares. In the latter days of the coal trade a large five-master had one of her shares sold in excess of $2,000, which was not a small sum at that time, and excluded any shipmaster not given to frugality and the exercise of sound business judgement.

The salary of the captain of a large collier was in the neighborhood of $50 a month and he was usually paid about 5% of the gross freight. When this was added to his share of the vessel dividend, it could build into a tidy sum for the captain who was inclined to hustle and as a result the position of captain was eagerly sought after.

Some captains, more enterprising than others, invested their earnings in additional vessel property and gradually built around themselves a fleet of vessels which they more or less owned or over which they exercised a managing interest. Such a man was Captain Magnus Manson, of New Haven, Connecticut. The history of the Manson fleet was generously made available by Mr. H. Sherman Holcomb, a descendant of the Manson family, in a privately printed booklet written by H. Sherman Holcomb entitled, "Magnus Manson and the Benedict Manson Marine Co."

Magnus Manson was born June 25, 1829, the son of Thomas and Mary Manson of North Roe, Shetland Islands, Scotland. Around 1850 he arrived in New Haven, Connecticut, as a crew member on a vessel carrying coal. At New Haven, following a dispute, he jumped ship and went inland to find work as a farm hand until he was sure that his ship had sailed. He then returned to New Haven where he went to work on a vessel owned by H. W. Benedict & Son, coal dealers. Mr. Benedict took an interest in Magnus Manson and within a very short time he was given command of the "J. W. Hine", a small vessel owned by the Benedicts.

On March 2, 1859, Magnus Manson became a naturalized citizen of the United States. On June 14, 1860, he married Margaret Robertson Mowatt, of North Mavin, Shetland Islands, a girl he had known as a youngster and to whom he had written a proposal asking that she come to America and marry him. They were married upon her arrival at which time Captain Manson was in command of the schooner "Merritt".

He continued to command vessels in the coasting trade and in 1889 had his first schooner built which he named the "Agnes E. Manson", after his second child. From 1860 until February 1906, when the firm of Benedict-Manson Marine Company was formed, Captain Manson commanded or acquired an interest in many vessels owned by the firm of Benedict and Downs. Prior to the launch of the "Agnes E. Manson", Captain Manson was in command of the "James Boyce" and carried coal to Boston. Sailing in this trade often enabled a trip home to Connecticut while his vessel was being unloaded.

During the early 1890's, Henry W. B. Manson, the youngest son of Captain Manson, was at home and it was his job to see to the many chores around the house during the captain's frequent absences. One evening, an amusing incident occurred in the course of a visit with the family while his new vessel, the "Agnes E. Manson", was being unloaded. As the family was seated around the supper table, Captain Manson said Grace and did some quick checking on Henry, all in one breath:

"God bless this food to our use and us to Thy service, for Christ' sakes Henry have you greased the windmill?"

Upon the formation of the Benedict-Manson Marine Company, Captain Manson was elected its president and continued in this capacity until his death on October 24, 1909. The company was formed at a time when the competition from barges and steam colliers was being felt to an increasing extent and the new company was an effort of the existing sailing ship owners to meet this threat to their vessels. The Benedict-Manson Marine Company continued in business until December 13, 1916, when the stockholders voted to terminate its corporate existance. During the ten years of the company's operations they had control of no less than 27 schooners, all of which were three and four-masters, with the exception of the "Magnus Manson", a small five-master launched at Bath, Maine on April 2, 1904. The "Magnus Manson" was virtually ready for sea when launched and was commanded by Captain Daniel Tulloch of New Haven, who was Magnus Manson's brother-in-law. Although the vessels in the Benedict-Manson Marine Co., were primarily interested in the transportation of coal, they by no means held to this as an exclusive cargo. Any cargo that was an acceptable paying proposition was welcome, more especially towards the end of the company's career.

The last vessel owned by the company was the little four-master, "William E. Burnham", built by Cobb-Butler, in Rockland, Maine and launched in November 1909. She was sold to the Whitney-Bodden Shipping Co., of San Francisco in 1917 and foundered at sea on November 5, 1927 in Long. 21.9, Lat. 84.45.

A list of the Benedict-Manson Marine Company vessels is as follows:

| NAME | MASTS | GROSS TONS | WHEN BUILT | LAST REPORT |
|---|---|---|---|---|
| James Boyce | 3 | 453 | 1877 | Stranded Oct. 10, 1909, Maine |
| Bessie C. Beach | 3 | 341 | 1880 | Stranded Dec. 6, 1912, L.I., N.Y. |
| Zaccheus Sherman | 3 | 767 | 1880 | Stranded Feb. 28, 1913, N.C. |
| Helen H. Benedict | 3 | 770 | 1881 | Stranded Feb. 6, 1914, N.C. |
| James D. Dewell | 3 | 573 | 1882 | Lost prior to Sept., 1912 |
| Alice B. Phillips | 3 | 622 | 1883 | Sold April 15, 1916 |
| Childe Harold | 3 | 781 | 1886 | Torpedoed June 21, 1917 |
| Charles F. Tuttle | 3 | 776 | 1886 | Lost prior to Sept., 1912 |
| F. G. French | 3 | 184 | 1887 | Sold 1910 |
| Jennie E. Righter | 3 | 647 | 1887 | Sold 1916. Shelled by sub. Oct. 16, 1917. |
| George M. Grant | 4 | 1,252 | 1889 | Foundered Oct. 14, 1916, Bahamas |
| Massasoit | 4 | 1,377 | 1889 | Stranded Nov. 15, 1914, Va. |
| Lyman M. Law | 4 | 1,300 | 1890 | Sunk by sub Feb. 12, 1917, Mediterranean Sea |
| Howard B. Peck | 3 | 472 | 1890 | Stranded Feb. 15, 1908, L.I., N.Y. |
| Bayard Barnes | 4 | 1,005 | 1891 | Sold foreign Oct. 27, 1917 |
| James Davidson | 3 | 451 | 1891 | Foundered Aug. 26, 1911, S.C. |
| George E. Dudley | 3 | 407 | 1891 | Ashore Sept. 4, 1916, Iceland |
| Estelle Phinney | 4 | 922 | 1891 | Collision Dec. 27, 1907, N.J. |
| General E. S. Greeley | 4 | 1,306 | 1894 | Sold France Jan. 19, 1918 |

Benedict-Manson Marine Company Vessels (Cont.)

| NAME | MASTS | GROSS TONS | WHEN BUILT | LAST REPORT |
|------|-------|------------|------------|-------------|
| May V. Neville | 4 | 1,191 | 1901 | Foundered April 9, 1927 |
| Frank W. Benedict | 3 | 534 | 1902 | Sold foreign 1917 |
| Magnus Manson | 5 | 1,751 | 1904 | Sunk by sub May 25, 1917 |
| Dean E. Brown | 4 | 719 | 1907 | Missing Sept. 17, 1917 |
| Jessie A. Bishop | 4 | 754 | 1908 | Stranded Jan. 1, 1912, Fla. |
| Bertha L. Downs | 4 | 716 | 1908 | Sold Denmark in 1916 |
| Mary Manson Gruener | 4 | 715 | 1908 | Foundered Oct. 1, 1923 |
| William E. Burnham | 4 | 772 | 1909 | Sold 1917. Lost Nov. 5, 1927 |

A schooner captain with a little imagination and daring could raise himself to the position of principle owner or manager of a large fleet of vessels, if he were lucky and had the right backing. Captain Lorenzo Dow Baker, a coasting skipper of Wellfleet, Massachusetts, was one of those upon whom the glow of success shown brightly. In 1870, Captain Baker took a load of mining equipment on his first long voyage, to the tropical country of Venezuela in his newly purchased schooner "Telegraph". For a return cargo he picked up a load of bamboo on the island of Jamaica and while loading at Port Morant, he tasted a native fruit that was new and different to him. Captain Baker was very impressed with the taste of his discovery and thought upon the possibility of introducing the banana to North America. He accordingly bought a few bunches, but made the mistake of acquiring fruit that was already ripe and by the time he arrived at New York, they were completely spoiled.

Captain Baker was not a man to be easily discouraged and upon his return to Jamaica next year, bought a complete cargo of bananas, only this time he was sure to load only unripened, or green fruit. This second venture went from Port Antonio to Boston, arriving in good condition and immediately made a tremendous impression upon the people of the north, assuring the future success of Captain Baker.

Mr. George Baker, also of Wellfleet, was the financial backer for Captain Baker's second trip and when offered a choice of repayment on the loan, chose cash rather than stock in Captain Baker's newly formed company; much to the everlasting dismay of Mr. George Baker and his descendants.

During the course of the next ten years, Captain Baker added new vessels to his fleet and added coconuts to his return cargo as well as bananas. He prospered so well that in 1881 the Atlas Steamship Lines offered him a position as their agent. He took the job and henceforth shipped his cargos in their boats. Shortly after this he formed a partnership with his brother-in-law, Elisha Hopkins, also of Wellfleet, and they called their new enterprise, L. D. Baker & Co. Following this, Captain Baker organized the Standard Steam Navigation Co., of Boston, whose purpose was to supply bigger, faster boats for his perishable tropical cargos. Finally in 1885, the Boston Fruit Company was formed and anyone who held on to the stock purchased in this company eventually found themselves holding stock in the United Fruit Co., which was the final stage of Captain Baker's forethought and enterprise.

Not only did Captain Baker invest wisely in his own enterprise, but he also invested in the shipping activity of others and upon his death in 1908, he was found to be the largest single share-holder in the "Marie Palmer", the pioneer vessel in the famous Boston fleet of coasters, owned in part and managed by Mr. William F. Palmer. In fact Captain Baker and his estate owned shares in every single vessel of the Palmer fleet.

The vessels of the William Palmer fleet and those of the fleet of Nathaniel T. Palmer are often confused and it might be well to mention the fleet of Nathaniel T. Palmer before going on with the history of the Boston fleet. Mr. N. T. Palmer owned five four-masted schooners and one five-masted schooner. All of these were vessels built by him at Bath, Maine, for his own account and are listed in the following order, according to the year in which they were built:

| 1894 | four-masted schooner | Sarah E. Palmer | 1225 tons |
| 1894 | four-masted schooner | Augustus Palmer | 1287 tons |
| 1895 | four-masted schooner | Mary E. Palmer | 1526 tons |
| 1896 | four-masted schooner | William B. Palmer | 1805 tons |
| 1897 | four-masted schooner | Frank A. Palmer | 2014 tons |
| 1898 | five-masted schooner | Nathaniel T. Palmer | 2440 tons |

These schooners were primarily colliers and as can be seen were very large vessels, the "Nathaniel T. Palmer" being the second five-master to be built and much larger than her predecessor, the "Gov. Ames". Nathaniel T. Palmer died on March 18, 1904 and was buried at Brunswick, Maine. Following his death the vessels remaining in his fleet were taken over by J. S. Winslow & Co., of Portland, Maine. The last one to survive was the "Mary E. Palmer", which was lost at Casablanca, Morocco on Aug. 8, 1920. None of the vessels in Nathaniel T. Palmer's fleet, which was a Maine fleet, had anything to do with the fleet of William F. Palmer, which was a Boston fleet and which was not started until after the last of the Maine Palmers was built.

The story of the Boston fleet of Palmers is a most interesting one, especially since its managing owner, Mr. William F. Palmer appears to have had little actual contact with seafaring prior to his commencing as a ship owner. Mr. Palmer was a forty-one year old school teacher when he determined to go into the shipping business in 1900. During the 1890's he had been the headmaster of Bristol Academy at Taunton, Massachusetts, and as at that time Taunton was the center of the bituminous coal trade, it is entirely possible that the inspiration for entry into the coasting business came at that time. During his stay at Taunton he mastered the art of naval architecture, which was to be of great value to him later, for during his career as a shipowner and manager, he designed all but two of the vessels in his fleet.

Mr. Palmer was principal of the Malden High School in Malden, Massachusetts, when he decided in 1899 to take the plunge into the shipping business. One of the problems of any managing owner of a fleet of sailing vessels was not only to coordinate the activities of the fleet, but also to find backers for new vessels and Mr. Palmer seems to have been particularly adept at both. Besides Captain Baker of Wellfleet, Benjamin B. Crowninshield, designer of the huge

"Thomas W. Lawson", the firm of Yates & Porterfield. the Boston ship chandlery of James Bliss & Co. many personal friends in Taunton were all early backers of Palmer's vessels.

According to reliable historical record, Mr. Palmer's first vessel, the "Marie Palmer", did very well, paying her owners six dividends totaling $316 per 1/64 during 1900, which was her first year. This was a return of better than 27 percent. By 1906, she had paid for herself and by 1909, the year she was lost, she had returned 127 percent on a share to her owners. It has been stated that this was not untypical of schooners built through 1902. Large schooners built after that date were less likely to pay their way, unless they were lucky enough to last through the slow period prior to World War I.

William F. Palmer was most successful with his vessels. In 1908 following the launching of the "Fuller Palmer", the ownership of the vessels was vested in a corporation called The Palmer Fleet, with Boston listed as home port for all the vessels. All of the schooners were named so that the last part of each name ended in Palmer, with the first part, according to the scuttlebutt of the day, being named in honor of the vessel's largest backer. The vessels of the Palmer fleet devoted their time almost exclusively to the transportation of coal and thanks to Mr. Palmer's shrewd business judgement, managed to pay their owners a fair return on their investments, many of them paying a monthly dividend for years. It's interesting to note that the cost of a share in the four-masted "Maude Palmer", built in 1900 and the second schooner to join the fleet, was $1,080 a share and only three years later the five-master "Elizabeth Palmer" cost $2,125 a share.

With the launching of the "Fuller Palmer", by Percy & Small, the building of the Palmer fleet came to an end. Mr. William F. Palmer passed away in 1909 and the control of his fleet of white colliers went to J. S. Winslow & Co., of Portland, Maine, as had the fleet of Nathaniel T. Palmer almost five years earlier. The Winslow Company painted their vessels black with white trim and the vessels of the Palmer Fleet were altered in decor upon their acquisition by the Winslows. In 1917 the Winslow fleet was sold to the France & Canada Steamship Co.

The last of the Palmer vessels to survive was the "Dorothy Palmer", which was wrecked on Stone Horse Shoal, Nantucket Sound, on March 29, 1923. She was loaded with 4,000 tons of soft coal at the time and was bound from Norfolk to Portland. Her crew was taken off by the Coast Guard and the old five-master went to pieces.

In all, the Palmer fleet consisted of 15 schooners, two of which were four-masters, the other 13 being five-masters. George L. Welt of Waldoboro, Maine, built 6 of the Palmer vessels, Percy & Small of Bath, Maine, built 4, William Rogers of Bath, Maine, built the only 2 of the four-masters in the fleet, Cobb, Butler & Co., of Rockland, Maine, built 1, The New England Co., of Bath, Maine, built 1 and John M. Brooks of Boston, Massachusetts, built 1. The names and a few particulars on each vessel are as follows:

| NAME | RIG | YEAR & WHERE BUILT | GROSS TONS | YEAR LOST |
|------|-----|--------------------|-----------|-----------|
| Marie Palmer | 4 masts | 1900 Bath, Maine | 1904 | Dec. 17, 1909 |
| Maude Palmer | 4 masts | 1900 Bath, Maine | 1845 | Aug. 26, 1915 |
| Fannie Palmer (1) | 5 masts | 1900 Waldoboro, Maine | 2558 | July 11, 1914 |
| Rebecca Palmer | 5 masts | 1901 Rockland, Maine | 2556 | Sold Greece 1921 |
| Baker Palmer | 5 masts | 1901 Waldoboro, Maine | 2792 | Dec. 11, 1915 |
| Prescott Palmer | 5 masts | 1902 Bath, Maine | 2811 | Jan. 20, 1914 |
| Paul Palmer | 5 masts | 1902 Waldoboro, Maine | 2193 | June 15, 1913 |
| Dorothy Palmer | 5 masts | 1903 Waldoboro, Maine | 2872 | Mar. 25, 1923 |
| Elizabeth Palmer | 5 masts | 1903 Bath, Maine | 3165 | Jan. 26, 1916 |
| Singleton Palmer | 5 masts | 1904 Waldoboro, Maine | 2859 | Nov. 6, 1921 |
| Jane Palmer | 5 masts | 1904 Boston, Mass. | 3138 | Dec. 18, 1920 |
| Harwood Palmer | 5 masts | 1904 Waldoboro, Maine | 2885 | May 23, 1917 |
| Davis Palmer | 5 masts | 1905 Bath, Maine | 2965 | Dec. 24, 1909 |
| Fannie Palmer (2) | 5 masts | 1907 Bath, Maine | 2233 | Dec. 25, 1916 |
| Fuller Palmer | 5 masts | 1908 Bath, Maine | 3060 | Jan. 12, 1914 |

Another colorful owner-manager whose fleet hailed from Boston, was Captain John G. Crowley. Captain Crowley was born in Plymouth, Massachusetts, in 1856. He went to sea when he was only ten years old, being signed on as cook on the 150 ton schooner "Mount Hope", which was in command of his father, Captain Thomas Crowley. John G. Crowley worked his way up to a command in short order, holding his masters certificate when he was only twenty-one. He sailed out of Taunton, Massachusetts, in command of various three-masted schooners engaged in the coal trade, one of them being the "Henry S. Culver", built in Alexandria, Virginia, in 1883 by Charles Ward.

Captain Crowley's first four-masted schooner was the new "Mount Hope" launched by H. M. Bean in Camden, Maine in 1887 and the second vessel to carry that name. His second four-master was the beautiful "Sagamore", launched in Kennebunk, Maine in 1891 by Charles Ward, who had returned to Maine from Virginia. This able, new vessel was placed in command of Captain Arthur L. Crowley, the younger brother of Captain John G. Crowley.

The "Sagamore" went into the coal trade and she continued in this until the end of her career, which came violently on May 10, 1907. She was then under the command of Captain Trefry and was bound through Nantucket Sound with 2,200 tons of coal from Newport News to Boston. It was night and the schooner was clipping along at better than 10 knots with a strong north wester and everything was set and drawing. Suddenly lights loomed directly ahead of the bounding schooner. They were lights carried by a Norwegian steamer "Edda", loaded down with plaster and bound from Nova Scotia to New York.

With a rending crash, the bow of the steamer cut deeply into the port bow of the helpless "Sagamore". The force of the collision caused the schooner's bowsprit to swing inboard over the badly damaged steamer. The long jibboom was sweeping the open bridge of the "Edda", just about waist high and was heading directly for her amazed Captain. Before it could bowl him over, he attempted to vault the swinging spar and instead of going over it, landed directly on top of its tip end.

In another second he was carried out over the black waters of Nantucket Sound, where he helplessly watched the lights of his command receding from him, full astern.

He then scrambled back along the jibboom and reached the deck of the "Sagamore" where he had the unhappy task of identifying himself to Captain Trefry, whose command was rapidly showing signs of going under. The yawl boat was launched and all hands, including the terribly embarrassed skipper of the Norwegian steamer, rowed ashore at Oak Bluffs, on Martha's Vineyard.

The next morning the "Edda" was seen to have been run ashore at Squash Meadow, but all that could be seen of the beautiful "Sagamore" were her topmasts sticking above water with her topsails set.

The vessels under the management of Captain John G. Crowley were all engaged in the transportation of coal, loading many of their cargos at Philadelphia. As his managerial responsibilities continued to increase, Captain Crowley "swallowed the anchor" in the late 1890's and moved to Boston. In 1903 his schooners were incorporated into one big fleet known as the Coastwise Transportation Company, with Boston as their home port and Captain Crowley being retained as manager.

The Captain will probably be best remembered as the man who thought BIG when it came to having schooners built, for it was his imagination and daring that ordered the building of the first six-master and the one and only seven-masted schooner; the "Thomas W. Lawson". The three six-masters under his control were the "George W. Wells", "William L. Douglas" and the "Mertie B. Crowley", which was the last schooner that Crowley had built. Some of the five-masters which he managed were the "Van Allens Boughton", John B. Prescott", "Margaret Haskell", "T. Charlton Henry", "Samuel J. Goucher", and although not built for Captain Crowley the "George P. Hudson", ex "Fannie Palmer", which came under his control around 1907, as did the "Marcus L. Urann", which came under his managership in 1910. Besides the "Mount Hope" and the "Sagamore", the four-masters "Henry W. Cramp" and the "J. C. Strawbridge" were also Crowley managed vessels.

Around 1910, the Coastwise Transportation Company, having prospered under Captain Crowley's direction, started to build steam colliers, commencing with two vessels, the "Coastwise" and the "Transportation". These did well and were soon followed by more, plainly indicating that the sailing vessels were running out of time, being unable to compete with the punctual steamers.

One of the last big schooner fleets to operate from Boston was that managed by Peter M. Crowell and Lewis K. Thurlow, which was known far and wide as Crowell & Thurlow. Starting around the turn of the century, they built up a fleet of ten or twelve big Maine built schooners, chiefly engaged in the coal trade from Norfolk, Virginia to ports in New England. Around 1912, as had the "Coastwise Transportation Company, Crowell & Thurlow became interested in steam colliers and started a separate company called the Crowell & Thurlow Steamship Company.

However, with the beginning of World War I, a new lease on life was given to the sailing ship and Crowell & Thurlow added some more schooners to their fleet. In 1916 the Atlantic Coast Company was formed with Crowell & Thurlow owning the controlling interest. The new company started building vessels for its own account at recently acquired yards in Thomaston and Boothbay Harbour, Maine. Schooners were also built for this company at Stockton Springs, at Harrington and at Rockland, Maine. Another corporation, the East Coast Ship Company, was also organized by Crowell & Thurlow and associates and this company built four vessels for their own account. In 1921 the Boston Maritime Corporation was formed to acquire all the vessels that were operated by Crowell & Thurlow and the East Coast Ship Co., numbering about 20 vessels in all. Around 1923, the Atlantic Coast Co., was reorganized as the New England Maritime Co., and the vessels therein continued under the management of Crowell & Thurlow.

About this time the Florida land boom was beginning and the railroads soon found that they were unable to handle the demand for southbound freight, so lumber and building materials from the north were loaded on anything that would float and headed south. In 1926 several of the vessels belonging to the G. G. Deering Co., of Bath, Maine, were added to the Crowell & Thurlow fleet. Following this period, schooners were desperately in search of cargoes, and with the collapse of the Florida trade around 1928, most of them were laid up, cut down to barges, sold abroad or broken up. Around 1927 about 25 of the larger schooners found employment for awhile carrying railroad ties from southern ports such as New Orleans and Savannah to Boston and New York, however this traffic did not last long. By the end of the 1930's, the fleet of Crowell & Thurlow was all but wiped out.

During the period in which they were managing vessels, Crowell & Thurlow had control of no less than 71 sailing ships. Of these, two were barks, one was a barkentine and the rest were schooners. Of the schooners, four were five-masters and eight were three-masters, one of these being the big "Bradford C. French." The rest of the schooners in the fleet were rigged as four-masters. Although many coal cargos were hauled by the vessels in this fleet, they were by no means as dependent on this cargo as were the fleets of Palmer or Crowley.

The last vessel to survive of the once great fleet of Crowell & Thurlow, was the four-masted "Herbert L. Rawding", which was built by the Atlantic Coast Co., in 1919 at Stockton Springs, Maine. The "Rawding" measured 1,220 gross tons, 1,109 net tons, was 201.7 feet long, 38.5 feet beam and 21.9 feet in depth. She had been laid up in Boothbay Harbor for several years until 1937 when she was bought by Mr. Bernard Baruch of New York and completely overhauled and put back to work as a commercial carrier. She was finally sold to Canada. After having one of her masts removed and diesel engines installed, she made a trip to the Mediterranean with lumber in the spring of 1947. On the way back, during June, 1947, she went down off Gibralter.

The "Sally Persis Noyes" was another Crowell & Thurlow four-master that had a long and interesting career. Built in Harrington, Maine in 1919, she was used as a general trader, carrying coal, lumber, salt, molasses and whatever came along. She was finally laid up around 1929-30 along with other Crowell & Thurlow vessels in Boothbay Harbor and there she lay until 1932 when she was bought by Mr. Robert L. Royall of East Boothbay, who renamed her "Constellation". He intended her for a school ship, but the idea fell through. In 1934 she was sailed to Washington, D.C., where she was put to use as a restaurant open for dining and dancing. In 1935 the "Constellation" was chartered to demonstrate a new diving bell and eventually to take a treasure seeking group to the Carribean under the technical direction of Lt. Harry E. Rieseberg. Financial difficulties followed and the schooner was sold in July, 1936, to the Empire Marine Engineering & Salvage Corporation of New York who intended using her to raise sunken treasure supposed on board the liner "Merida" sunk in collision off the Virginia Capes in 1911.

The "Constellation left Jersey City on August 20, 1936, upon her "secret mission" which was thoroughly blurted to the world through the microphones of Lowell Thomas and Edwin C. Hill. She arrived on location on August 27 and two days later while at anchor, was hit by bad weather which so damaged the schooner that she had to set sail for New York. Upon her arrival at New York she was laid up and later moved to New Jersey. From the time when she was sailed to Washington, until being laid up in Perth Amboy in the middle thirties, she had been under the command of Captain Lawin Loesche, who after having gone through several marshal sales with the schooner, finally left her.

The "Constellation" was finally acquired by Captain A. W. Schoultz, President of the Intercontinental Steamship Co., of New York, and in December, 1942, began loading cargo for Europe. She started but never made the crossing, piling up on the rocks off Bermuda near the end of July, 1943, and becoming a total loss.

Along with the large schooner companies that had their home offices in Boston, there existed many small ones. These small fleet owners could be found in all the major ports on the eastern coast and at one time made up a great portion of the coasting fleet on this seaboard.

One such fleet which had its headquarters in Boston was started by Captain Harold G. Foss and operated under the management of two firms: Foss & Crabtree, and the Superior Trading & Transportation Company. These firms both used the same offices in Boston, both had the same set of officers, both directed the financial course of the same vessels, and both were under the complete control of Captain Foss.

Captain Foss, often referred to as "Mr. Schooner", by sailing ship enthusiasts, was until recently one of the few surviving members of the coasting fraternity. He made his way to the command of a sailing vessel at a very early age, and had a tremendous knowledge of the coasting trade. This stems from the fact that he was literally brought up with it as a way of life. Both his father and grandfather were men of the sea and Captain Foss, who was born in Hancock, Maine in 1882, went to sea for the first time with his father and mother at the age of twelve. It was common for coasting captains to take their families along with them on coastal trips during the pleasant summer months. This first voyage for young Foss was from New York to Cuba on the three-masted schooner "John Paul". The "John Paul" had been built for Captain Foss's father two years earlier and was one of three vessels for the elder Foss in which he owned a part as well as held command.

Within a very short time, after his father had retired from the sea, young Harold Foss was mate of the "John Paul", and after six months as mate, was placed in command of the schooner and charged with the responsibility of taking a cargo to the Gold Coast of Africa. At this time the new captain was 19 years old.

Captain Foss returned to New York with a cargo of palm oil and made three more trips to Africa in the "John Paul", before going on to other commands. He had, at one time, command of the "Pendleton Satisfaction",ex "Myra B. Weaver", which had previously dragged on to Handkerchief Shoals off Nantucket and drowned her former captain, the captain's wife, sister-in-law, the cook and three seamen. The last schooner in which Captain Foss went as master, was the four-masted "Sallie C. Marvil". The "Marvil" was a pretty little vessel, measuring 568 gross tons, 546 net tons, was 173.9 feet long, 37.2 feet beam and 18.3 feet in depth. She had been built in 1901 by the Sharptown Marine Railway Company, at Sharptown, Maryland. Shortly after 1905, the "Marvil" stranded in a N.E. gale at Cape Canaveral, Florida, and her master, Captain James Harvey, was washed overboard and drowned. She was bought by A. H. Bull & Company of New York, who refloated her and placed her in command of Captain Foss, who also bought an interest in the vessel.

She was used as a general trader until 1911, when Captain Foss chanced to carry a small quantity of goat manure, to the States, to test the possibility of using it as a commercial fertilizer. He managed to work out an agreement with a Florida concern, the E. O. Painter Fertilizer Co., and shortly thereafter began carting what they preferred to call "goatina", from Venezuela. In 1915, Captain Foss sold his interest in the "Sallie C. Marvil". Shortly after that, during the same year, the "Marvil" was lost on the island of Buen Aire, Venezuela, while bound for the port of Le Vela de Coro, to load.

When World War I broke out, Captain Foss, who had been staying in Venezuela, returned to the United States, joined the navy and was placed in command of a transport with the rank of lieutenant commander. After the war was over he went back to Coro, where he was appointed American Consular Agent and where he again picked up and continued the goat manure business. Shipments were made to ports on the east coast from Boston to Tampa.

The Superior Trading & Transportation Company was formed in 1925, as near as Captain Foss can remember, and when he bought it they only had one asset, the schooner "Edna Hoyt". He added more vessels to it, finally closing the Boston office in 1940. During the intervening time, it had owned the following schooners:

"MABEL", ex "ADELAIDE BARBOUR" built in 1901 at Newburyport, Massachusetts. Was abandoned at sea in 1929.

"GENERAL LEON JURADO", ex "ALICE MAY DAVENPORT" built in 1905 at Bath, Maine, which was wrecked in 1931 on the coast of Santo Domingo.

"HAROLD G. FOSS", ex "THOMAS N. BARNSDALL" built in 1920 at Camden, Maine and was stranded at Venezuela in 1932.

"EDWARD L. SWAN", ex "M. VIVIAN PIERCE" built in 1919 at Thomaston, Maine. This vessel fell over in a dry dock at Perth Amboy, New Jersey about 1936. She was then used as a breakwater near New York.

"EDNA HOYT" built in 1920 at Thomaston, Maine and was damaged in the Bay of Biscay in 1937. She was towed to Lisbon, Portugal and sold for use as coal hulk.

"DUNHAM WHEELER" built in 1917 at Bath, Maine. This vessel sank off Cape Canaveral, Florida in 1930.

The last two vessels in the foregoing list were five-masted schooners and the rest were four-masters. The "Edward L. Swan" was half owned by Mr. Swan of New York. All six of the schooners were engaged in the trade with Venezuela at one time or another.

After about 25 years ashore, Captain Foss went back to sea during World War II as master of some large steamships: "I had ten good sized ships and had some very interesting experiences. In 1948 in the SIR JOHN FRANKLIN we took some rubber from Singapore up to Vladivostok, Russia. At that time the United States and Russia were not friendly. In the THEODORE FOSTER we were the first convoy, (I was the commodore) from Saipan to Yokohama, Japan."

Following the war, Captain Foss went back to the town of Hancock, Maine, where he was born, and very generously gave of his time to those who are interested in the days when sailing ships ruled the seas. He died on October 2, 1965 and is buried in Hancock.

Besides being the location for the builders of many coasting vessels, Maine was also the home of many fleets of coasters and many of these fleets were owned and managed by the firms who built schooners. Percy & Small of Bath, the builders of the giants, built 15 schooners for their own account. These included two six-masters, the "Eleanor A. Percy" and the "Wyoming", the five-masters "M. D. Cressy", the "Helen W. Martin", the "Martha P. Small", the "Cora F. Cressy", the "Grace A. Martin" and the "Governor Brooks", the four-masters "Charles P. Notman", "William H. Clifford", "S. P. Blackburn", "Florence M. Penley", Robert P. Murphy", "Dustin G. Cressy" and the "Carl F. Cressy", which was launched in 1915 and was the last vessel built for the account of Percy & Small.

The "Carl F. Cressy" was another of those vessels having a short life span. On August 22, 1917, she left La Pallice, France, in company with the big six-masted "Edward J. Lawrence". Once outside, the schooners split tacks, the "Lawrence" heading to the northwest and the "Cressy" holding to her original course. At daylight of the next day, the "Cressy" was intercepted by a German submarine and sunk by shell fire in Lat. 45.53 N., Long. 11.13 W. Her crew of nine were able to launch the yawl boat and were later picked up by the French bark "Quevilly". The "Lawrence" made a 35 day passage back to Norfolk, Virginia untroubled by enemy activity.

Percy & Small at one time owned as much as 25,000 tons of fore and aft shipping, capable of moving 400,000 tons of coal to New England ports in a single year. They managed their vessels until 1917, when their fleet was sold to the France & Canada Steamship Company at a tremendous profit. The "Wyoming" was reported to have brought $400,000 alone. After the war the huge schooner was bought by A. W. Frost & Co. of Portland, Maine, and re-entered the coastwise trade until she was lost in 1924.

The last vessel owned by Percy & Small was the little three-masted "Mary E. Olys", built by the New England Co., at Bath in 1891. The "Olys" had the misfortune of celebrating New Years Day, 1920, by going ashore on Cape Porpoise. The last vessel launched by Percy & Small was the four-master "Cecilia Cohen", a 1,102 ton vessel, built for New York owners in 1920. With the passing of the year 1920 the history of the builders and owners of giant schooners came to an end.

Another famous down east firm of ship owners and builders was that of Gardiner G. Deering and William T. Donnell, known as Deering & Donnell. This partnership was formed in Bath in 1866 and built 70 schooners, 54 being two-masters and the remaining 16 being three-masters. Of the three-masters, seven were built for their own account. In 1886 the partnership was dissolved and after dividing the vessel property, both of the ex-partners continued building vessels on their own. Gardiner G. Deering seems to have been the most ambitious of the two builders, turning out 29 more schooners before he stopped construc-tion in 1919. Seven of the 29 were five-masters, 16 were four-masters, 4 were three-masters and 2 were two-masters. Twenty-four of the 29 of G. G. Deering's vessels were built for his own account. He died on October 24, 1921, but the G. G. Deering Company remained in existence until about 1930. The last of its schooners, the "Gardiner G. Deering" was burned at Brooksville, Maine on July 4, 1930.

One of the most interesting of G. G. Deering's vessels was the last one he built; namely the five-masted "Carroll A. Deering", launched in 1919 from his yard in Bath. This vessel measured 2,114 gross tons, 1,879 net tons, was 255.1 feet in length, 44.3 feet beam and 25.3 feet in depth and was listed for a crew of eleven.

In September, 1920, the new schooner, barely a year old, set sail from Boston bound for Buenos Aires in command of Captain F. Merritt. While off the Delaware Capes, Captain Merritt became ill and put in at Lewes, Delaware where he was replaced by Captain W. T. Wormwell, a veteran shipmaster. She then proceeded to South America without further incident. On December 2, 1920, the "Carroll A. Deering" cleared from Rio de Janiero bound home for Norfolk, Virginia without cargo. On her way north she made one stop at Barbadoes in the West Indies. A month went by after the "Deering" left Rio and not much thought was given to the schooner. Indeed not too many people knew that she even existed. This was soon to change.

The night of January 30, 1921, was a stormy one off Diamond Shoals, North Carolina, and before a sunset a spectator might have looked out over the wild, yet lonely scene and watched the huge combers as they burst with a roar over the shifting sands on the shoals. Nothing more was there to be seen.

However, as dawn broke on the morning of the 31st, surfman C. P. Brady was astonished to behold a five-masted schooner, upright and with sails set on every mast, firmly aground in the white water off shore.

Two boats were quickly manned and launched in the rough surf. They managed to reach the vicinity of the stranded vessel about mid morning, however due to the shallowness of the water and the breaking "greenbacks", the surfboats were able to get no closer than a quarter of a mile to the big schooner. She appeared utterly abandoned, being without any boats and with a jacobs ladder hanging over the side. The lifesavers still did not know the identity of the vessel which lay before them. The weather looked ominous and the surfboats put back for shore without being able to get aboard.

Not until February 4th, four days later, did the seas subside enough to permit a boarding of the big five-master. It was then learned that the name of the stranded vessel was the "Carroll A. Deering", from Bath, Maine. By this time the "Deering" had become a sodden wreck. The seas that had swept over her had opened up her seams and she was full of water. Her steering gear was smashed and it did not take long for those aboard to realize that there was no hope of salvaging the stranded schooner.

On going into her after cabin, charts were found strewn about the captain's bath room. Food was still setting on the galley table and there was food on the stove. However, there was not one sign or apparent reason why the crew should have left a perfectly able vessel; assuming of course, that they left before she struck the shoals.

To this day no one knows what happened to the officers and crew of the "Carroll A. Deering". Neither the yawl boat nor any bodies were ever found, either on the coast of North Carolina, or anywhere else. Many ideas have been put forth; mutiny, piracy, abandonment at sea, abandonment when she struck — but no one knows for sure, for dead men tell no tales and the crew of the "Deering" must surely have died soon after leaving their vessel.

The wreck of the "Deering" caught the fancy of the public and all sorts of press came out on the loss of the big five-master. Wreckers took off what they could and the remains of the schooner were then dynamited to prevent its breaking away and becoming a menace to navigation. The stern section stayed on the shoal, but the bow came free and drifted on to the beach at Ocracoke, North Carolina where for many years it remained visible for visitors to come and stare at — and wonder.

A very well known firm of owner-managers of sailing ships, was J. S. Winslow & Company of Portland, Maine. This firm was started during the Civil War and from that time until the 1880's, Captain Jacob S. Winslow built up a fleet of 25 ships, barks, barkentines and brigs for the general freight trade all over the world. Many of the smaller vessels in this fleet were engaged chiefly in trade with the West Indies.

92

In 1889 the Winslows had their first four-masted schooner built, the "Jacob S. Winslow" and the next year she was followed by another, the "Major Pickands". Both of these vessels went into the lumber and coal trade and signaled the change-around about to take place in the Winslow fleet. Within a few years there were over 20 fore and aft rigged vessels and only one bark and one barkentine, with major emphasis being directed towards the coastwise, rather than the foreign trade.

Of the 41 schooners that were built by Percy & Small, 12 were built for J. S. Winslow & Co. Of these, 5 were six-masters, 2 were five-masters, and 5 were four-masters. The 5 six-masters were: the "Addie M. Lawrence", "Ruth E. Merrill", "Alice M. Lawrence", Edward J. Lawrence" and the "Edward B. Winslow", all being engaged in carrying bituminous coal and making this company the owners of some of the largest sailing vessels afloat. The 3 vessels whose names ended in Lawrence, were named after members of a family from Fairfield, Maine, who controlled the cotton mills at Waterville, Maine, and who also had extensive interests in Winslow vessels.

The firm eventually passed from the control of Captain Winslow to Mr. Eleazer W. Clarke, under whose direction the fleet became the most prosperous floating property on the coast. After the death of Mr. Nathaniel T. Palmer in 1904, the vessels remaining in his fleet were taken over by the Winslow fleet and following the death of Mr. William F. Palmer in 1909, the vessels left in his fleet were also acquired. At this time, the tonnage of the 34 vessels in the Winslow fleet grew to the staggering sum of 54,993 tons, making it the largest fleet of its kind in operation.

In 1917, as with the fleet of Percy & Small, the vessels belonging to the J. S. Winslow Company were sold to the France & Canada Steamship Company at high prices brought on by the war. After 55 years, the blue "W", on a white background, the house flag so well known on the east coast, was hauled down and not seen again.

The Pendleton Brothers, of New York and Isleboro, Maine, also was a firm with a large number of vessels. They had in addition to their many schooners, the barkentines "John C. Meyer", a four-master built on the west coast, and the "Marsala", a five-master of ugly appearance, built on the Gulf coast. The Pendleton vessels were engaged in general freighting and were not aimed at any one trade in particular as, for example, were the Winslow vessels meant for the coal trade during the latter part of the company's existence.

In 1903, the handsome three-masted schooner "Frank Huckins" went down the ways of Kelly, Spear & Co., at Bath, Maine. With her launching was signaled a change in the standard ownership and management of sailing property. Heretofore, a company or individual, responsible for the management of a vessel or vessels, would "get up" shares and have a schooner built, which in turn was chartered or otherwise made available to someone wishing to transport a cargo.

This chartering of vessels was often a very big expense to a lumber or a coal company, for example, and problems such as demurrage, long passages due to lay overs and the inability to directly charge the captain of a vessel were wrankling factors. The Hirsch Lumber Company, of New York felt that some of these problems could be overcome by owning their own vessel and accordingly had the "Frank Huckins" built with themselves as sole owner, and with no 64ths being considered.

The "Frank Huckins" measured 545 gross tons, 457 net tons, was 152.8 feet long, 35.8 feet beam, 13.2 feet in depth and carried a crew of seven men. The new vessel was placed in command of Captain Hunter, of Tennants Harbor, and proved a great success, with the result that many other companies soon followed the example set by the Hirsch people.

The "Frank Huckins" not only did well financially, but kept herself out of trouble, never becoming involved in any serious accidents while owned by the lumber company. In 1918, as had so many others, the Hirsch Lumber Company could not resist the high war time prices for vessels that were being offered by foreign powers and the "Huckins" was sold to France.

It would not be right to close this chapter on the owners of coasting vessels without mentioning something about some of the colorful skipper-owners, whose numbers were legion along the entire coastline. By skipper-owners, I refer to those captains who owned out-right the vessel of which they were in command, or who held at least the major portion of her shares. Most of the vessels controlled in this way were usually no larger than three-masters and in the vast majority of cases were found to be two-masted schooners. A lingering few of them were sloop rigged. The townies in practically every port on the Atlantic coast could at one time recall the name and antics of some skipper and his little vessel that used to haul in freight up until the mid 1930's.

Nantucketers in particular, recall the names of "Cap'n Zeb", from the Vineyard, or firey old Park Hall from Maine, and when they do, they invariably bring up the name of the "Alice S. Wentworth", for the three were inextricably entwined.

The "Wentworth" in command of Captain Zeb, was a frequent visitor to this island during the '20's and '30's and carried her age quite well. Although listed in the "List of Merchant Vessels of the United States" as being built in 1905, this is not quite the case. This little two-master was originally built in South Norwalk, Connecticut in 1863 as the "Lizzie A. Tolles". She was named after the builder's daughter and was built to carry 55,000 brick on deck and for many years sailed on Long Island Sound and in the Hudson River.

Around 1890 she was bought by Arthur Stevens who sailed her for almost 14 years and who then took her to Wells, Maine in 1904, where she was rebuilt. In 1905 she went back in the water under the new name of "Alice S. Wentworth", being named after Captain Stevens' niece, a pretty young lady from the state of Maine. At this time Zebulon Northrup Tilton, later known far and wide as "Cap'n Zeb", joined Captain Stevens and stayed with him on board the "Wentworth" until 1909.

After leaving the "Wentworth" in 1909, Captain Zeb bought the "John B. Norris" a little two-master which measured 49 gross tons, was 66.5 feet long and had been built in Fairhaven, Massachusetts in 1868. Once when the "Norris" was laying at anchor off Stapleton, Long Island, with a load of coal that was bound for the Vineyard, a knot in the centerboard trunk came loose during the night. Captain Zeb was awakened when water rising in the cabin came in contact with his hand which was hanging over the side of his bunk and he and his crew barely had time to get clear of the schooner before she slid under. Captain Zeb had hands the size of hams and feet to match and it was rumored at the time that it took several days to find a pair of shoes on Staten Island that would fit the captain, as in his haste, he had come ashore barefoot. He dutifully sent a telegram to his wife on the Vineyard which said:

"The John B. Norris sunk, without a word of warning."

During 1921 Captain Zeb and other Vineyard parties bought the "Alice S. Wentworth" from Captain Stevens, who in turn bought the three-masted "Frank Brainerd". Perhaps Captain Stevens should have held on to the "Wentworth", for not long after buying the "Brainerd", his three-master went ashore sustaining damage amounting to $17,000. This Captain Stevens was unable to pay, and he lost the "Brainerd". She finally wound up in the Cape de Verdes packet trade and in June, 1941, foundered on a voyage from the United States to the islands. According to Charles Sayle, those in charge of the "Brainerd" at that time, left her centerboard laying on the wharf at New Bedford, feeling she didn't need it. After running into bad weather in mid-Atlantic, they found much too late, that the centerboard would have made quite a difference to the success of the voyage had it been on board rather than on the dock at New Bedford.

Captain Zeb used the "Wentworth" for general freighting and did well with her, paying her owners an annual dividend of between 15 and 20 percent. Once during 1923 the "Wentworth" was anchored inside the breakwater at Point Judith and her anchors let go. The wind was blowing near 90 miles an hour and would have blown the little schooner on the rocks had not Zeb put the foresail on her and sailed on to a nearby strip of sandy beach. Her long pole bowsprit was broken upon this occasion and when she was repaired Zeb evened off the broken end of the bowsprit and added a flying jibboom. At this time the measurements of the "Alice S. Wentworth" were as follows: 68 gross tons, 65 net tons, 73.2 feet in length, 23.7 feet beam and 6.1 feet in depth. She drew 5.6 feet of water light and 8 feet of water when loaded. With the centerboard all the way down, she could draw as much as 17 feet. Her main mast was 71 feet, the foremast 70 feet, main topmast 33 feet, fore topmast 32 feet, main boom 50 feet, fore boom 23 feet, bowsprit 22 feet and flying jibboom 15 feet. She could carry 100 tons of cargo, or 400 bbls. of oil, or 60,000 board feet of lumber. She carried a flying jib, main jib, foresail, mainsail, main topsail, and for a short while a fore topsail, her fore topmast being removed in her later days.

Although Captain Zeb usually carried one hand besides himself to sail his 73 foot schooner, he made two trips from the Vineyard to Providence alone. He was born at Chilmark on the Vineyard in 1867 and had four or five brothers, most of whom followed the sea. These were Willard, Welcome, George Fred, the famous whaleman, and John R., all coming from Chilmark. Zeb went to sea with Captain Josiah Cleveland on the little schooner "Eliza Jane", when Zeb was only 15 years old. He also sailed on the anchor dragger "Wilfred W. Fuller" at an early age.

Captain Zeb was married three times and his third marriage, to Grace Stubbs McDonald, took place in the early 1940's at the Seamen's Bethel on Martha's Vineyard and proved to be quite an affair. He was bound that he'd be married by the wheel of his vessel, but the wedding took place during the month of February and it had snowed. The deck of the schooner was full of slush and slippery and certainly not in the proper condition for such a ceremony. Not to be foiled, Captain Zeb took off the wheel and hauled it up to the Bethel where his fondest wishes were fulfilled. Charles Sayle, who brought a wedding cake from Nantucket, was there and remembers that people had come from far and wide for Zeb's wedding and that the Bethel was so packed, people were standing in the aisles and had climbed up and were peeping through the windows.

In 1939, or thereabouts, Zeb was finding it tough sledding and he was forced to sell the "Wentworth". She was bought by Captain Ralph Packer for $724. A stock company was formed and 150 shares were sold at $10 a share in order to repay bills and repair the old "Wentworth". After this was done Captain Zeb was placed in command again and for the next three years the stockholders' meetings were held in the summer on board the schooner and the various members of the firm were treated to a free sail.

Around June, 1943, the "Wentworth" was sold for $600 to Captain Parker Hall, who stayed on Nantucket until fall and then set sail all by himself for Maine. Off Gloucester the foresheet carried away and Captain Hall and the schooner nearly went on the rocks of Norman's Woe. She then stayed at Gloucester where Parker Hall sold her to Maine parties during the following winter. She was used in the pulpwood trade for a while and once was reported to have sunk. She was, following this, bought by Captain Fred Guild for use as a dude schooner and was in turn bought from him by Captain H. Hawkins for the same purpose. Hawkins sold her to Miss Ann White in 1960 and in 1962 she came back to Nantucket with dude sailors during the summer. In 1963 she filled and sank at Woods Hole on Cape Cod, but was raised within a few days. In 1964, she went down again at Woods Hole and stayed under for several months. She was raised in the spring and was beached near the town wharf. She has since been sold at auction and is being used in connection with a restaurant in Boston.

After selling the "Wentworth" Captain Zeb bought the little schooner "Coral" from Captain Tucker, with the intention of fixing her up and going back coasting. He succeeded in replacing her bowsprit, but never got beyond this and the poor little "Coral" went to pieces in Fairhaven.

In 1944, when he was 77 years old, Zeb, his son-in-law and 16 year old grandson, Donald, sailed the three-masted "Lucy Evelyn" from Boston around Cape Cod to New Bedford. This happened after the schooner had been repaired in Boston following damage suffered when she struck the breakwater at Vineyard Haven. The "Lucy Evelyn" then went into the Cape de Verdes packet trade and eventually wound up at Beach Haven, New Jersey as a tourist attraction and gift shop.

In his 86th year Captain Zeb died on the Vineyard from the effects of a broken hip suffered from a fall on the ice the previous winter.

96

Parker Hall, who had a home at Sandy Point, Maine died during the summer of 1948 at the age of 87 years. He, like Captain Zeb, had early followed the sea. He was born at Kinston, Massachusetts where his father was the keeper of the Gurnet Light. When Parker was 15, he sailed a 15 foot catboat named the "Annie Fuller" to Kennebunk, Maine and then home again. At 19 he was the skipper of a mail and passenger sloop running from Cedar Keys to the Florida mainland. He was skipper-owner of the following vessels: "Robert P. King", "Addie J.", "George R. Smith" ex "Nellie Doe", "Angler", "Carrie J.", "Howard Russell", "Mizpah", a 32 foot schooner he used for partying in 1910, "George Gress" ex "Peter Merhoff", a Hudson River schooner, and the "Alice S. Wentworth". He also had the sloops "Rosewood", "Flying Mist" and "Joseph G. Hamlin", but he didn't think much of the sloops. When he was in the "Angler", he brought over material from the mainland to build the Muskeget Life Saving Station. The "Robert P. King" was an ex slaver that had been built as a half brig in 1847 at Philadelphia, however when Captain Hall bought her in 1898, she was schooner rigged.

It was probably while he was in command of the "King", that the crew mutineed when in New York and tried to rob Parker Hall. He shot two of them, killing one. This happened around 1907 and he never carried a crew after that, sailing alone.

He obtained the "George R. Smith" after the "King". The "Smith" was a 136 gross ton, 129 net ton, two-masted schooner built in 1867 at Orrington, Maine and she measured 89.2 feet in length, 25.8 feet beam and 8.0 feet in depth and carried two topmasts. Captain Hall sailed this vessel from ports in Maine to Philadelphia and places in between until 1920, and sailors of today take notice, he did this all alone.

While he was master and crew of the "George R. Smith" he had to improvise and use much ingenuity. He would lash wooden fenders to the windlass brakes on one side, for example, and he would work the other side. He said that the crews he could get at the time would not heave up or down, but the weight of the fenders would at least heave down. Parker had a bad speech impediment, stuttering terribly and when asked why he did not carry a crew, he explained in his sputtering way that in the time it took to make some one understand what he was saying, he could do it himself. However, there were those who said it was Parker's fierce temper that kept him from carrying a crew. When he flew off the handle, his anger knew no bounds, so he preferred to play it safe and go it alone.

He made, as did Zeb, many trips to Nantucket carrying general freight and as the prevailing wind on the island is S.W. and the wharfs are almost upwind after rounding Brant Point, he would head for them with sheets eased off and at the last minute slack them off entirely, tossing someone on the dock a line asking them to, "mmmummm-mmake it ffuff-fast".

As luck would have it one day, Parker came in and one of the "townies" was standing on the wharf, whose nickname was "Gapple Dumplin'". "Gapple" got this name when some one asked him what he was going to have for dessert one evening — he too had his troubles communicating.

Parker eased alongside the wharf and tossed a line saying, "Here, mmmumm-mmake it fffast."

"Woo wwwhere, woo wooww-wwwilll I ppp pput it?" queried Gapple, as he deftly caught the line.

"Ah-ah- ah- ah-roun' yyyer Gug-gug-gug-God da-da damn n-n-neck!", raged the indignant skipper, as he climed the spiles with blood in his eye.

Luckily for Gapple Dumplin' there were people standing around on the wharf who knew both parties and they quickly stepped in between before any blood was shed and after making everything fast and cooling Parker down, explained the situation.

It is said that Parker and Gapple became friends after that, although anyone trying to join in on their conversation, soon gave it up as a bad job.

*Schooner Ashore*

## Chapter XIV

## THE DANGERS OF THE TRADE

As one goes through the histories of the various sailing vessels that were engaged in carting freight along the American coastline, it soon becomes apparent that few of them terminated their careers quietly or peacefully. It was only towards the end of the era that any number of schooners were laid up or abandoned. These vessels, still capable of earning a living but lacking work, were towed into some creek or back bay and allowed to quietly fall apart. However, in the hey-day of the trade a violent end was the rule and those serving aboard often shared the fate that was accorded their vessel.

When comparing coasters to deepwatermen, it is found that both suffered from many of the same difficulties, however not in the same degree. For example, the life on a coasting schooner was less humdrum, as a rule, than the life on board a deepwaterman, because the coaster was more frequently in port. This allowed the crew of the coaster more of a chance to blow off steam or to leave if conditions or officers did not suit them. Mutinies were therefore comparitively rare, although some did occur on coasting vessels.

In the fall of 1905, the four-master "Harry A. Berwind" was bound from Mobile, Alabama, to Philadelphia, when four colored members of her crew murdered Captain Rummill, the mate, the cook and the engineer. Their bodies were thrown overboard and the mutineers then took over the operation of the vessel. Off the coast of North Carolina the "Berwind" very nearly ran down the four-masted "Blanche H. King", arousing the suspicions of her master, Captain Taylor, who ordered his mate to board the "Berwind" with a prize crew. After subduing the mutineers, the prize crew, with the "King's" mate in charge, sailed the "Berwind" into Southport, North Carolina, where they turned the mutineers over to the authorities. Their trial was held at Wilmington, North Carolina, and they were sentenced to be hanged on January 26, 1906.

Another mutiny which attracted international attention, occurred on a three-masted schooner in 1875, back in the days when it was fairly common for schooners to be making deepwater voyages in addition to their coastal passages. The vessel was the "Jefferson Borden" and at the time of the mutiny she was bound on a voyage from New Orleans to London with a cargo of oilcake.

The "Borden" was a 563 ton vessel built in Kennebunk, Maine, by David Clark in 1867, and was owned in Boston, Massachusetts. She left New Orleans on March 5, 1875, in command of Captain Wm. Manson Patterson, two mates who were relatives of the captain, a steward, four seamen and a French boy from Calais. One of the crew, a Russian with the unlikely name of Miller, behaved insolently toward the captain and the officers from the start, and on the eighth day of the voyage, threatened them, so he was put in irons and confined for 48 hours. This seemed to take some of the starch out of Miller and he was released when he promised to behave and so stated in the log, which he then signed.

About 12:30 a.m., on April the 20th, Miller came to the captain's cabin and told him that one of the crew had fallen and broken his leg and he requested the captain to go forward and assist the injured man. Captain Patterson called for the second mate, who was supposed to be on watch at the time, but received no answer. Miller came from behind the house and asked the captain why he did not go forward, saying, "for God's sake, help the man, he is dying." Captain Patterson noticed that Miller was carrying something in his hand and wisely stepped back into his cabin and refused to go forward. Miller tried to get the steward to go, but the captain restrained him.

When daylight came, the captain saw three men forward and called them aft, but they refused to obey. He got his shotgun and fired it at the mutineers, but they were not frightened and threw iron and bottles back at him. The situation turned into a stalemate and all the rest of the day the schooner slopped along with the wheel lashed and no one controlling or directing her course. After dark the mutineers tried to launch the yawl boat but found it too heavy for the three of them to handle, so they went forward to the forecastle. Captain Patterson managed to slip forward and shut them in, but they refused to give up. He then shot at them through a port with his pistol, during the course of the next day, until they finally surrendered. They had all been wounded.

They then confessed to killing both of the mates and throwing them overboard. After clapping them in irons, two of them who were less seriously injured, were forced to pump the vessel which had been unattended for two days. The third being badly wounded, was of no help whatever. Due to this extreme shortage of able hands, Captain Patterson experienced great difficulty in properly working his vessel.

Eight days after the mutiny they fell in with the Norwegian bark "Brevig" and one of the sailors from that vessel was sent to Captain Patterson to help him get his schooner to port. With the help of this man, the "Jefferson Borden" finally arrived at London and the mutineers were removed to the London Hospital under police guard.

Under the Extradition Acts and Treaties, the men were returned to the United States and were tried for murder in Boston. The three of them were convicted and two were sentenced to hang; the third, because of his youth, was sentenced to five years. Later the President was prevailed upon to commute the death sentences of the two and they went to prison for life at Alfred, Maine.

In 1883, the "Jefferson Borden" was sold and renamed "Arcana". On January 28, 1885, while bound from Portland, Maine, to Bear River, Nova Scotia, to load lumber, she struck a ledge on Quaco Reef, at St. Martins, New Brunswick, during a wild snow storm. Of her crew of ten men, all were lost with the exception of one man named Patrick Lyons. Three of her crew had managed to reach the abutment of an old lighthouse, but due to rising tide, could not get all the way to shore as Lyons had. They tried to keep themselves alive by constantly moving about the top of the abutment, but finally collapsed from exhaustion. When found they were frozen to death and completely encased in ice.

Mutinies such as those that occurred on the "Harry A. Berwind" and on the "Jefferson Borden", were most unusual on coasters and violence on the part of crews was seldom resorted to. There were, of course, times when disputes arose between officers and crew, but these were more often troubles that might be classified as labor-management problems and were usually settled by the captain without the use of force.

An interesting story is told about Captain Ben Paschal when he was in command of the three-masted schooner "Melissa Trask". He was bound from the West Indies to New York and the "Trask" was leaking so badly that her crew had to be kept working constantly at the pumps. Finally one night the mate knocked on the door of the cabin and informed Captain Paschal that the men were all worn out and that they had refused to go on pumping. Captain Paschal told the mate to go forward and tell the crew it was perfectly all right with him if they stopped pumping. In fact, if they wanted to, they could throw the "blankety, blank, blank, pump brakes overboard, for he had just as many friends in hell as they did!"

After having made his point on the somewhat dull minds of his crew, the captain was relieved to see them go back to the pumps, enabling their safe arrival in New York. If Captain Paschal had tried to get tough with his balky crew they probably would have given him an argument, and sunk in the process.

Fire was another enemy of the deepwaterman that did not occur as frequently on coasting vessels; at least not from the same causes. Spontaneous combustion of coal cargos was responsible for the loss of many square rigged vessels, due to the longer time they remained at sea, however there were few cases of coal catching fire for the same reason on coastal traders. There were schooners that burned due to other causes; carelessness, explosions, dock fires, and in the case of the little lime schooners running from Maine; if they leaked and water came in contact with their cargo, they were very apt to go up in flames. However, for the most part, fire can be discounted as one of the major causes of disaster in the coasting fleets. Collision and shipwreck, caused by stress of weather, were the major terrors confronting those who went to sea in a coaster.

Frequently schooners were blown off shore and literally torn apart by the force of wind and waves. Fortunate indeed were those aboard such craft when rescue chanced along, usually in the form of a passing steamer and plucked them from the door of eternity, often just in the nick of time. Countless men were not so lucky and either went down with their vessel or abandoned it and were overwhelmed while adrift in a small boat. There are also cases on record of where crews became panicky and left their vessel which they expected to founder and the vessel then went on, staying afloat for months and in some cases, even years, without sinking or breaking up.

These floating derelicts, some barely awash, then became things of deadly consequence to those who chanced across their paths. They could easily cause the destruction of any vessel unfortunate enough to blunder into them. During the years 1887 to 1891, there were 957 derelicts between the 52nd meridian of west Longitude and the east coast of America that were reported to the Hydrographic office at Washington, D.C. Of these, 332 were identified by name and the remainder were either capsized or battered beyond recognition. On the average, there were about 20 derelicts drifting aimlessly about the North Atlantic at any given moment during this time, with a life expectancy of about one month. A very large proportion of these were coasting vessels, many loaded with cargos of lumber so that it was impossible for them to go down. As many as 1,000 had been reported in a single year, according to an article by Gilbert A. Grosvenor in the September, 1918 issue of the National Geographic Magazine, and the majority of these were in or near the Gulf Stream. Obviously these menaces to navigation had to be dealt with.

The Hydrographic Office of the Navy Department kept a careful check on derelicts, requesting every sighting to be reported to the department giving its exact location, direction of drift, appearance, and if possible, its name. The office gave each derelict a serial number and plotted its position on a map. After cross checking several reports on the same wreck, it was possible in some cases, to guess its direction of drift and enable government vessels to intercept and destroy it. Derelict information was published in weekly Hydrographic bulletins and on monthly pilot charts. Revenue cutters, and after 1915, Coast Guard cutters on patrol were also charged with keeping an eye out for abandoned vessels, either towing them to port whenever possible or blowing them up when salvage was impractical.

As diligent as these various governmental services were in the performance of their duties, many of these derelicts seemed to have been guided by ghostly hands and truely led a charmed existance, staying afloat for great lengths of time and traveling prodigious distances with none but the wind and the sea for company. According to the records of the Hydrographic Office, one finds that in six years, 25 derelicts were reported as having drifted at least 1,000 miles each, 11 have 2,000 miles apiece to their credit and 3 each, sailed the astounding distance of 5,000 or more rudderless miles.

In 1884, the "W. L. White", a 660 gross ton, three-masted schooner, was launched at Rockland, Maine. Four years later, during the big blizzard of March, 1888, she had to be abandoned just east of the Delaware Capes. The crewless vessel then started a drift towards the banks of Newfoundland, where she remained for many days. wandering back and forth in the path of trans-Atlantic shipping. She finally took a slant to the northeast and eventually drove ashore on Haskeir Island, one of the Hebrides, after traveling about 6,000 miles in 310 days. Her cargo of timber, which was the means of her staying afloat, was salvaged by the islanders and found to be in fairly good condition.

In 1895, the 522 ton, three-master, "Alma Cummings", built and owned in Boston, was abandoned in February off Chesapeake Bay. After the month of May had passed, nothing further was heard from the derelict schooner and most people presumed that she had gone ashore on some lonely beach and broken up. However, she turned up a year later in March, 1896, and was reported as being 800 miles off the Cape Verdes Islands. She was totally dismasted, had evidently been set on fire by some passing vessel and her deck was level with the sea. In August of the same year, she was finally observed ashore on an island off the San Blas coast, Isthmus of Panama, with the natives hard at work stripping anything they could from her wrecked hull.

The story of the big Canadian four-masted schooner, "Governor Parr", built in 1918 at Parrsboro, Nova Scotia, is an interesting account of a vessel that refused to meet her end gracefully. This 912 net ton coaster was claimed to be the most handsome vessel launched in Atlantic Canada and was named after an early governor of Nova Scotia. On September 25, 1923, she left from Ingramport, Nova Scotia, bound for Buenos Aires in command of Captain A. D. Richards, with a load of lumber. Soon after sailing she ran into a North-Atlantic snorter and lost her mizzen and spanker masts and suffered other extensive damage. On October 3rd, she was abandoned, her crew being taken off by the American liner, S.S. "Schodack", several hundred miles south of Newfoundland. A chronological account of her meanderings was reported in Sea Breezes Magazine in October, 1924.

"November, 1923. — Boarded by a boat from the "Saxonia" and found water-logged, but otherwise in good condition, with two of her masts standing.

"December, 1923. — United States coastguard cutter "Seneca" sent out to deal with the derelict. She got on the track, but was disabled and had to return. Just before Christmas the United States cutter "Tampa" left New York with orders to destroy the "Governor Parr". She found her on New Year's Day some 33 miles east from where she was abandoned. The derelict was taken in tow, but the "Tampa" ran short of fuel and had to abandon her.

"February, 1924. — Sighted another 300 miles eastwards, drifting strongly. The derelict doubled on her track, and was reported by the White Star liner "Majestic", who saw her in broad daylight in the middle of April, 330 miles nearer America.

"Middle of June. — Seen by the American steamer "Olen", who stated that her bowsprit, anchors and deckhouses were intact, and that she was floating on an even keel.

"July. — Haunting the Canaries route off the coast of Portugal. A Lisbon tug was sent out to destroy her on "no-cure, no pay" terms. Bad weather forced the tug to return home.

"August 8th. — Encountered by the West African liner "Zaria", who found her water-logged and awash amid-ships. It was decided to finish her this time. She was boarded and two drums of paraffin were used to start two fires — one in the forecastle and the other amidships. As soon as she was well ablaze the liner proceeded on her voyage.

"August 11th. — Seen burning by the "Umtali".

"August 13th. — Seen by the "Iberia", who reported that she was 'not on fire'".

She was last sighted on October 14, 1924, off the Canary Islands, still afloat and some 2,000 miles east from where she had been abandoned, although the exact mileage covered by her wanderings greatly exceeded 2,000 miles. Captain Richards and one of the seamen from the "Parr" lost their lives on this last voyage of the big schooner and where she finally settled her bones after this unusual passage, no one knows.

Again quoting from the October, 1924 issue of Sea Breezes:

"It had been found that ships abandoned along the Atlantic seaboard of the United States are carried south by the Labrador current for some distance until, getting into the Gulf Stream, they proceed on a northeasterly course. Near the Azores the sea surface current opens out fanwise, and should a ship get into the southern portion, as the "Governor Parr" evidently did, she may be months covering a hundred miles. Once well into the northern stream, however, she will probably fetch up somewhere on the north coast of Scotland.

"Probably now that the where-abouts of the "Governor Parr" have been so closely defined, steps will be taken to bring her career to an end. How great is the derelict's capacity for mischief was shown in the spring of 1900 when the Allan liner "Ionian" struck one and limped into port with a gash 40 feet long in her side."

The schooner "B. B. Hardwick" was reported abandoned in October, 1919, south of the Azores and unlike the "Governor Parr", she headed west instead of east. A year later she was sighted 2,000 miles west of the spot where she had been deserted by her crew.

The vessel, however, that set the record for wandering the greatest distance, going in all directions, and for the longest period of time, is the 296 gross tons, 120 foot schooner "Fannie E. Wolston", built in 1882 at Bath, Maine. The "Wolston" was abandoned on October 15, 1891, off Cape Hatteras and started her lonely traveling by heading north in the Gulf Stream. Off Norfolk, Virginia, she suddenly changed course and went out across the Atlantic, towards Africa. On June 13, 1892 she was sighted half way across. She then headed southward for more than 300 miles; then shifted her course to the northeast for another 200 miles, retraced her track for several hundred miles and then turned again and went in the opposite direction. Then she took another tack and headed west for nearly 400 miles; then shaped a course to the north for 300 miles, then east again for 700 miles, so that in January, 1893, she was almost in the same Latitude and Longitude that she had been in during the previous June. In May, 1893, she was 1,000 miles away from where she had been in January, on the border of Cancer and midway between Florida and the coast of Africa.

Again the "Fannie E. Wolston" headed toward America for a passage of 600 miles and again began many months of erractic zigzagging back and forth.

Finally, thirty-one months after she had been abandoned to the elements, she was sighted for the last time 250 miles off Savannah, Georgia, having traveled the amazing distance of better than 7,000 miles with no living hand to guide her.

Those responsible for eliminating derelicts found it was one thing to plot the location of an abandoned vessel on a chart and another to go out and find it. And then once found it was not always easy to get rid of the menacing hulk, as one cutter was to discover while trying to dispose of the wreck of a 248 ton schooner. After failing in an attempt to tow the derelict to port, three 30 pound bombs of gun cotton were attached to the keel of the lumber laden vessel and set off. She remained still in one piece following this and five more bombs were placed on board which broke her back and split frames, but she stubbornly refused to break up or sink. The cutter then rammed the hulk amidships and broke her in two, releasing her cargo. After this, it still took several shells to drive the after section of the staunch three-master down to the depths of Davey Jones' locker.

Not all discoveries of derelict schooners ended unfavorably for the derelict. For example, the three-masted schooner "Frederick Roessner", a 406 ton vessel built in Bath, Maine, in 1890, was abandoned on June 9, 1912 in Lat. 35.48 N., Long. 74.05 W. She was reported to the derelict hunting Revenue cutter "Seneca", which immediately set out to find the disabled schooner. Four days later the "Roessner" was discovered in Lat. 37.40 N., Long. 68.50 W., having traveled a distance of no less than 285 miles in 96 hours.

In appearance the helpless schooner was a shambles with all of her masts gone and her decks awash. The men on the "Seneca", however, did not jump to the conclusion that the condition of the schooner was hopeless and investigated to determine how badly she was damaged about the hull. Their examination indicated that there was a possibility of saving the "Roessner" and accordingly a tow line was put on board and she was successfully towed to New York, where she was repaired and put back in service.

Since being placed in commission in 1908, the "Seneca" had cleared 40 obstructions to navigation, including the "Frederick Roessner", up to the middle of the year 1912, and of these 40 obstructions, six were abandoned vessels which she was able to tow back to port for repair.

Another of the schooners salvaged by the "Seneca" was the three-masted "Sadie C. Sumner", a 672 ton vessel, 176 feet long, built in 1890 at Thomaston, Maine. On February 8, 1910, the Dutch steamer "Prins Wilhelm III" arrived in New York and reported having spotted a waterlogged and dismasted sailing vessel drifting aimlessly at sea. Word of this sighting was immediately sent to the "Seneca", which succeeded in finding the derelict three days later on February 11th, southeast of the position reported. She was loaded with cypress lumber which kept her afloat, however her rudder had carried away, her masts were snapped off with only the stumps of the fore and main sticking above the deck, her bowsprit was broken off and she was full of water.

The "Seneca" took the derelict in tow and headed for the Virginia capes, but that night a northeast gale caught the two vessels and made it impossible for the cutter to continue towing. The "Seneca" led her tow line forward and tried to use the water-logged hulk as a sea anchor, but the line parted and it wasn't until February 13th that the cutter was able to get a line back aboard the "Sumner" and continue the trip toward land. Although the line parted again, the cutter and tow finally arrived at Hampton Roads, Virginia, on February 15th, where the dismasted schooner was anchored.

The "Sadie C. Sumner" was repaired and rerigged by the Newport News Shipyard and again put to sea. However, she was another of those vessels to which fate accorded much bad luck. On July 5, 1916, after leaving St. Andrews, Florida, with a cargo of hard pine for San Juan, she was caught in a hurricane. In an effort to save themselves and their vessel, her crew cut away the masts of the laboring schooner and while this prevented her from capsizing, her seams opened up and she sank so low in the water that the crew of nine had to take refuge atop the after cabin. Here, exposed to the full fury of the elements, they lashed themselves to keep from being washed overboard by the huge seas that were continually sweeping their wrecked schooner.

When the storm finally subsided, the men on the drifting wreck found that in order to survive, they had to dive down into the murky waters inside the vessel to get at the canned food stored below in the food lockers. The "Sumner" was once more a derelict, only this time was carrying her crew with her. After five days of aimless wandering in the currents of the Gulf, the unfortunate band finally drifted on to soundings, between Pensacola and St. Andrews Bay, where the crew of the "Sumner" were able to anchor their vessel. The dingy, which had been damaged in the storm, was repaired and all those aboard succeeded in reaching shore.

The "Sadie C. Sumner" was later picked up and towed to Mobile, where once again her wounds were patched up, but this time she went back to work as a barge, in November, 1916.

In August, 1917, due to the heavy wartime demand for shipping, the unlucky old coaster was once more rigged as a three-masted schooner. In 1918 she was sold to France for a high price and was renamed "Monte Grande", hailing from Le Havre.

Her change of flag, however, did little to change her bad luck, for on January 10, 1920, while bound from LeHavre to Haiti, she went ashore at East Wittering, England and went to pieces.

The history of derelicts floating along our Atlantic coast line is a long one and lasted as long as there were sailing coasters. On looking back even further into the past, stories such as the following were reported prior to the time when the United States had patrols searching for abandoned vessels.

In May, 1823, the "Integrity" fell in with a derelict close to Jamaica, the decks and hull of which were showing a rich crop of barnacles. Her cabin was full of water, but a trunk was fished up which when opened, contained coins, rings and watches to the value of 3,000 pounds.

In August, 1872, the schooner "Lancaster", sighted a dismasted derelict, the "Glenalvon", on board of which was found several skeletons, surmised to be the remains of her crew. There was not one morsel of food to be found anywhere.

106

An open Bible was reported to have been found laying face downward on the cabin table alongside a loaded revolver and a bottle which contained a paper upon which the following was written:

"Jesus guide this to some helpers! Merciful God, don't let us perish!"

All the bodies were reverently committed to the deep and the derelict "Glenalvon" was left to face whatever the future had in store for her.

In 1908 occurred the very unusual instance of a schooner rescuing the crew of another schooner and then turning around and salvaging the abandoned vessel by towing her to port. This was an experience accorded to Captain Harold G. Foss when he was in command of the four-masted "Sallie C. Marvil", owned and managed by A. H. Bull & Co., of New York.

In October, 1908, the "Marvil" sailed from Mobile, Alabama, with a cargo of hewn timber bound to Boston, Massachusetts. They had a good run up to Cape Hatteras where they ran into a heavy gale and were forced to reduce sail to a reefed fore, main and mizzen, the spanker and all other sails being furled. They headed off, close hauled on the port tack and did their best to ride out the terrible weather, as the wind gradually increased to hurricane force and seas built up to mountainous height. About 4:00 a.m. they wore ship and headed to the west and although the weather showed no signs of moderating, they seemed to be doing all right in their tussle with the elements.

At 7:00 a.m., the man at the wheel called Captain Foss's attention to a three-masted schooner that was to windward and heading down toward them with only a part of its foresail set. Through binoculars the Captain noticed that she was steering badly and had the American flag hung in the mizzen rigging, union down. Obviously she was in trouble and needed help.

When the distressed schooner got closer it was seen that her lifeboat had been lost and all the sails, with the exception of the foresail, were in shreds. Running dead before the wind, she passed close astern of the "Marvil", and the name of her bow, which read "Florence Shay", was plainly visible. The captain of the "Shay", using a megaphone, hollered over to those on board the "Marvil"; "Take us off; we're sinking!"

Captain Foss replied to those on the "Shay" telling them to lower their foresail, which after some discussion, they did, letting it go on the run. Realizing that the weather made the use of a lifeboat extremely dangerous, Captain Foss thought that he would try and put a line aboard the drifting schooner and hold her into the wind until the weather moderated enough to transfer the crew. After passing hairraisingly close to the windward side of the "Shay", a heaving line was put aboard the three-master and a towing hawser was then hauled over. As soon as a strain was placed upon the hawser, it parted and most of it was lost.

They then got the lifeboat on the "Marvil" ready and the mate and one other hand volunteered to go over after the crew on the other vessel. An oil slick was let out which helped calm the breaking seas somewhat and the lifeboat with the two men in it was cast adrift up wind of the "Shay". Within five minutes the boat was fast to the stern of the wallowing schooner.

All nine men on the "Shay" managed to get in the lifeboat, and the "Marvil" then ran down to them, came into the wind and picked them all up, leaving the lifeboat towing astern on a long painter. When Captain Gilbert of the "Shay" came on board the "Marvil" he handed Captain Foss his sextant saying, "Here, Foss, take this as a present, because if I ever get my feet on dry land once more then I will never go to sea again".

Captain Foss told him to keep his sextant and go below, have a good stiff drink and have some dinner which had been prepared for them. After eating, Captain Gilbert was shown to a spare room where he was able to get some much needed sleep.

During all this time, the "Marvil" had been standing by the "Shay" and Captain Foss noticed that she did not seem to be going down very fast. The thought of salvage came into his mind. At 4:00 the mate came on watch and Captain Foss put the idea up to him, pointing out that the weather was getting better and the barometer was on the way up. Captain Foss told the mate that he could take the crew from the "Marvil" and go back on board the "Shay", pump her out and then they would try and tow the abandoned vessel to Norfolk, Virginia. The mate went for the idea at once and so did the rest of the crew of the "Marvil", when they were asked.

Leaving Captain Foss, the cook and the donkeyman, plus the rescued men on board the "Marvil", the mate and the rest of the crew managed to get back aboard the "Shay" and set to their labors of getting the schooner ready for a tow next day. As soon as his men were safely aboard the other vessel, Captain Foss went aloft on his own schooner and cut free the wire topping lifts on the fore, main and mizzen masts. These lengths when shackled together made a very strong towing cable 400 feet long, to which a heavy rope, doubled up, was attached at each end. The "Marvil" then stood by as her crew continued throughout the night, pumping the laboring "Shay".

The next morning, after three tries, the towing hawser was hauled aboard the "Shay" and made fast around the foremast. Then easing his vessel off the wind, Captain Foss began towing his prize towards Cape Henry at the rate of 4 knots.

When Captain Gilbert came on deck soon after, he was understandably astounded to find one of his own men at the wheel of the "Sallie C. Marvil" and his late command, the "Florence Shay", dogging along astern at the end of a tow line.

About noon a large passenger liner, the ss "Prinz Eitel Freidrich", came up with the two schooners and offered assistance, which Captain Foss declined, thanking them and asking if they would please send a wire to his owners, A. H. Bull & Co., telling them he was heading for Hampton Roads. The liner replied that the wire would be sent immediately and wished them luck, hoping they would make it all right. By sundown they were about 73 miles away from Cape Henry, however the weather did not look good to Captain Foss and the glass had started slowly falling.

Around 2:00 a.m., the lights of another vessel were approaching them and soon turned out to be lights carried aboard the ocean going tug "Walter E.

Luckenbach". They had "gotten wind" of the rescue through the radio message sent to the "Marvils" owners and the skipper of the tug tried to con Captain Foss into taking his tow line by telling him he had authority from A. H. Bull & Co., to tow the "Marvil" and the "Shay" into port. Captain Foss doubted that this was the case and told the tug to go back where it came from.

After much haggling back and forth, Captain Foss told the tug that he would agree to giving him one third of the salvage money, but the tug boat captain would have none of this and steamed off in a huff. He only went away a mile or so before he turned around and came back, asking Captain Foss if he had changed his mind.

"No", replied the Captain, "but probably you have, or else why did you come back?"

Captain Foss's offer was finally accepted and at 9 o'clock both vessels were safely anchored in Hampton Roads. The crew of the "Marvil" returned to their own vessel and Captain Gilbert and his crew went back on board the "Shay". Captain Foss telephoned his owners in New York, who complimented him on a job well done and the next day the "Sallie C. Marvil" got under way and continued with her trip to Boston.

The men on the "Florence Shay" were lucky. If rescue hadn't come along in the form of the "Sallie C. Marvil", they might otherwise have been lost; their vessel either going under or being swept ashore on some remote part of the Atlantic coastline. Many an unfortunate coaster had finished her career in this way.

The United States Life Saving Service which began its existence with the establishment of a few crude refuge shelters on the Jersey coast in 1848, eventually played a great role in saving the lives of mariners cast ashore or otherwise in peril on our eastern coastline. The establishment of huts was extended to the shores of Long Island and Rhode Island and eventually all of the dangerous areas of our eastern coast had manned stations which were always on the alert for ships in distress during the dangerous times of the year. Mr. Sumner I. Kimball took charge of the Service in 1871 and brought it to a wonderful state of efficiency providing for beach patrols, surf boats and breeches buoy apparatus with paid and thoroughly trained men residing at the stations. Although the number of vessels going ashore continued high, the loss of life on those vessels showed a great decrease due to the efforts of the new service. In 1915 the Life Saving Service merged with the Revenue Cutter Service into one organization which became known as the United States Coast Guard under the jurisdiction of the Department of Treasury.

In 1875, Congress passed an act requiring records to be kept at the various life saving stations and ordered an annual report prepared listing the activities of the service for each preceeding year. These reports make interesting reading and plainly indicate how large were the numbers of coasting vessels that came to grief on our eastern shoreline; most of the endings being violent ones, as mentioned earlier.

In the Annual Report of the United States Life Saving Service for 1912, is found listed for April 30th, a report typical of many found throughout this and the many reports that were filed both before and after that date.

While "making the midnight to 2 a.m. patrol north, a surfman from Cape Henlopen, (Delaware) Station discovered a schooner dangerously near the beach. He burned two successive signals in an effort to warn her off, but she paid no heed to the warnings and soon stranded, striking 50 yards from the shore near the point of the Cape. The weather was thick, with a strong east-northeast gale blowing and a high sea running, which explains the inability of the vessel to keep out of danger.

"The surfman sent in a call to his station by telephone from the halfway house on the beach. He also notified the station at Lewes on the opposite side of the cape. The crew of the two stations met abreast of the vessel at 2:00 a.m. and put off to her in the Cape Henlopen station surfboat. They found her to be the 187 ton schooner "James Duffield," from Portland, Maine, for Philadelphia, with a cargo of brownstone. She had filled soon after grounding, and when the service boat pulled alongside, the waves were breaking clean over her. Notwithstanding the state of the wind and sea, the rescuers succeeded in boarding her, taking her crew of five safely off and getting back unscathed to shore. The vessel and cargo were totally lost."

The "James Duffield" was a three-masted, centerboard schooner, which was built at New London, Connecticut in 1889 by James Davidson & Son. She measured 187 gross tons, 177 net tons, 112.3 feet in length, 28 feet beam and 8.8 feet in depth and at the time of her loss was owned in Hartford, Connecticut. She was 23 years old at the time of her stranding, which was considered to be a fairly long life span for a wooden vessel. Although there were many wooden sailing craft that lasted more than three times that long, fifteen years of active service from such vessels was about all that one could safely expect as an average. Indeed, many vessels never lasted to complete their first voyage. There are many accounts of new vessels sailing away on their maiden voyages which were never heard from again. Others were swept ashore and dashed to pieces only a short while after leaving port.

One of the last of the big four-masted schooners to be built in Canada managed to set a record for being the schooner with the shortest sea going career. This was the 820 net ton "George Melville Cochrane", which was launched at Port Greville, Nova Scotia in 1919. The new schooner was taken to Saint John to be rigged and after this was completed, loaded a cargo of lumber at the same port. On February 24, 1919, she was towed out of Saint John, bound for Buenos Aires under command of Captain Arthur Conrad. When she cast off her tow and set sail the weather was fine and there was every indication that things would go well for her first voyage.

As darkness approached the breeze began to pick up and blew quite hard, however, this in itself was nothing out of the ordinary. A little later the watch on deck noticed that the lee rigging had suddenly gone slack, but before anything could be done to remedy this situation, she was struck by a squall and her masts went over the side. She was drifting in the high swells and strong tidal currents off Brier Island, Nova Scotia, and in short order was washed ashore and pounded to pieces, making her life span upon the high seas something that was numbered only in hours rather than in days.

Another coaster which did not last long was the big 2,638 gross ton "Washington B. Thomas", built in 1903 at Thomaston, Maine. The "Thomas" left Newport News, Virginia, on June 3, 1903, on the last leg of her second voyage. She was bound for Portland, with a cargo of 4,226 tons of coal and carried fifteen people on board, including Mrs. Lermond, the wife of Captain Lermond who was master of the "Thomas". Captain Lermond was a veteran square rig captain with much deep water experience.

On the afternoon of June 11th, after a somewhat slow passage, the fog cleared and Richmond's Island on the Maine coast was sighted, whereupon Captain Lermond stood the "Thomas" to sea. At 7:00 he changed tacks and once more headed inshore, finally dropping his starboard anchor in nineteen fathoms of water. The weather was calm, but they were surrounded by an exceedingly thick fog.

The big schooner lay at anchor all night and all the next day due to the heavy fog and only once did they get a clear spot in the soupy weather about them. They were then barely able to make out Wood Island lighthouse, which bore north by east, just before the fog shut in again. At 9:00 p.m. on the 12th, the breeze sprang fresh from the southwest and continued to increase until it had worked itself into a regular gale. A sea made up and in a short time the "Washington B. Thomas" was found to be dragging. The port anchor was let go and for a while she brought up to her anchors. It was discovered soon after this, when she began to drag a second time, that the starboard anchor had carried away from its chain. Captain Lermond tried to raise the port anchor and get to sea, clear of the dangerous lee shore, but they were unable to start the anchor, nor could they, on account of the sweeping seas that were breaking aboard, get at the shackle and slip the cable.

The deeply laden schooner continued to drag until around 10 or 11 p.m., when she was carried onto one of the outlying reefs off Stratten's Island, where she started to break up. Mrs. Lermond was caught in the after cabin and drowned in spite of everything Captain Lermond tried to do to save her. The shipwrecked crew were spotted next day and late in the afternoon a surfboat was able to remove nine of the survivors in spite of the tremendous seas that were running. Captain Lermond and the remainder of his crew had to remain aboard the rest of the night, clinging to the wave washed forward section of the schooner. They were finally taken off by the returning surfboat at 8:00 the next morning, making a total of 14 lives that were saved. Several of those rescued were badly injured and Captain Lermond was never the same after the loss of his wife and his vessel. The "Washington B. Thomas" soon broke up completely. She had been in operation for only 60 days.

Some schooners that went ashore were fortunate enough to survive the ordeal, eventually being hauled off and resuming their careers. This happened to the "Nathaniel T. Palmer", when she went ashore at Beach Haven, New Jersey on March 11, 1901; to the "George P. Hudson", ex "Fannie Palmer", when she stranded at Southhampton, Long Island on April 9, 1908; to the Canadian four-master "Ada Towers", when she went ashore in 1926 at Sayville, Long Island, and to the three-master "Thomas B. Garland", when she went ashore at Great

Point, Nantucket on Dec. 16, 1910; all of these vessels, and many more, were hauled off, only to be lost in another place at a later date.

The flush decked four-master "Katie J. Barrett" was a 967 gross ton, 191 foot vessel, built in Bath, Maine, in 1887. On February 24, 1890, she went ashore on Nauset Beach, Cape Cod, and by the end of the next month, it looked like she was finished. Her masts had gone over the side and her jibboom was broken off at the cap. She was exposed to the full fury of the surf and many times had to take a terrible pounding, with waves breaking and flying clean across her long deck. However, she just sat there and refused to break up.

The following September she was bought as she was for next to nothing by a man named Green, from Boston. Green hired some salvage experts and to the wonder of many, the "Barrett" was hauled off the beach and towed to Boston. It was said that before the tow arrived inside Boston Light, Green had been offered $15,000 for the staunch old schooner. At Boston she was repaired and put back in service under the new name "Star of the Sea". Under this name she repaid Green's gamble by staying active in the trade for over the next twenty years.

Some stranded vessels seemed to exhibit an almost human quality for cussedness or stubborness and although not damaged by their stranding, would repeatedly foil every effort made to set them afloat again. Witness the following.

On December 18, 1887 the "Lewis King" came ashore a mile and a half southwest of Montauk Point, Long Island, at a spot called Stony Brook. The "King" was a 150 gross ton, two-master, built in 1883 at Ellsworth, Maine and was also owned there. Her stranding did not injure the vessel and T. A. Scott, of Scott Wrecking Company from New London, Connecticut, came over and succeeded in getting her back in the water. She immediately went back on the same spot during a storm and was then sold to New York people who were successful in launching her a second time. Another storm came up before she could be taken away, and back she went to the same spot on the rocky beach. Some people from Greenport then took her over and again managed to get her back in the water, however, she went back on the beach a fourth time. Finally, two years after she first went ashore, the "Lewis King" was burned to get her out of the way.

The "Alice E. Clark", a 1,621 gross ton four-master, launched in 1898 at Bath, Maine, by Percy & Small, foiled all attempts to save her after she ran onto a rocky ledge off Coombs Point, Islesboro, Maine. This happened when the captain of the coal laden vessel misjudged her location on July 1, 1909, and ran inside of the buoy off the ledge. After she struck she filled with water, but her owners, J. S. Winslow & Co., thought there was a chance of saving her and called in salvage experts. However, the "Clark" refused to cooperate and rolled over. Following a heavy gale which struck the coast on December 5, 1909, she broke into pieces and disappeared.

There definitely were parts of the eastern coastline which proved more prone to shipwreck than others and of course these places earned unfavorable reputations with mariners. Nantucket, Cape Cod and the Vineyard, together with their surrounding shoals, accounted for hundreds upon hundreds of losses among the coasting fleets. Long Island, especially at its eastern end, had more than its share of wrecks and the coast of New Jersey and Delaware figured in the loss of a great many coasters.

The one place though, that was the most dreaded by coastwise and deepwater sailors alike, was Cape Hatteras, often referred to as, "The graveyard of the Atlantic". David Stick in his book dealing with the history of the coast of North Carolina, lists over 399 schooners lost between 1815 and 1942, and this does not include vessels of other rigs that were engaged in coasting, nor does it take into account the fact that many vessels struck bottom off those dreaded shoals and were beaten to small pieces before they could be identified as to name or rig.

There were two schooners listed as lost on the coast of North Carolina in 1942, the last year in which any coaster losses were reported from that state. One was the "Anna R. Heidritter", which was lost at Ocracoke on March 2nd, and the other was the "Mayfair", lost on Carolina Beach on November 9th.

The loss of the "Anna R. Heidritter" is described by her master, Captain Bennet D. Coleman, in a letter he sent to his sister, Jennie Hamlin. This letter and information on Captain Coleman and the "Heidritter" was kindly supplied by Mrs. Allan F. Robbins of Teaticket, Massachusetts. Mrs. Robbins states that Captain Coleman was from Cotuit, Massachusetts, and came from a long line of seafarers, originally from Nantucket. He was at one time master of the three-masted schooner "Francis B. Goudnow" and prior to the "Heidritter", had command of the three-masted "George Edmonds", which he took over when she was brand new and sailed until she was lost during World War I.

The "Anna R. Heidritter" was originally built as the four-masted "Cohasset" in Bath, Maine, in 1903. On January 22, 1907, she caught fire at Baltimore and was all but destroyed, burning to the waters edge. What was left was later towed to the Sharptown Marine Railway Company at Sharptown, Maryland, where she was rebuilt as a four-master, renamed "Anna R. Heidritter", and launched in 1910.

The "Heidritter" measured 694 gross tons, 610 net tons, was 185 feet long, 37.1 feet beam and was 13.5 feet in depth, and carried a crew of eight. Captain Coleman's letter follows:

"My dear Jennie and all: I am sure this will do for all as I have so much to attend to.

"No doubt you have heard that my old schooner is no more. Well, we sailed from Charleston on a Friday and on Sunday had a good run to Hatteras on our way to the Delaware where we were bound with logwood from Haiti. Of course on account of the enemy submarines which were operating around Hatteras and north it was not, according to Naval orders, wise to get around the shoals only in daylight. When we got up here the wind came ahead from N and N.E so no chance to dodge around to any kind of safety so we anchored E.S.E. of Ocracoke light (in) an inlet in 13 fathom, nice place to be in a N.E. wind and storm but we were of course exposed to any sub that would be lurking around, and there was, for while we were ashore at a fisherman's home after our wreck they sank a steamer inside of where we were only 2 miles off Ocracoke bar. Anyway a heavy S.E. gale came on, we gave her all anchors and chains and the kedge anchors with 150 fathoms of hawser, but she lost the anchors and chains, came for the beach and sails would not stand and in fact we could not do anything as the fires all washed out the boiler in the engine room, cleaned out the forward house. When she neared the bars which were breaking masthead high, every man got into the rigging and lashed himself, and the sea broke above us and we shifted up to about 40 ft. from the water. There was plenty flying over us there, but after pounding over she rested more easily, her head wobbled around in a most distracting manner. There was too much sea on the beach for the life savers to get near, but at low tide the next afternoon both stations got to work and got a line across which we got to the mast head and we all came ashore in the breeches buoy. We were able to get off to the vessel only once for the week, the sea and wind so bad. Saved my sextants and chronometer and some clothes that we dug up out of the mud and water in the cabin; 4 ft. of water at low tide, but standing on the bed in rubber boots we raked up some, had them cleaned so got a change of clothes from oil skins on Saturday.

"Well, it don't look very good to start again. One of my owners suggested buying me another vessel that can be bought, but I guess I'll give it a trial ashore. Seems to bad to lose the old schooner as it would have been better to have sold her to someone, got something to use to start life anew ashore. That's what it amounts to. However, we were lucky to get out. If the masts had gone on the shoals we would have gone with them, but she was a strong old craft. Has weathered many gales with me and died honestly. I did not run her ashore. We tried our best for two hours to keep her off.

"I am writing this to you and if there is anything of interest to the others pass it along. I may go to New York from here. Much love to all.

Bennett

"A sailor without a ship the first time in 48 years, that is for any length of time."

According to a letter from Mrs. Robbins:

"Captain Coleman never got a chance at shore life as he was killed about three days after he had written this letter. He headed for Jersey City to a relative's house, took a cab from the railroad station, which was involved in an accident about two miles from his destination."

As mentioned earlier, collisions at sea were a common cause of loss for many in the coasting fleet. Not only were the coasters working in the confines of coastal waters, but in addition, were constantly passing or entering busy ports where foreign shipping was also passing, increasing the possibility of collisions. Although coasters occasionally ran into coasters, it was steamships which were more often at fault. Liners bent on keeping to a strict schedule and barreling through thick fog, or officers aboard who underestimated the speed of a nearby coaster, often caused the loss of the unlucky sailing craft. The right of the way in many of these cases belonged to the sailing vessel, but most of the time it was the sailing vessel that was lost.

To go into a detailed account of the many collisions and sinkings that occurred would be repetitious, suffice to say that they happened both upon the open sea as well as in protected waters and if a schooner was fully loaded with a cargo such as coal, it usually meant the end of the coaster then and there.

There is at least one case on record of where a fully loaded schooner was rammed and sank and it later rose to the surface. This happened to the four-masted schooner "A. Ernest Mills", which had been built in Stockton Springs, Maine in 1919 and was owned by the famous firm of Crowell & Thurlow.

The "Mills", in command of Captain Carl Chaney of Medford, Massachusetts, had loaded a full cargo of salt at Turks Island and was bound north for Norfolk, Virginia. On the night of May 3, 1929, the "Mills" was very close to her destination, the weather was good, the night clear and everyone aboard the four-master expected to be in port the next day.

Three United States destroyers came steaming out of Norfolk in straight formation and while the first one managed to miss the heavily laden schooner, the second, named "Childs", cut deeply into the hull of the four-master. Instead of keeping her bow in the gaping hole she made, the "Childs" backed away full astern, and the "A. Ernest Mills" went straight to the bottom.

A month later, the salt cargo aboard the sunken schooner had dissolved sufficiently to allow her to float to the surface and she became a menace to navigation. The Coast Guard took charge of the derelict and blew it up, part of the wreckage drifting ashore on the coast of Virginia.

One of the weirdest cases involving the loss of a schooner happened to the three-masted "Peaceland", in 1943. The "Peaceland" was built in Annapolis, Nova Scotia in 1919 and was the last three-master to operate out of the Bay of Fundy. On February 2, 1943, she was sold to the United States and her first voyage under the American flag, loaded cement and machinery at Norfolk, Virginia. Soon after leaving port she ran into a bit of winter weather and began to leak, so her master, Captain Walsh, ran back to a sheltered anchorage behind the point of one of the Virginia Capes. While she was waiting there for the weather to change, a Coast Guard cutter came alongside to see if everything was all right. Those on the schooner informed the cutter that everything was fine and requested them to take the cook ashore to mail some letters and to get some new lenses for his glasses. The cutter consented to this and when the cook left the schooner, his comrades lined the rail to wave him a good bye. The cook later said that when he left the "Peaceland", she was wallowing deep, "like a pig in a mudhole!"

The cook was gone from his vessel for twenty-four hours and when he tried to return, he found to his amazement and dismay, that the "Peaceland" with his six shipmates aboard, had vanished. To this day no one knows what happened to the old schooner, other than the fact that she had probably gone down. Where or why she went down is still a mystery.

World War I and World War II, both caused an increase in the use of sailing coasters and both also caused the decrease in the numbers of these vessels. Prior to the First World War, many of the vessels on the east coast were being laid up, sold, or were carrying cargos that afforded little profit, and very few were being built, when compared to a decade before. However, with the arrival of the war in Europe, all things changed and a great demand developed for shipping. Foreign powers were paying fantastic prices for practically anything that would float across the Atlantic. Whole fleets, as with the Winslows and Percy & Small, were sold abroad and more were ordered built. People who had hung on to their schooners, made big money during the war years.

The United States, under President Wilson, did its best to stay neutral and tried not to become actively involved in the struggle going on in Europe. However, continuing efforts made by the United States to trade with Europe slowly but surely helped in drawing America into the middle of the struggle.

On Thursday, February 15, 1917, The New York Times ran a headline that read:

"AUSTRIAN SUBMARINE DESTROYS AMERICAN SCHOONER; BERLIN REPEATS U-BOAT WAR WILL BE UNRESTRICTED".

The article dated Washington, February 14th, went in part, as follows: "The American sailing schooner "Lyman M. Law," enroute with a cargo of lumber from Maine to Italy, was destroyed by an Austrian submarine off the coast of Sardinia, in the Mediterranean, last Monday, according to official information which reached the state department today in a dispatch from Roger Culver Treadwell, American Counsul at Rome.

"Captain S. W. McDonough and his crew of nine men have landed at Cagliari, Sardinia. Seven of the crew are Americans and two are British."

The "Lyman M. Law", formerly belonging to the Benedict-Manson Marine Company, had been sold by them prior to the war, and belonged at the time of her sinking to a syndicate at Stockton Springs, Maine, headed by Mr. George A. Cardine. Her agents were the Maritime Transportation Company of New York. She was a 1,300 ton vessel, 211 feet long and had left Stockton Springs on January 9th, loaded with a cargo of box shocks and was bound to Palermo. The schooner was boarded by the sub at 9:00 on Monday, February 12, and was sunk very near the zone designated by Germany on January 31st, as the boundary between the zone in which shipping bound for Greece would be exempt from attack and the barred area in which all shipping was to be subject to attack without warning. After the attack, the "Law" was observed in flames in Lat. 38.32 N., Long. 7.58 E., southwest of Sardinia.

In another article in the same issue of the Times, this paragraph was printed:

"Today news comes that the American sailing ship Lyman M. Law has been sunk by an Austrian submarine under circumstances that may lead this Government to conclude that it is useless to be patient longer with Germany and her Teutonic ally."

Within a very short time the fat was in the fire and German war vessels, mainly submarines, were actively engaged in sinking American vessels of all types. In 1917, at least thirteen schooners belonging to the United States were sunk by enemy action, and in 1918 at least fourteen, or more, United States sailing coasters went to the bottom from the same cause.

Between May 15, and October 20, 1918, no less than six German submarines had arrived off the coast of the United States and were sinking our merchant vessels by bombs, mines and torpedo. These subs were the U-151, the U-156, the U-140, the U-117, the U-155 and the U-152. Had not the armistice been impending, another, the U-139, would have joined in the attack upon our vessels.

The first U-boat, the U-151, in command of Commander von Nostitz, claimed the American schooners "Hattie Dunn", "Hauppauge" and "Edna", which they sunk or damaged with TNT bombs on May 25, 1918. On June 2nd, the same U-boat sunk the schooners "Isabel B. Wiley", "Jacob B. Haskell" and "Edward H. Cole". On June 4th she sunk the "Samuel G. Mengel" and on June 5th, set off TNT charges on the "Edward R. Baird Jr.", however the lumber on board the "Baird" kept her from going down and she was later towed to port and repaired.

The "Hauppauge" was a new vessel at the time she was attacked by the German U-boat, having just been launched at Wilmington, North Carolina, and she, like the "Baird", did not go down. She carried no cargo at the time, which is probably why the four-master was able to stay afloat. She was eventually hauled in and repaired. She was renamed the "Alice L. Pendleton", sometime during the early 1920's. She ended her days as a rotting hulk in Noank, Connecticut.

After sinking or severely damaging the vessels mentioned above, plus a large number of steamers, the U-151 left the coast of the United States on June 13th and headed home for Germany. For a considerable part of her stay on the coast of the United States the submarine kept the crews from some of the sunken coasters as prisoners aboard the sub, however they were all released unharmed, before the sub left the coastline. On her way back she overhauled and sank the schooner "Samoa", of Christiania and also bagged several steamers, finally arriving safely at Kiel at 9:30 a.m. on July 20, 1918.

Only a short time after the end of the war, it's interesting to note than an American submarine "got into the act" and bagged a coasting vessel. This occurred on November 24, 1919, when the "R-3" and the schooner "Oakwoods" were in collision off the Cape Cod Canal. The "Oakwoods" was a two-masted, 173 gross ton vessel that had been built in Kennebunkport, Maine, in 1880 and was 96 feet long. The schooner came off second best, with the two crewmen on board being saved.

When the United States became involved in the Second World War, the few coasting vessels that were still in operation were having all they could do to survive and many were on their last legs. Schooners had been laid up in bone yards along the coast all during the 1930's and those that were thought at all suitable were again hauled out, quickly repaired and put to sea. The casualty rate for these old timers was very high and by the end of the war, there were not many left. Although enemy submarines accounted for the loss of a few, most of them were lost by foundering, abandonment, stranding, or other natural causes. In 1940 there were at least a dozen American and Canadian four-masted schooners still in operation. By the end of the war there were only two of these remaining, most of them having been lost between 1940 and 1943. There were also about two dozen three-masters operating in 1940 and they too, were cut down to a very small number by 1945. Of these three dozen vessels only three are definitely known to have been attacked by German submarines, although several left port and went missing and may have been victims of Hitler's undersea raiders.

The "George E. Klinck" is a typical of the schooners that were taken out of retirement during the war and put back to work. The "Klinck" was built in 1904 at Mystic, Connecticut, by M. B. McDonald and was a regular three-masted coaster, with nothing special about her except the fact that she was still around in 1941. In the 1930's, the "Klinck" had been laid up with a sister ship in Rockland, Maine, and by 1937 was no more than a derelict. With the arrival of the war she was taken over by new owners, fixed up and again went to sea. She was a single decked vessel measuring 560 gross tons and was 152 feet in length.

On March 7, 1941, while bound from Jacksonville, Florida, to Portland, Maine, under Captain Lewis McFarland, she ran into a mean southwester off Cape Hatteras which tore her apart and she started to founder. Fortunately the aircraft carrier, U.S.S. "Wasp" came along and dramatically rescued the crew of the doomed schooner just before she went down. She sank in Lat. 35.02 N., Long. 74.21 W., ESE. off Cape Hatteras, carrying down with her the high hopes of some who thought that coastal sail might be revived.

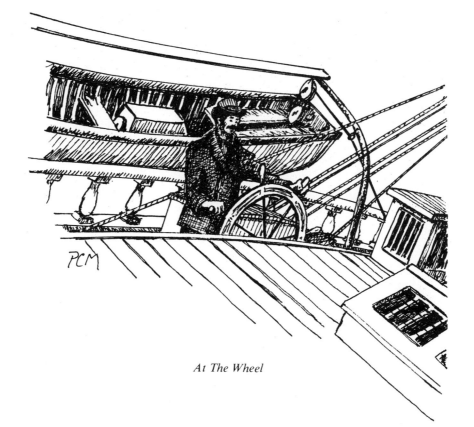

*At The Wheel*

## Chapter XV

## THE MEN AND THE TRADES

In only a few ways was the life on a coasting schooner like that on a deep-waterman. The crew was divided into two watches, the first mate being in charge of the port watch and the second mate, generally called the "Bosun" on coasting vessels, taking charge of the captain's, or starboard watch. The watches lasted four hours on, and four hours off, but were broken up by the dog watches from 4:00 p.m. to 6:00 p.m. and from 6:00 p.m. to 8:00 p.m., alternating the times that a particular watch would be on deck each succeeding day.

Generally speaking, the crew on a schooner was numbered at two men per mast, plus the captain. However, this was not a fixed rule and frequently that number was exceeded by one or two on larger vessels and quite often fewer were found on small ones. In addition to the captain and two mates, there was usually an engineer and cook, plus the hands in the forecastle. A typical four-master then, would carry nine people on board and there would be only three people in one watch, the cook and engineer not being required to stand regular watches. Each of the two sailors in the watch would be required to spend two hours of each four, standing their trick at the wheel. There was supposed to be a lookout kept forward at all times, but during daylight hours this worthy was usually called off the forecastle-head by the officer in charge and put to work doing something more useful.

The days work commenced at daylight and usually was begun by washing off the decks with the pumps and then swabbing them down. Officers most always prided themselves on the appearance of their vessel, and cleaning, scraping and painting were the routine jobs that frequently occupied those on watch. Any major sail changing was saved, if possible, until the switching of the watches when all hands would be on deck and could be called upon to turn to and help with the job. Of course this was not always possible. If an emergency arose in the middle of a watch, then those off watch would be called on deck and all hands, including the officers, would pitch in together to get the job done.

There was no overtime paid for work done while "off watch". In the 1880's a seaman's pay was in the neighborhood of $16 to $18 per month in the winter, and nearer $20 per month in the summer. With the influence of the unions being felt around the turn of the century, a seaman's pay rose to around $30 per month and finally reached $60 a month for those few who were still sailing in 1940.

During the mid 1890's, the engineer, cook and first mate were each paid about the same wage, which was somewhere between $50 and $55 per month. The engineer was responsible for having steam up in the donkey boiler at any time, day or night, that there might be a call for power and also had to keep all the machinery in working order. The cook started his work at half past 3:00 in the morning so that he might have coffee ready for the watches which changed at 4'00. He had to serve three meals a day and did not have the benefit of refrigeration. He had to keep the cabin and galley clean and the things therein polished. He also had the duty of keeping the lamps aboard in working order with their wicks properly trimmed and chimneys cleaned. Next to the mate, he was probably the hardest working individual on the vessel.

Over half of the captains in the coasting fleet came from the state of Maine. In 1900 a capable master might earn as much as $2,800 a year, which in those days meant a great deal more than it does today. The officers usually were native Americans or Canadians and in the early days of the trade, the crews were also made up of Yankees. After the turn of the Twentieth Century, fewer New Englanders were to be found among the crews and by the time the First World War came upon the country, very few native Americans were in the forecastles of our large coasting vessels. More often, the smaller vessels were more apt to carry a larger number of Americans than did the bigger vessels.

The crews usually signed on for a round trip on a coaster before a United States Shipping Commissioner and were required to perform their duties until the termination of the voyage. They could then stay or leave, depending upon their whim, providing the vessel was ready to sign on a new crew. If not, they were kicked out whether they wanted to stay or not.

Sailors were a happy-go-lucky lot, who were used to facing up to a way of life that was full of hardships. They frequently had to dodge the grim reaper, or watch helplessly as one of their shipmates was carried away. A sailor had a great many shipmates, but seldom developed strong, close friendships. A friend was a responsibility and very often a man before the mast was a man who shunned responsibility.

The crew lived in the forecastle which was located on the port side of the for-

120

ward end of the forward house on the bigger vessels. This room was lined with double decked bunks and was also the place where the crew ate their meals. The meals were brought to the forecastle from the galley in a "dog basket" by the junior member of the crew. In off duty time the men smoked or chewed, slept, read, washed clothes, played cards and had long bull sessions which usually were about ships or women and the various good and bad points of both.

When in port, while the vessel was loading or waiting to load, it seldom took the foremast hands long to find out where the nearest "gin mill" and "cat house" were located. Occasionally a good fist fight in either of these establishments livened up shore leave and often before a loaded vessel could get under way, her captain would have to bail his crew out of the local calaboose.

Although a skilled able seaman on a schooner was a sailorman in every sense, he still was not required to know as much as the skilled able seaman on a square rigged vessel. Marlinspike seamanship was more often performed by riggers in shipyards then by sailors aboard a coaster. If a vessel was dismasted in the coasting trade, she was usually close enough to some port to enable a tug to tow her in for repairs; this was not so in the case of the deepwater voyagers.

Even the voyages to the West Indies or South America could not compare in length to those taken by the square riggers and a coaster sailor had much greater opportunity to junp from ship to ship, if he so desired. There were literally hundreds of vessels of all sizes, carrying a great variety of freight, that were constantly working their way along the coast.

Holme's Hole, or Vineyard Haven, as it is now called, used to be a favorite place for coasters to lay over while waiting for a change in wind or weather. Located on the northwestern side of Martha's Vineyard, it commanded one of the important and most frequently used entrances to Nantucket Sound. Less than one hundred years ago this little port had a custom house which could boast of over 7,000 entries in a single year. Many of these vessels were from foreign ports, but the vast majority were coasters. The coasting trade in those days was truly of great proportions and employed a vast number of people.

In October, 1893, the Seaman's Bethel was opened at Vineyard Haven, in charge of a dedicated man named Madison Edwards. By the year 1906, between 80,000 and 100,000 seamen had benefited from the efforts of those in charge of the Bethel. Madison Edwards was more than just the first chaplain of the Seaman's Bethel at Vineyard Haven, for it was he who founded and first gave the Bethel its breath of life. In 1888, he had opened a sailor's reading room in a farmhouse at Tarpaulin Cove on Naushon Island, one of the Elizabeth Islands, southwest of Cape Cod. This cove was also a favorite lay over spot for coasters and Edwards once wrote:

"I am very busy among the seamen at Tarpaulin Cove: one day there were 400 men ashore there. Last evening there were near 100 vessels at anchor and we had a very pleasant meeting in the room ashore."

Mrs. Gardiner Greene Hammond offered to build a reading room on the Vineyard for Mr. Edwards and he moved to that location in 1893. Chaplain Edwards found that he needed a boat to bring sailors ashore and obtained a steam launch, which he named "Helen May" after his two daughters. The "Helen May" was consecrated at Woods Hole. It was eventually changed from steam to gasoline power. The society called the launch its "little devil chaser" and indeed, it chased the devil right out of Vineyard Haven harbor. In command of Chaplain Edwards, ably assisted by Austin Tower, the "Helen May" would visit every vessel at anchor, winter and summer, in storm or calm, picking up the crews of the coasters and bring them ashore for a visit at the Bethel.

In a letter to the Vineyard Gazette, printed on Jan. 17, 1964, C. Harrison Dwight comments upon the Bethel and its chaplain and at the same time paints a vivid word picture of the anchorage at Vineyard Haven around the turn of this century.

"Your editorial on Chaplain Edwards was excellent. So, alas, was the letter regarding suitable memorials.

"Chaplain Edwards, the Bethel, the Helen May, the Aransas, Austin Tower! What a flood of memories extending back to at least fifty years!

"I can see Vineyard Haven Harbor towards dusk of a summer's evening. At anchor are a dozen schooners and a cluster or two of barges. There mother tugs, huge oceangoing vessels, are tied up tandem at the wharf. The lights of the Uncatena can be seen as she moves across the mouth of the harbor from the dock at West Chop to her overnight berth at Edgartown, touching at the Bluffs. The wind is from the southwest and the barges and schooners lie partly into the wind and partly against the tide which is making out into the Sound. Anchor lights glow from each craft and maybe a dim beam comes from cabin or fo'c'sle.

"Chaplain Edwards is at the forward end of the cabin of the Helen May, in a diminutive wheelhouse, calling orders aft to the second in command at the Bethel, his splendid co-worker Austin Tower. The engines grind and, with the Bethel flag and yacht ensign flying, the sturdy craft heads out around the wharf.

"The first call is at a three master, with a towering deckload of lumber from the Provinces. The captain waves his hand and three sailors swing themselves over the side and on to the cabin roof of the Bethel launch. Off we go towards a cluster of barges, dirty and deep-laden with coal from Philadelphia. 'Tis but a slight outward jump from the deck to the launch.

"The next is a "big boy", a four master in ballast, westward bound in the morning. The harbor waters ripple around her anchor chain as she gently responds to the fickle combination of tide and wind. And so the Helen May gathers the congregation for the evening meeting at the Bethel.

"All have shore leave for a time and then return to the cheery room for a simple, heart-to-heart talk by Mr. Edwards, gospel songs are sung (a favorite being "Does Your Anchor Hold In The Storms Of Life?"). Miss Helen Edwards probably plays the piano, testimonies are given and then the meeting concludes. Maybe two or three fellows have joined the chaplain's Hold Fast Club — a world wide fraternity of Christian sailors. Then it's all hands aboard the Helen May and the harbor cycle is repeated.

"For many years there was a second launch, given to the Bethel by a Downeast steamship company as a token of appreciation for the men at the Bethel which aided some shipwrecked sailors from their coastwise steamer Aransas.

"May the work of Chaplains Edwards and Tower never be forgotten and may the Bethel always be a reminder to Vineyard folks, old and new, of what can be accomplished by dedicated men.

C. Harrison Dwight

Madison Edwards dedicated his life to the welfare of sailors and in 1926 passed to his reward. The Bethel was then taken over by his assistant Austin Tower, who had also become his son-in-law; however, with the opening of the Cape Cod Canal in 1914, the number of vessels anchoring in Vineyard Haven rapidly began to diminish.

The trades that most coasters were engaged in during the late 1800's and early 1900's, were largely those in which bulk cargos were carried. There was often a large turn-over in the crew over short periods of time as most voyages did not last very long. In the coal trade for example, the "King Phillip" made the round trip from Portsmouth, New Hampshire to Newport News and back in 12 days in 1892. The "Eleanor A. Percy" in 1903, ran from Boston to Newport News and back in 13 days. In 1906 the "Ruth E. Merrill" carried 14 coal cargos during the year, between Baltimore and Portland, Maine, averaging 5.4 days southbound and 6.2 days northbound. Between 1886 and 1887, the four-masted "Sarah W. Lawrence" from Taunton, in command of Captain John Farrow, set an all time record by delivering 26 cargos of coal from the Chesapeake to Boston and was on its way with the 27th when the year was out. Unfortunately it is reported that the vessel was towed on several trips, making it an unfair record when compared to those who sailed without any help from a tow boat.

As mentioned before, Taunton, Massachusetts was the home of the early large schooners and practically all of these were engaged in the coal trade. Captain Jacob B. Phillips was one of the early organizers of a fleet of vessels for the coal trade and his cousins, Captains William H. Phillips and J. Marshall Phillips also were associated with fleets of vessels employed in hauling coal. Although only four coal laden vessels had left Philadelphia in 1822 bound for eastern ports, in 1837 over 3,200 vessels were reported as leaving and most of these were small two-masters. After the Civil War, Taunton took the lead in developing larger three-masted, centerboard coal schooners which were much admired along the whole coast. In the 1870's, the vessels in the trade had outgrown the river in Taunton and moved to Boston and Fall River. These big three-masted "Taunton Flyers" were the forerunners of the huge multimasted schooners destined to compete for the coal trade in another 25 years.

In the 1880's the railroads had brought the coal fields in contact with tidewater ports such as Newport News and Norfolk, Virginia. From then on competition was keen to figure faster and more efficient ways for hauling coal for the industrialization of the north. Bigger and bigger vessels were built and captains made every effort to cramb as many trips into one year as possible.

It would, however, be incorrect if one were to infer that the coal trade was the only lasting one of major importance. One of almost equal importance in the latter days of coasting was the lumber trade. Immediately after the Civil War, the north-

123

ern United States embarked upon a period of industrial expansion. People began to concentrate around urban areas and a great demand grew for southern hard pine necessary to build dwellings and other structures needed for the advancement of the industrial process. As the expansion continued, growing to great proportions, more and more vessels were needed to carry timber from such ports as Savannah, Georgia, Georgetown, South Carolina, Fernandina, Florida, Pensacola, Florida and Mobile, Alabama. This in turn meant that shipbuilding materials were needed as well as materials for buildings. Lumber was shipped in many forms and for many different purposes all through the history of the lumber trade. Latches, box shooks, shingles and even scraps to be used for fire wood made up cargos for vessels that ranged in size from sloops to large four and occasionally, five-masted schooners. The very large vessels, the mammoths of the coasting trade, were designed primarily as coal carriers and did not enter into the lumber trade to any appreciable extent.

Maine had hundreds upon hundreds of small vessels that did nothing more than cart wood from one place to another on the coast. One great source of employment was the lime kilns at Rockland and Rockport, where thousands of cords of wood were burned in the production of lime. From time to time these little lumber vessels would alter their routine with a load of coal, grain or brick and sometimes a trip to the West Indies.

Trade to the West Indies remained as an important part of the coastal picture until the final phase in the history of the sailing vessels. Salt from Turks Island and Logwood from Haiti and Jamaica were important cargos right up to the very end. Salt was a necessary curing and preservative agent needed by the northern fishing industry, for example, and was hauled in bulk. Logwood was used for the making of dye and was usually taken to Baltimore, Maryland or Chester, Pennsylvania, during the waning days of the trade. Sugar and molasses also were brought north from Barbados and other West Indian ports. Often various schooners would go from one cargo to another and an examination of the cargo manifests of the later, large three, four and five-masters would show lumber, salt, logwood, coal and anything that would turn a dollar, carried as the opportunity presented itself. The three-masted "Frederick P. Elkin", originally built as the "Seaman, A.O." at Cape D'Or, Nova Scotia, in 1919, was sold to Bridgetown, Barbados in 1946, and in 1947 brought the last cargo of Barbados molasses north for a Bangor, Maine wholesaler. On July 3, 1948, she was the last schooner to carry a cargo of coal from Newport News, Virginia taking this cargo south to the West Indies. The tired old schooner did not last long after this, being dismantled in the Barbados in the early 1950's.

Ice was another export from America that the state of Maine had a monopoly on and for a long time this was a very important part of the winter economics in that state. The natural ice formed on the fresh water rivers and ponds in Maine was cut during the winter and stored in huge ice houses awaiting summer. This ice, which was of a much more durable quality than artificial ice due to the fact that it was frozen at a much lower temperatures, was then slid down large chutes to the loading cribs built in the various Maine rivers and from there was loaded into the holds of waiting coasters. Dunnage ice, or small pieces of ice, then completely covered the closely packed large cakes of ice and the vessel then headed south. Not only were the southern states supplied with northern ice, but South America was also supplied. Captain J. W. Balano, of Thomaston, Maine, in the schooner "Mabel Jordan", for 17 consecutive years took cargos of ice to Rio de Janerio, Brazil, planning always to get there just before Christmas. The export ice business grew to a thing of great importance for those in the state of Maine, but was finally eclipsed by artificial refrigeration. Many ship owners refused to let their vessels haul this perishable cargo because of the damaging effect that the fresh-water had upon the hulls of their vessels.

Mention has been made of the many vessels engaged in carrying lime from ports in Maine to such ports as Boston and New York. These were usually small, two-masted schooners and due to the inflamable nature of the cargo, had to be tight. Vessels that were prone to leaking soon went up in smoke in this trade. Once smoke or the odor of lime being slacked by water was detected coming from the hold of a lime schooner, the only way to save her was to completely close up all the openings to the hold and by making them air tight, hope to smother the fire. If this did not work, scuttling the craft was the only other course open and frequently, when water hit the entire cargo, the lime would swell, bursting the casks containing it and the continued swelling would often do more damage to the timbers of the coaster than the fire.

*A Night "Buy Boat"*

## Chapter XVI

## YO-HO-HO AND A BOTTLE OF RUM

Although the schooner barges managed to take over the major portion of the coal trade and the steam colliers which followed proved to be the successors to the barges, coasting schooners valiantly kept up the struggle to stay in existence. Vessels that had been built early in the boom years of World War I paid their owners a handsome profit, but those that were launched in the later years proved to be losing propositions. Many schooners launched near the turn of the 1920's found it tough sledding and a few were able to make only one or two voyages before being laid up for want of cargos. Although lumber cargos in various forms remained important, there still were not enough to fill all the coasting vessels that were looking for work. The days of the sailing coaster seemed definitely on the way out.

Two things, however, happened in the 1920's that slowed down the disappearance of these sailing vessels. One was the passing of prohibition into law by the American public and the other was the great land boom in Florida which reached its peak in 1925.

Prohibition, called "the noble experiment" by many, was destined to bring about the use of a number of small coasters and fishing schooners on the east coast, but did not effect many of the larger vessels. The law went into effect on January 17, 1920 and the United States Coast Guard was given the tremendous job of en-

126

forcing the embargo on any alcohol being sent to the shores of the United States by way of the sea. The Coast Guard was at first not properly equipped to do their job and for a few years rum runners made capital of the situation and shipped in large quantities with impunity.

During the prohibition it was against the law for any American vessel to be found with alcoholic spirits, however any foreign vessel, as long as it stayed outside the twelve mile limit, could be loaded to the gunwales with alcohol and was not liable to seizure. Consequently, many Canadian, Bahamian, or vessels from French owned St. Pierre et Miquelon, off the south coast of Newfoundland, began to make up part of a fleet lying off the shores of the United States which came to be called "rum row". These schooners, mostly two and three masters, were loaded at ports in the above mentioned places and would then sail to a predestined spot just outside the legal limit, off the American coast line and there proceed to sell their cargos to bootleggers who came out to them in fast speed boats.

The field was open to anybody with enough money to obtain a vessel and a cargo and if successful, the profits were huge. Naturally this led to fierce competition amoung rival rum runners and bootleggers with the result that much hijacking, or just plain piracy, began to flare up on the eastern seaboard after almost a century had passed since the last recorded act took place in the 1830's. Piracy, for a while, was much more to be dreaded by those in rum row than seizure by the ill-equipped men of the Coast Guard. Some of the pirates were what was termed "go through guys", who would wait until a vessel off shore had sold out most of its cargo and then would board it under the guise of prospective buyers and seize at gun point all the cash that had accumulated on board. Others were more interested in obtaining a free shipload of whiskey and made off with whole cargos before anything was sold. In either case, these piracies were often accompanied by pitched battles. Stories reminiscent of the old days on the Spanish Main began to appear in Twentieth century newspapers.

Near the end of March, 1923, the Coast Guard cutter "Manhatten" was bound in to New York, when off Fire Island she found the two-masted British schooner "Patricia M. Beman" without lights. The schooner's anchor was overboard and was dragging and she had her sails set. This unusual situation naturally aroused the interest of the men on the cutter who boarded the schooner where they found evidence of a violent battle having been fought. Bullet holes were everywhere and rifle cartridge cases were all over the deck, but not a person was found on board, alive or dead. The hold of the schooner was empty, save for some straw bottle wrappings; however, records found on board indicated that the vessel had sold or disposed of 3,918 cases of liquor between January 12 and March 27. It was theorized that the "Patricia M. Beman" had been boarded by pirates who were resisted by those on the schooner and in the battle that followed, the pirates had won, killing the crew and throwing their bodies overboard. The cutter thereupon took the unfortunate schooner in tow and hauled her into the barge office in New York.

The little 70 ton schooner "Victor" was discovered 12 miles south of Ambrose Lightship, stripped of her sails and rigging, lifeboat gone and not a soul on board. Below decks the boarding party found a freshly cooked meal and the table set for dinner and that was it. Piracy seemed the only logical conclusion that could be arrived at in this case.

On another occasion, the Canadian schooner "J. Scott Hankenson" was boarded by two men from the speedboat "Grayhound", while lying about 15 miles off Rockport, Massachusetts. The "Grayhound" had been a previous customer of those on board the schooner and not much concern was given the men from the motorboat until one pulled out a gun and shot the captain of the "Hankenson". This was a signal for seven more armed men to jump from concealment off the "Grayhound" and when the cook on the schooner made a move to defend himself, he too was shot. The rest of the crew on the schooner were locked in the forecastle and the pirates then proceeded to loot the vessel of all the whiskey that was left on board plus over $25,000 in cash. The men who were shot fortunately did not die and the pirates were later apprehended at Gloucester. These three cases of piracy that have been described are representative of a great many more.

Out of a total of 65 vessels seized as rum runners by the Coast Guard cutter based at New London, Connecticut in 1924, seven were schooners, fifteen were sloops and four were barges. It was of interest to learn that not all the schooners in the rum running fleet were foreign vessels which hung around rum row. Some, instead of waiting outside the twelve mile limit, would try and sneak through disguised as ordinary merchantmen and unload their cargos at some out of the way spot on the coast. A great many were successful. Many also were caught and as the Coast Guard began to warm up to its task, fewer sailing vessels were able to get away with this.

The pretty little two-masted schooner "Mary Langdon" was a 78 foot vessel that had been built in 1845 at Thomaston, Maine and in 1925 was owned in Rockland. During June, 1925, she was spotted at anchor by the patrol boat "GC-282", about two miles off Nobska Light, Cape Cod. The little schooner was deeply weighted down with an innocent looking deck load of lumber. She was ordered to move by the Coast Guard vessel but rather stupidly refused to comply and the patrol boat then went in to Woods Hole to request further orders. The Coast Guardsmen came back and sent the "Langdon" to Tarpaulin Cove, where two men from the patrol boat boarded and searched the balky schooner. After moving some of the lumber piled up on deck, access was gained to the hold where 2,000 cases of scotch came to light. This was a little too much for the captain of the "Langdon" to pass off with a. "Well I wonder how that got there?" The "Mary Langdon" was immediately seized, her crew of six arrested and the schooner was taken in tow to New Bedford.

Usually when a rummy was seized and towed into port, her crew was arrested and if tried and found guilty, stiff prison terms would be meted out to the offenders and their vessel was sold at public auction. Often the vessel would be bought back by the same syndicate that had owned her in the first place, or she would go to another with similar intent and shortly after the sale would make her appearance once more on rum row with a new load of whiskey.

Canada adopted prohibition during the 1920's and whiskey laden schooners were also seized by Canadian officials, making the lot of the rum runner even more difficult. The three-masted "St. Clair Therault", built in Belliveau Cove, Nova Scotia in 1919, was seized in 1927 and towed into Halifax where she was put up for auction by the Canadian Exchequer Court. This vessel finally ended her days as a legitimate trader in January, 1939, when she sank in the eastern North Atlantic after having been abandoned and set on fire by her crew.

On December 5, 1933, the 21st amendment went into effect and prohibition with all its good intentions and bad effects came to an end. By this time however, the Coast Guard had so effectively done its job, that few schooners of the coaster type were to be found operating in rum row.

*Schooner Graveyard*

## Chapter XVII

## THE LAND BOOM AND GOODBYE

About the same time that prohibition was being felt in the early 1920's, something was beginning to happen in Florida that was going to have a much more profound effect upon larger coasting schooners. Visionary land speculators and promoters had fired the imagination of the American public with the idea of living in a semi-tropical paradise and everyone seemed to be trying to buy land; as long as it was in Florida. Centering around Miami, the Florida land boom reached its peak in 1925.

Miami Beach had formerly been a mangrove swamp on Biscayne Bay, until Mr. Carl G. Fisher cut down the trees, buried the stumps under five feet of sand, fashioned lovely lagoons and islands, built villas and hotels and reportedly made forty million dollars selling lots. The population of Miami jumped from around 30,000 in 1920 to over 75,000 in 1925. There was a mad scramble to get property in this "tropical paradise" of the south, and most of the people involved had but one idea in mind; that was the making of a fast dollar. Prices for real estate were climbing to incredible heights and the fever had spread to other Florida cities. The entire strip of coast from Palm Beach southward was being developed into an American Riviera; for sixty odd miles it was being staked out into fifty foot lots.

130

A lot in the business center of Miami which had sold for $800 in the early days of the development, had resold for $150,000 in 1924. A piece of land near Miami that had cost a poor woman $25 in 1896, sold for $150,000 in 1925. Any piece of coastal Florida swampland had suddenly acquired tremendous monetary value. Fifty by one hundred foot lots that were ten and fifteen miles outside of Miami were selling for $8,000 to $20,000; waterfront lots were going for $15,000 to $25,000 and seashore lots were sold for the tidy sum of from $20,000 to $75,000.

By 1925 the city of Miami was bursting with people, and the skyline of the city was rapidly undergoing a change. Towering hotels were stretching skyward in the new Venice of the tropics and a building boom was under way that was completely beyond the scope of the railroads. Building materials were wanted in a hurry and anything that would carry a load to the bustling state was pressed into service. The rough, unpaved wharves and docks of Miami began to look like old scenes of South Street in New York City in bygone days, as the timber bowsprits of dozens of big coasting schooners stuck inland over crews of men feverishly unloading as other schooners lay at anchor in the harbor, awaiting their turn.

In the mid-twenties, the Royal Palm Hotel, the Dallas Park, the McAllister Hotel, the Columbus Hotel, the Miami Colonial Hotel, the Everglades Hotel, the Alcazer Hotel, and the News Tower, were all skyscraper type buildings that were either up or going up near the Miami waterfront behind a forest of fore-and-aft rigged masts. Vessels that had been pushed into the mud in some northern creek were hauled out, given a quick refit, loaded with building materials and sent to Florida. The fleet of Crowell & Thurlow of Boston was going full blast. It was at this time that they acquired a large portion of the fleet of the G. G. Deering Co., of Bath.

However the bubble that had lifted those coasters out of disuse and decay did not last long. It was at its height during the winter of 1925-26 and after that it started to go down. By 1927 it was all over, and unwanted coasting schooners were either cut down to barges, sold abroad or shoved back in the mud.

In the Kill van Kull, which separates Staten Island from New Jersey, about half way between Bergen Point and Constable Hook, lies Port Johnson, which became famous as a graveyard for rotting ships.

Previous to this, Port Johnson had been for many years a busy trans-shipping point for coal. Trainloads of coal from Pennsylvania and Virginia had been shipped to the yards of the Central Railroad of New Jersey at Port Johnson and from there carried by barge to points north. In the early 1900's the docks were razed by fire and received only superficial repair. In 1919 the business of the port was moved to the railroads newly constructed Pier 18, in Jersey City, and Port Johnson fell into disuse.

From this time on, many ship owners who wished to abandon unwanted vessels would request permission of the railroad to tie up their outmoded sailing craft at the crumbling wharves of Port Johnson. These requests were always granted and all through the twenties the port grew famous as a place of dead ships with gaunt masts rising at giddy angles from empty hulls. Gradually these vessels settled into the mud and for the most part crumbled to pieces where they sat.

Practically every large port had its bone yard where during the 1930's, vessels that still had a good many years left in them when laid up, could be found in an advanced stage of decay with none but sea gulls and others of their own kind for company. Boston, New York, Noank, Boothbay, Wiscasset, all had collections of schooners that had no place to go.

The depression of the early 1930's also helped to thin out the ranks of coasting vessels and by the time the European situation had caused an increase in available cargos during the late thirties, there were but few schooners left to carry them. Sea Breezes Magazine, all during this time, kept a running account of the activities of many of the last American and Canadian sailing coasters in a section in the back of the magazine called "The Signal Station". Practically every month, with each new issue, one would read not only of the departures and arrivals, but also of the losses of some of these gallant old vessels who were still trying to hold on to a vestige of the past. The last issue to contain this list was in September, 1939, and 14 coasting vessels belonging to American and mainly Canadian owners were mentioned. This of course did not include vessels that were enroute or in port waiting for cargos and it is probably safe to say that there were three times that many, or more, still in operation. As mentioned earlier, these were not destined to last very long.

People often wonder why more auxilary schooners weren't used with success. In as much as the wind is free, they reason, why wouldn't sails still be practical? In answer to this; the unions would undoubtedly classify such a vessel in much the same way they would any other power driven vessel and the number of extra hands that would have to be carried would make the proposition unprofitable. Secondly, the railroads, modern tankers and the tremendous fleet of trucks in the United States would leave little material for such coasting vessels to haul.

The plain fact is, as with the horse and carriage, the day of the sailing coaster is gone. Today in 1973 there is not one sailing vessel left that is carrying freight along the Atlantic seaboard as in the past. The dude schooners alone give todays landsman a chance to glimpse at a part of our history that has, regretably for some, sailed over the horizon forever.

## PHOTOGRAPHS OF
## AMERICAN SAILING COASTERS

The following are part of the collection of sailing ship photographs that I have made over the past 30 years. They have been selected from the 5,000 photographs in my collection as best representing the material in the text. Most of these photographs were taken by unknown photographers between 1880 and 1930.

*Paul C. Morris*

The "Rachael Emery", a barkentine built in 1883 at Waldoboro, Maine. She was 167 feet long and owned in Boston, Massachusetts.

A watercolor painting of a typical "Baltimore Clipper" built in this country in the late 1700's and early 1800's.

Above, the "Kremlin" was a big barkentine built at Bath, Maine in 1890. She was owned in Boston, Massachusetts and was intended for deep water work as well as coastal trips.

Below, the "Eugene Hale", a brigantine built in 1883 at Calais, Maine. This vessel was 124 feet long and was used in deep water as well as coastal work.

136

Above, the "Frances Anne", a sloop built in 1859 at Hempstead, New York, and typical of the type that was employed on Long Island Sound and the Hudson River.

Built in 1859 at East Haven, Connecticut, the 66 foot "W. O. Nettleton" was at one time a Boston-Nantucket packet.

Left, the sloop "Nena A. Rowland", built in 1883 at Norwalk, Conn., and the "Wm. P. Boggs" are shown ashore on Commercial Wharf, Nantucket, following a winter gale in the early 1900's.

Right, the "Joseph I. Thompson" built in 1867 at Nyack, New York, is shown ashore at New Rochelle, New York. Notice the old style wooden davits on the stern.

138

Above, the "Storm Petrel", built in 1870 at Ellsworth, Maine, is shown with a deck load of wood.

Stern view of the "Silver Wave".

Above, side view of the "Silver Wave".

Below, the "Only Son", an early type schooner hauled out on the ways. This particular vessel is one thought to have been built in 1866 at Staten Island, New York, and owned in New York City.

Above, the "St. Leon" was built in 1871 at Penobscot, Maine.

Looking aft on the "St. Leon".

Above, the "E. T. Hamor", a small schooner built in 1889 at Eden, Maine.

The "Louise Hastings" frozen in the ice off Hyannis, Massachusetts, January 1888. The "Hastings" was built in Brewer, Maine in 1885 and for some time was owned in New England after which her ownership was transferred to Key West, Florida.

142

Above, the "Herman F. Kimball" was a lime schooner owned at Rockport, Maine. She had been built in 1888 at Boothbay, Maine.

The "Annie and Reuben" was a stone schooner built in 1891 at Bath, Maine.

Above, the "Annie and Reuben" unloading.

Below, the famous "Alice S. Wentworth" as she was snapped during one of her stockholders cruises at Nantucket.

144

A view from the bowsprit of the "Wentworth".

Captain Zeb Tilton at the wheel of the "Wentworth".

Captain Parker Hall

The "Thomas H. Lawrence" built in 1891 at Boston, Massachusetts, is shown discharging coal at Nantucket.

146

The "Lois M. Candage", built in 1912 at Bluehill, Maine, is shown in the early 1950's carrying a load of dude sailors out of Camden, Maine.

Stern view of the "Candage".

The "Charles Luling" was a "laker" built in 1873 at Manitowoc, Wisconsin. She was brought east through the Welland Canal as were many other lake built schooners. She is shown at Commercial Wharf, Nantucket in 1904, after having gone ashore near the western jetty at the entrance to Nantucket harbor.

The "W. H. Oler", was built in 1880 at Bath, Maine and was one of the types of three masters which was built with the long quarter deck.

Above, the "L. T. Whitmore" built in 1874 at Rockland, Maine is shown in New York after a collision.

View of the foc'sle head of the "L. T. Whitmore".

The "Nantisco" shown unloading barrels of kerosene at Nantucket. She was originally named the "Emily S. Baymore" and was built in 1884 at Dennisville, New Jersey.

The "Damietta & Joanna" built in 1890 at Yarmouth, Maine.

Looking forward on the main deck of the
"Damietta & Joanna".

The "Rebecca R. Douglas" built in 1894
at Bath, Maine.

Above, detail of the "Thomas H. Lawrence" showing the jibboom and dolphin striker.

Detail of the "Thomas H. Lawrence" showing the bow.

152

Above, detail of the "Thomas H. Lawrence" showing the foc'sle head.

View of the "Thomas H. Lawrence" showing the forward house.

Above, view of the "Thomas H. Lawrence" looking aft showing the well deck
with the hatch open.

Detail of the "Thomas H. Lawrence"
showing the main cabin aft.

The "Thomas H. Lawrence" under way.

The "James M. W. Hall" built in 1916 at Phippsburg, Maine by F. S. Bowker, was the last of eight such vessels built for the management of Rogers & Webb of Boston.

Above, the Canadian schooner "Carib II" was built at Shelburne, Nova Scotia in 1901.

Below, the "Coralleaf" built at Spencer's Island, Nova Scotia in 1902.

View of the fore, main, and mizzen masts of the "Thomas H. Lawrence".

The "Frank Huckins" was built in 1903 at Bath, Maine. She was the first vessel to be entirely owned by a single company and was built for the sole purpose of hauling the owner's product.

157

Above, the "Annie Marcia" built in 1914 at Bridgewater, Nova Scotia.

Below, the "Hiram D. MacLean", shown in tow, was built in 1919 at Economy, Nova Scotia. She was later renamed the "St. Pierraise".

Above, the "Peaceland" built in 1919 at Annapolis, Nova Scotia, had a mysterious ending to her long career.

The "James William", the only steel sailing vessel built in eastern Canada, was launched in 1908.

The "T. K. Bentley", built in 1920 at Advocate, Nova Scotia, is shown sailing through Long Island Sound with a load of piling in the late 1930's.

The "Florence B. Phillips" unloading lumber at Port Chester, New York in 1921. She was built in 1917 at Camden, Maine by Robert L. Bean.

160

Above, the "Agnes Manning" was one of the early four masters. She was built in 1892 at Camden, New Jersey.

Below, the Portland, Maine owned "James W. Elwell" was originally built as a four masted barkentine in 1892 at Bath, Maine.

Above, the "Frank A. Palmer" was one of the largest four masters. She is shown just after being launched in 1897 at Bath, Maine.

Below, the "Anna R. Heidritter" was originally built as the four master "Cohasset" at Bath, Maine in 1903. In 1907 she caught fire at Baltimore and burned to the water's edge. In 1910 she was rebuilt at Sharptown, Maryland. She was one of the last sailing vessels to be lost on Cape Hatteras.

Above, the "Kennebunk", a flush decker, is shown outward bound after being launched. She was built in 1918 at Kennebunkport, Maine and was the last large vessel to be built there.

Below, the "Lillian E. Kerr" was originally built in 1920 at Pocomoke City, Maryland, as a three master. Here she is shown in Long Island Sound in the late 1930's shortly after being rerigged as a four master.

A beautiful view of the after section of the "Lillian E. Kerr".

The "Lillian E. Kerr" as seen from astern.

164

The scrollwork at the bow of the "Albert F. Paul".

The "Alcaeus Hooper", built in 1920 at Stockton, Maine, is seen bound south in ballast.

Above, the outward bound "Dolly Madison" with a load of coal. She was built in 1920 at Newcastle, Maine.

Below, the "Constellation", (ex "Sally Persis Noyes") was one of the later four masters and had a checkered career.

The last four master to be built in Canada was the "Whitebelle", launched in 1920.

The second east coast five master was the "Nathaniel T. Palmer". She is shown ashore at Beach Haven, New Jersey after stranding on March 11, 1901. She was later hauled off.

Above, the "Laura Annie Barnes" was the last big windjammer to be wrecked in Nantucket Sound.

Below, the "Gov. Ames", built at Waldoboro, Maine in 1888 was the first five master on the east coast.

Above, The "Nathaniel T. Palmer" ashore at New Jersey.

Below, the "Nathaniel T. Palmer" ashore at New Jersey.

Above, the "John B. Prescott" shown ready for launching, was launched only a few weeks after the "Nathaniel T. Palmer".

Below, the "Dorothy Palmer" shown at anchor and light, was the last of the famous Palmer fleet to survive.

Above, the "Rebecca Palmer" shown when under the management of J. S. Winslow Co.

Below, the "Cora F. Cressy" deeply laden with coal. Full loads often left little freeboard on the big schooners and decks were frequently awash.

Above, the "Magnus Manson" under sail with everything set.

Below, this view of the "Helen W. Martin", a big five master, gives an excellent chance to see how much of these vessels were under water when loaded.

Above, the "Dustin G. Cressy" hauled out on a marine railroad.

Below, "Dorothy Palmer", a big five master unloading at New York.

Above, the big schooner "Grace A. Martin" is traveling light and is dickering with a tug for a tow into port.

The "Kineo" built in 1903 at Bath, Maine, was the only steel five master built on the east coast.

Courtesy of the Peabody Museum of Salem

174

Above, the big "bald headed" west coaster, "Nancy", ashore at Nantasket Beach in 1927. She never got off.

Below, the "Bright", a Big west coaster, spent her entire life on the east coast, ending her days as a barge.

Above, the "Edna Hoyt", at anchor, was the last American five masted schooner in operation on the east coast.

Below, the "George W. Wells" launched at Camden, Maine in 1900, was the first six masted schooner. She is shown shortly after launching with the rigging still unfinished.

Above, the "Alice M. Lawrence" going south in ballast.

Below, the "Mertie B. Crowley" fully loaded at anchor.

Above, the big "Eleanor A. Percy", built at Bath, Maine in 1900, is shown being fitted out for sea.

A deck view of the "Edward B. Winslow".

Above, a beautiful shot of the "Edward B. Winslow" under way, fully loaded, in a strong breeze.

A deck view of the "Wyoming" under construction.

Above, the mighty "Wyoming" with everything but her topmast staysails set. This was the largest wooden vessel ever to carry a cargo.

Below, the "Dovrefjeld", sunk at Stapleton, Staten Island, 1917.

Above, the "Thomas W. Lawson" as she appeared in ballast. She was the only seven masted schooner ever built.

Below, the "Delaware Sun", ex "William L. Douglas, was the only steel six master.

Above, South Street, New York around 1900 with square riggers and coasters unloading together.

The harbor at Port Jefferson, New York, in the late 1890's.

Above, the four masted schooner "Jacksonville" shown under construction at a yard in Jacksonville, Florida in 1906.

A wooden ship under construction.

Above, the "Magnus Manson" ready to be launched at Bath, Maine 1904.

The "Grace A. Martin" being launched at Bath, Maine 1904.

184

Above, the launching of the "Marie Gilbert".

The "Belle O'Neil", built in Bath, Maine in 1881 and owned at New London, Conn., is shown lumber laden and water logged 300 miles off Sandy Hook on December 17, 1905. She was short of provisions and is flying the flag upside down signalling her distress. She was taken in tow and safely arrived at Norfolk, Virginia three days later.

The launching of the "Marie Gilbert" at Mystic, Conn., 1906.

The stern of the "Perry Setzer" with lines taught as a tug attempts to haul her free.

186

Above, while loaded with salt, the "Austen Locke" went ashore on Nantucket on December 9, 1885.

Below, the "Oregon", shown ashore on the east side of Nantucket in 1885, was loaded with granite curbing and soon went to pieces.

The lumber laden "Clara Jane", built in 1864 at Pembroke, Maine, is shown stranded on Eastern Point, Gloucester, Mass. on January 10, 1913. The surf boat from the Lifesaving Service is shown along side rescuing the crew.

On December 18, 1887 the "Lewis King" came ashore southwest of Montauck Point, Long Island. She was refloated and came ashore three times in the same place before being burned two years later.

Above, the "Mola", built in 1892 at Black River, New Brunswick, shown ashore. She was refloated and sold to Mexico in 1905 and renamed the "Minerva".

The "Frederick Roessner", shown here ashore on a breakwater, became a wandering derilect in the Atlantic in 1912.

Above, the "John F. Kranz" ashore off Mantoloking, New Jersey on March 21, 1903.

Below, the "James Duffield" ashore off Cape Henlopen, Delaware on April 30, 1912.

Above, the "Ada Tower" was built in 1916 at Port Greville, Nova Scotia. A view of her ashore at Sayville, Long Island in 1926. Surviving this event she was later lost October 28, 1929 at Jacksonville Beach, Florida.

Below, the "Alice E. Clark" hit a ledge and sunk off Maine in 1909.

Above, the "Jennie French Potter" sunk in Vineyard Sound on May 18, 1909.

The British schooner "Canaria", in the left foreground, was among twenty-one schooners and one barkentine that were driven ashore in a terrible storm that hit Vineyard Haven harbor on November 27, 1898. In addition, four other schooners were totally dismasted and two sunk, one bark and three barges were sunk, and four other vessels were badly damaged.

A side view of the "Canaria" ashore in Vineyard Haven harbor.

Below, the "Dorothy B. Barrett" is shown being sunk by a German U-boat on August 14, 1918 off Cape May, New Jersey.

Above, the big "Independent" was one of the early vessels built specifically as a sailing barge. She is shown stranded near Riverhead, Long Island on November 26, 1898.

Below, the barge "P. J. Carleton" was originally a bark built in Camden, Maine, in 1870.

## ACKNOWLEDGEMENTS

As in all works of this sort it comes time for the author to say thanks to those who lent a helping hand in getting this vessel "launched". I am indeed grateful to my good friend "Charley" Sayle for much information and some of the photos used in this book. I'll never be able to personally say thanks to Captain Harold G. Foss, of Hancock, Maine. We corresponded for three years while I was putting all this together and in one of his last letters to me, just before he died, he said, "Paul, I'm counting on you". Well, I hope that what I have done would have pleased him. There are multitudes who helped in many ways; Mr. H. Sherman Holcomb, Mrs. Allan Robbins, Mr. Robert B. Applebee, my good friend Ed. Stackpole, Mr. "Danny" Poor, Mr. Howard I. Chapelle and Mr. Melvin Jackson, both from the Smithsonian, for their efforts and encouragement, Mr. Philip C. F. Smith, of the Peabody Museum, and to the many people who wrote to me, sent me pictures, who spent time and talked to me — all I can say truthfully, is this. Thank you from the bottom of my heart. Without your help, it just never would have been done.

*Paul C. Morris*
Nantucket, Massachusetts

# APPENDIX I — HISTORY

## AMERICAN SCHOONERS ON THE EAST COAST
## WITH FIVE, SIX AND SEVEN MASTS

### SEVEN MASTS

Name

THOMAS W. LAWSON — Home port was Boston, Massachusetts. This was the only seven-master built and was constructed of steel. On December 14, 1907 she was wrecked on Hellweather Reef, off the Scilly Islands, England, while trying to ride out a gale at anchor. Only two men survived.

### SIX MASTS

ADDIE M. LAWRENCE — Home port was Portland, Maine. On July 12, 1917, she stranded at Les Boeufs, France, near the mouth of the River Loire. She was bound from Boston to St. Nazaire, France, with general cargo.

ALICE M. LAWRENCE — Home port was Portland, Maine. On December 5, 1914, she stranded on Tuckernuck Shoal, Nantucket Sound. She was bound from Portland, Maine to Norfolk, Virginia in ballast. On November 27, 1915, while still aground, she was burned by vandals.

DOVREFJELD — Home port was New York, New York. This vessel was originally built as the paddle steamer "Rhode Island". Between 1911-13 she was converted to a 1,706 ton barge owned at Greenport, New York. In 1917 she was rebuilt as a six-masted schooner at New York, New York. On February 28, 1919, she foundered 32 miles east of Cape Hatteras, North Carolina, bound to the River Plate with lumber. Thirteen were saved, with none lost.

EDWARD B. WINSLOW — Home port was Portland, Maine. While loaded with cotton, she was burned off St. Nazaire, France, on July 10, 1917.

EDWARD J. LAWRENCE — Home port was Portland, Maine. On December 27, 1925, she was burned at Portland, Maine.

ELEANOR A. PERCY — Home port was Bath, Maine. She was the second six-master. On December 26, 1919, while bound from Buenos Aires to Copenhagen with wheat, she foundered in Lat. 48.30 N., Long. 17.45 W., with the loss of 13 lives.

GEORGE W. WELLS — Home port was Boston, Massachusetts. She was the first six-master. On September 3, 1913, she was lost by stranding at Ocracoke, North Carolina after a severe buffeting by a storm. At the time she was headed for Florida.

MERTIE B. CROWLEY — Home port was Boston, Massachusetts. On January 23, 1910, she was lost by stranding on Wasque Shoal, near Muskeget Channel, an entrance to Nantucket Sound. She was bound from Norfolk, Virginia to Boston, Massachusetts with coal.

RUTH E. MERRILL — Home port was Portland, Maine. On January 12, 1924, she foundered in Vineyard Sound off Vineyard Haven, Massachusetts losing her entire crew. She was bound from Norfolk, Virginia to Boston, Massachusetts with coal at the time of her loss.

WILLIAM L. DOUGLAS — Home port was Boston, Massachusetts. She was the only steel six-masted schooner built as such. In 1912 she was renamed "Delaware Sun", and converted to a tanker for the Sun Oil Co. On December 28, 1917, she was wrecked on the jetty off Sabine Bar, Texas.

WYOMING — Home port was Bath, Maine. During the night of March 11, 1924, while anchored in a severe gale near Pollock Rip Lightship, Nantucket Sound, she was lost. It is supposed she struck bottom at low water while fully loaded with coal. 14 men were lost with no survivors. Wreckage came ashore next morning on the north side of Nantucket and Tuckernuck Islands. She was the largest wooden sailing vessel ever to carry a cargo and was bound from Hampton Roads, Virginia to St. Johns, New Brunswick.

## FIVE MASTS

ARTHUR SEITZ — Home port was Rockport, Maine On May 25, 1902, she stranded on Skiff Island Reef, five miles S.W. of Muskeget Island and broke up. One large section of the starboard side floated over to Coatue, Nantucket, and is still there in the sand.

ASTA — Home port was New York, New York. This vessel was an auxiliary baldheader, and carried a yard on the foremast, West Coast style. She was renamed "Robert L. Linton", in 1926. She was reported as abandoned in the 1933 "List of Merchant Vessels of the U. S."

BAKER PALMER — Home port was Boston, Massachusetts. On December 11, 1915, she foundered at sea, Lat. 34.21 N., Long. 64.47 W.

CARROLL A. DEERING — Home port was Bath, Maine. On January 31, 1921, she came ashore on Diamond Shoals. Her sails were set, her boats were gone and she was abandoned. No trace of her crew has ever been found nor the reason for their having abandoned the vessel. The wreck was dynamited and part of it floated off and came ashore on the coast.

CHARLES E. DUNLAP — Home port was San Juan, Puerto Rico. This vessel was originally built as a four-masted schooner named "Myrtle Tunnell". The name was changed in 1907 to "Forest City". She was damaged by fire in Puerto Rico in 1916. She was rebuilt as a five-masted schooner in 1919 at San Juan and renamed "Charles E. Dunlap". She was lost by stranding on Fire Island, July 22, 1919.

CORA F. CRESSY — Home port was Bath, Maine. In 1929, she was converted to a night club in Boston and renamed "Show Boat". On March 19, 1938, she was towed from Boston to Medomak, Maine to the lobster wharf of B. T. Zahn, Inc., for a hulk. She is now used as a breakwater to protect a lobster pound.

COURTNEY C. HOUCK — Home port was Bath, Maine. In 1921 she was used for the filming of P. B. Kynes' "Cappy Ricks" and was named "Retriever", for the filming. She was abandoned in Boothbay Harbor, Maine in 1940. On the night of August 14, 1945, she was burned during the celebration of the end of the war with Japan.

DAVIS PALMER — Home port was Boston, Massachusetts. On December 26, 1909, she struck Graves Ledge at the entrance to Boston Harbor and foundered with all hands.

DOROTHY B. BARRETT — Home port was Bath, Maine. On August 14, 1918, she was intercepted by a German sub off Anglesea, Cape May, New Jersey. After the crew were permitted to take to the boats, she was set on fire and sunk by shell fire.

DOROTHY PALMER — Home port was Boston, Massachusetts. On March 29, 1923, she struck on Stone Horse Shoal, Nantucket Sound, and became a total loss. The crew were taken off by the Coast Guard.

DUNHAM WHEELER — Home port was New York, New York. On November 8, 1930, she was abandoned and sank during a storm off Cape Canaveral, Florida.

EDNA HOYT — Home port was Boston, Massachusetts. On November 25, 1937, she was discovered in distress and towed into Lisbon, Portugal, where she was condemned as unseaworthy. In February, 1938, she was sold to J. Vasconcellos of Lisbon, to be used as a coal hulk, She was the last of the five-masted schooners to be built and launched as such and was the last of the east coast vessels of that rig to be in operation.

ELIZABETH PALMER — Home port was Boston, Massachusetts. On January 26, 1915, she collided with the ss "Washington", and sank off Fenwick Island Lightship, Cape Henlopen, Delaware.

ELVIRA BALL — Home port was Mystic, Connecticut. On February 8, 1909, she was abandoned 130 miles east of Cape Charles, Virginia. Her wreck drifted from there across to the coast of Africa. She was the smallest of the east coast five-masters.

FANNIE PALMER — Home port was Boston, Massachusetts. She was renamed "George P. Hudson" around 1907. On July 11, 1914, she collided with the ss "Middlesex" and sank at Great Round Shoal, Nantucket, Massachusetts. Part of the wreckage floated to the beach at Nantucket. She was considered the least lucky of the Palmer fleet.

FANNIE PALMER — Home port was Boston, Massachusetts. She was the second vessel in the the Palmer fleet to carry this name. On December 25, 1916, she foundered at sea.

FULLER PALMER — Home port was Boston, Massachusetts. She foundered during the night of the disastrous storm of January 12, 1914, off Highland Light, Massachusetts.

GARDINER G. DEERING — Home port was Bath, Maine. She was burned at Brooksville, Maine on July 4, 1930. She was the last vessel of the G. G. Deering Co., which went out of business in 1930.

GOV. AMES — Home port was Providence, Rhode Island. On December 13, 1909, she was lost by stranding off the Chicamacomico Station, Wimble Shoals, Cape Hatteras, North Carolina with the loss of 11 lives. She was the first five-masted schooner on the east coast.

GOVERNOR BROOKS — Home port was Bath, Maine. On March 23, 1921, she foundered off Montevideo, Uruguay.

GRACE A. MARTIN — Home port was Bath, Maine. She foundered during the storm of January 12, 1914, thirty miles south of Matinicus Island, Maine. She was the second largest of the five-masted schooners.

198

HARWOOD PALMER — Home port was Boston, Massachusetts. On May 23, 1917, she was torpedoed by a German sub 5 miles SW., of La Blanche Island, France.

HELEN J. SEITZ — Home port was Boston, Massachusetts. On February 9, 1907, she stranded at Beach Haven, New Jersey.

HELEN W. MARTIN — Home port was Bath, Maine. She was abandoned by owners around 1916-1917.

HENRY O. BARRETT — Home port was Bath, Maine. Was sold foreign, renamed "Monte Finigu", and hailed from Le Havre, France in 1918.

JAMES W. PAUL, JR. — Home port was Portland, Maine. On June 28, 1918, she stranded off Rio de Janiero, Brazil. This schooner was unusual in that she carried a spike bowsprit.

JAMES PIERCE — Home port was Boston, Massachusetts. On November 9, 1912, she collided with the ss "Fram", 600 miles off the Bahamas.

JANE PALMER — Home port was Boston, Massachusetts. On December 18, 1920, she was abandoned at sea, Lat. 36.06 N., Long. 65.31 W. She was the largest five-masted schooner built.

JENNIE FLOOD KREGER — Home port was Boston, Massachusetts. Around June 15, 1940, she was raised from the mud of Boston Harbor and taken out and scuttled off the Boston Lightship.

JENNIE FRENCH POTTER — Home port was New York, New York. On May 18, 1909, she was lost by stranding in Nantucket Sound.

JENNIE R. DUBOIS — Home port was New Haven, Connecticut. On September 5, 1903, she sank following a collison with the ss "Schoenfels", off Block Island.

JEROME JONES — Home port was Bath, Maine. She was renamed "Frank M. Deering". On February 6, 1923, she was wrecked near Cobb Island, Virginia.

JOHN B. PRESCOTT — Home port was Fall River, Massachusetts. On February 23, 1902, she foundered at sea.

JOSEPH S. ZEMAN — Home port was New York, New York. On February 3, 1922, she was lost by stranding on Martinin Ledge, Penobscot Bay, Maine.

KINEO — Home port was Bath, Maine. She was the only steel five-masted schooner built as such and carried a spike bowsprit. She was renamed "Maryland" and was still afloat as a tanker in 1945.

LOUISE B. CRARY — Home port was New York, New York. On the evening of December 17, 1902, she foundered following a collision with the "Frank A. Palmer", close to Cape Ann, Massachusetts Bay.

M. D. CRESSY — Home port was Bath, Maine. On April 19, 1917, she foundered at sea, Lat. 39.31 N., Long. 7.58 E.

MAGNUS MANSON — Home port was New Haven, Connecticut. On May 25, 1917, she was sunk by a German sub, 50 miles SW., of Cape St. Vincent, while bound from Pensacola, Florida, to Genoa, with lumber.

MARCUS L. URANN — Home port was Boston, Massachusetts. On November 3, 1916, while loaded with lumber, she was abandoned at sea with a loss of nine lives. Three of the crew survived, landing at the Azores.

MARGARET HASKELL — Home port was Boston, Massachusetts. On February 28, 1916, while on a voyage from Pensacola, Florida to Genoa, with lumber and rosin, she was abandoned off the Tortugas in Lat. 26.35 N., Long. 76 W.

MARTHA P. SMALL — Home port was Bath, Maine. She was reported in Montevideo, Uruguay in 1920, in need of extensive repairs. She was sold there and scrapped.

MARY F. BARRETT — Home port was Bath, Maine. She was reported abandoned in Robinhood Cove, Maine, and dismantled on February 12, 1929.

MARY H. DIEBOLD — Home port was Boston, Massachusetts. She was reported abandoned and dismantled at Eastport, Maine in 1936.

MARY W. BOWEN — Home port was Fall River, Massachusetts. On July 7, 1917, she was torpedoed and sunk by a German sub in Lat. 47.20 N., Long. 8.10 W.

MOHAWK — Home port was New York, New York. This vessel was originally built as the passenger side wheeler "Penobscot". The name was changed to "Mohawk" and she was used as a passenger steamer on the Hudson River. In 1918, she was rebuilt as a five-masted schooner at Mystic, Connecticut retaining the name "Mohawk". She went missing on a voyage from New York City to Gulfport, Mississippi in 1918, her sailing career therefore lasting less than one year.

NATHANIEL T. PALMER — Home port was Portland, Maine. She was the second five-masted schooner built on the east coast. On December 1, 1911, she was abandoned at sea in Lat. 32.59 N., Long. 62.45 W.

OAKLEY C. CURTIS — Home port was Portland, Maine. She was abandoned in Portland harbor in the 1930's.

PAUL PALMER — Home port was Boston, Massachusetts. On June 15, 1913, she burned off Race Point, Cape Cod, Massachusetts. She was the smallest of the Palmer fleet.

PRESCOTT PALMER — Home port was Boston, Massachusetts. On January 20, 1914, she was abandoned at sea in Lat. 34.08 N., Long. 66.46 W.

REBECCA PALMER — Home port was Boston, Massachusetts. In 1921 she was sold to Greek interests, who dismantled her.

ST. JOHNS N. F. — Home port was New York, New York. She was later renamed "Edward B. Winslow", (the second vessel to bear this name) and owned in Portland, Maine. On December 27, 1928, she was abandoned 700 miles off Cape Hatteras, in Lat. 40.27 N., Long. 71.51 W.

SAMUEL J. GOUCHER — Home port was Boston, Massachusetts. On November 12, 1911, she grounded on a ledge off the Isle of Shoals, Portsmouth, New Hampshire in calm weather. She was loaded with 4,000 tons of coal and at low tide split completely open.

SINGLETON PALMER — Home port was Boston, Massachusetts. On November 6, 1921, she was rammed and sunk by the ss "Apache", off Fenwick Island, Delaware coast.

SINTRAM — Home port was Portland, Maine. This vessel was a Ferris steamer hull rigged as a five-masted schooner. She was lost in collision with the ss "David McKelvy", on November 19, 1921, north of Highland Light.

T. CHARLTON HENRY — Home port was Boston, Massachusetts. On June 23, 1907, she sank following collision with British ss "Cheltson", off Fire Island, New York.

VAN ALLENS BOUGHTON — Home port was Boston, Massachusetts. On September 4, 1917, she foundered 150 miles off Brest, France.

WASHINGTON B. THOMAS — Home port was Thomaston, Maine. On June 12, 1903, only 60 days after her launching, she was wrecked on Stratton's Island, Maine.

WILLIAM C. CARNEGIE — Home port was Portland, Maine. On May 1, 1909, she went ashore at Moriches, Long Island, New York, and became a total loss.

# APPENDIX II — STATISTICS

## AMERICAN SCHOONERS ON THE EAST COAST
## WITH FIVE, SIX AND SEVEN MASTS

| Name | Year and Where Built | G. Tons | N. Tons | L. | B. | D. | Crew | Masts |
|------|---------------------|---------|---------|-----|-----|-----|------|-------|
| Thomas W. Lawson | 1902, Quincy, Mass. | 5,218 | 4,914 | 375.6 | 50.0 | 22.9 | 18 | 7 |
| Addie M. Lawrence | 1902, Bath, Me. | 2,807 | 2,195 | 292.4 | 48.3 | 22.2 | 12 | 6 |
| Alice M. Lawrence | 1906, Bath, Me. | 3,132 | 2,230 | 305.1 | 48.2 | 22.6 | 13 | 6 |
| Dovrefjeld | 1882, Noank, Conn. | 1,858 | 1,858 | 332.2 | 46.2 | 16.4 | 14 | 6 |
| Edward B. Winslow | 1908, Bath, Me. | 3,424 | 2,482 | 318.4 | 50.0 | 23.7 | 12 | 6 |
| Edward J. Lawrence | 1908, Bath, Me. | 3,350 | 2,483 | 320.2 | 50.0 | 23.9 | 12 | 6 |
| Eleanor A. Percy | 1900, Bath, Me. | 3,401 | 3,062 | 323.5 | 50.0 | 24.8 | 15 | 6 |
| George W. Wells | 1900, Camden, Me. | 2,970 | 2,743 | 319.3 | 48.5 | 23.0 | 13 | 6 |
| Mertie B. Crowley | 1907, Rockland, Me. | 2,824 | 2,410 | 296.5 | 48.4 | 23.8 | 14 | 6 |
| Ruth E. Merrill | 1904, Bath, Me. | 3,003 | 2,359 | 301.0 | 48.2 | 23.7 | 12 | 6 |
| William L. Douglas | 1903, Quincy, Mass. | 3,708 | 3,470 | 316.0 | 48.0 | 28.9 | 12 | 6 |
| Wyoming | 1909, Bath, Me. | 3,730 | 3,036 | 329.5 | 50.1 | 30.4 | 12 | 6 |
| Arthur Seitz | 1901, Camden, Me. | 2,207 | 2,000 | 272.3 | 46.4 | 23.6 | 11 | 5 |
| Asta | 1917, Noank, Conn. | 1,965 | 1,724 | 246.6 | 42.8 | 22.5 | 10 | 5 |
| Baker Palmer | 1901, Waldoboro, Me. | 2,792 | 2,240 | 284.9 | 46.5 | 21.9 | 10 | 5 |
| Carroll A. Deering | 1919, Bath, Me. | 2,114 | 1,879 | 255.1 | 44.3 | 25.3 | 11 | 5 |
| Charles E. Dunlap | 1904, Millbridge, Me. | 1,609 | 1,296 | 224.8 | 42.0 | 18.1 | 11 | 5 |
| Cora F. Cressy | 1902, Bath, Me. | 2,499 | 2,089 | 273.0 | 45.5 | 27.9 | 11 | 5 |
| Courtney C. Houck | 1913, Bath, Me. | 1,627 | 1,357 | 218.9 | 42.7 | 24.6 | 9 | 5 |
| Davis Palmer | 1905, Bath, Me. | 2,965 | 2,287 | 305.4 | 48.4 | 27.2 | 14 | 5 |
| Dorothy B. Barrett | 1904, Bath, Me. | 2,088 | 1,799 | 259.5 | 45.4 | 25.1 | 10 | 5 |
| Dorothy Palmer | 1903, Waldoboro, Me. | 2,872 | 2,315 | 294.6 | 46.2 | 22.8 | 12 | 5 |
| Dunham Wheeler | 1917, Bath, Me. | 1,926 | 1,765 | 254.5 | 44.2 | 23.0 | 10 | 5 |
| Edna Hoyt | 1920, Thomaston, Me. | 1,512 | 1,384 | 224.0 | 41.1 | 20.8 | 10 | 5 |
| Elizabeth Palmer | 1903, Bath, Me. | 3,065 | 2,446 | 300.4 | 48.3 | 28.3 | 7 | 5 |
| Elvira Ball | 1907, Mystic, Conn. | 869 | 726 | 200.8 | 38.5 | 16.9 | 8 | 5 |
| Fannie Palmer | 1900, Waldoboro, Me. | 2,258 | 2,075 | 266.1 | 44.6 | 25.1 | 11 | 5 |
| Fannie Palmer | 1907, Bath, Me. | 2,233 | 1,726 | 263.7 | 45.0 | 21.3 | 13 | 5 |
| Fuller Palmer | 1908, Bath, Me. | 3,060 | 2,361 | 309.4 | 48.9 | 27.4 | 12 | 5 |
| Gardiner G. Deering | 1903, Bath, Me. | 1,982 | 1,714 | 251.6 | 44.4 | 25.1 | 9 | 5 |
| Gov. Ames | 1888, Waldoboro, Me. | 1,778 | 1,597 | 245.6 | 49.6 | 21.2 | 10 | 5 |
| Governor Brooks | 1907, Bath, Me. | 2,628 | 2,019 | 280.7 | 45.8 | 21.5 | 11 | 5 |
| Grace A. Martin | 1904, Bath, Me. | 3,129 | 2,624 | 302.0 | 48.1 | 28.6 | 14 | 5 |
| Harwood Palmer | 1904, Waldoboro, Me. | 2,885 | 2,400 | 301.7 | 46.3 | 27.8 | 10 | 5 |
| Helen J. Seitz | 1905, Camden, Me. | 2,547 | 2,249 | 282.6 | 48.4 | 23.0 | 12 | 5 |
| Helen W. Martin | 1900, Bath, Me. | 2,265 | 2,020 | 281.6 | 44.8 | 20.9 | 11 | 5 |
| Henry O. Barrett | 1899, Bath, Me. | 1,807 | 1,564 | 244.7 | 42.9 | 24.0 | 12 | 5 |
| James W. Paul, Jr. | 1901, Verona, Me. | 1,808 | 1,653 | 250.0 | 43.0 | 21.9 | 12 | 5 |
| James Pierce | 1901, Thomaston, Me. | 1,664 | 1,520 | 236.0 | 43.0 | 20.3 | 11 | 5 |
| Jane Palmer | 1904, Boston, Mass. | 3,138 | 2,823 | 308.6 | 49.0 | 22.4 | 13 | 5 |
| Jennie Flood Kreger | 1919, Belfast, Me. | 1,838 | 1,614 | 243.7 | 42.2 | 19.5 | 10 | 5 |
| Jennie French Potter | 1899, Camden, Me. | 1,993 | 1,794 | 257.7 | 44.3 | 21.0 | 10 | 5 |
| Jennie R. Dubois | 1902, Mystic, Conn. | 2,227 | 1,952 | 249.0 | 46.0 | 20.7 | 10 | 5 |
| Jerome Jones | 1916, Bath, Me. | 1,892 | 1,631 | 249.6 | 43.3 | 24.7 | 10 | 5 |
| John B. Prescott | 1899, Camden, Me. | 2,454 | 2,249 | 300.0 | 44.3 | 23.0 |  | 5 |

| Name | Year and Where Built | G. Tons | N. Tons | L. | B. | D. | Crew | Masts |
|------|---------------------|---------|---------|-----|-----|-----|------|-------|
| Joseph S. Zeman | 1919, Bath, Me. | 1,956 | 1,812 | 253.2 | 43.2 | 23.7 | 10 | 5 |
| Kineo | 1903, Bath, Me. | 2,128 | 1,867 | 259.5 | 45.3 | 22.9 | 12 | 5 |
| Louise B. Crary | 1900, Bath, Me. | 2,231 | 1,998 | 267.1 | 46.2 | 21.1 | 8 | 5 |
| M. D. Cressy | 1899, Bath, Me. | 2,114 | 1,884 | 264.4 | 43.9 | 21.6 | 9 | 5 |
| Magnus Manson | 1904, Bath, Me. | 1,751 | 1,526 | 223.0 | 43.2 | 22.0 | 12 | 5 |
| Marcus L. Urann | 1904, Phippsburg, Me. | 1,899 | 1,576 | 251.7 | 44.3 | 24.1 | 10 | 5 |
| Margaret Haskell | 1904, Camden, Me. | 2,114 | 1,870 | 252.3 | 48.0 | 20.5 | 12 | 5 |
| Martha P. Small | 1901, Bath, Me. | 2,178 | 1,903 | 264.6 | 45.7 | 21.5 | 11 | 5 |
| Mary F. Barrett | 1901, Bath, Me. | 1,833 | 1,564 | 241.4 | 43.3 | 24.7 | 9 | 5 |
| Mary H. Diebold | 1920, Newcastle, Me. | 1,516 | 1,397 | 223.5 | 42.8 | 22.6 | 10 | 5 |
| Mary W. Bowen | 1900, Bath, Me. | 2,153 | 1,907 | 246.1 | 46.5 | 21.9 | 10 | 5 |
| Mohawk | 1882, Boston, Mass. | 913 | 804 | 255.0 | 38.0 | 13.0 | 12 | 5 |
| Nathaniel T. Palmer | 1898, Bath, Me. | 2,440 | 2,244 | 295.1 | 44.4 | 22.2 | 10 | 5 |
| Oakley C. Curtis | 1901, Bath, Me. | 2,374 | 2,000 | 265.0 | 46.2 | 22.9 | 10 | 5 |
| Paul Palmer | 1902, Waldoboro, Me. | 2,193 | 1,763 | 276.1 | 44.2 | 24.4 | 10 | 5 |
| Prescott Palmer | 1902, Bath, Me. | 2,811 | 2,307 | 288.0 | 46.2 | 22.2 | 12 | 5 |
| Rebecca Palmer | 1901, Rockland Me. | 2,556 | 2,125 | 260.4 | 46.1 | 23.1 | 12 | 5 |
| St. Johns N. F. | 1918, Bath, Me. | 2,046 | 1,906 | 254.1 | 43.3 | 23.9 | 10 | 5 |
| Samuel J. Goucher | 1904, Camden, Me. | 2,547 | 2,249 | 281.6 | 48.4 | 23.0 | 12 | 5 |
| Singleton Palmer | 1904, Waldoboro, Me. | 2,859 | 2,357 | 294.9 | 45.4 | 28.2 | 12 | 5 |
| Sintram | 1920, South Freeport, Me. | 2,259 | 2,085 | 266.5 | 46.0 | 24.0 | 12 | 5 |
| T. Charlton Henry | 1902, Camden, Me. | 2,421 | 2,149 | 273.7 | 48.5 | 23.0 | 12 | 5 |
| Van Allens Broughton | 1900, Camden, Me. | 2,129 | 1,905 | 264.4 | 46.5 | 22.5 | 10 | 5 |
| Washington B. Thomas | 1903, Thomaston, Me. | 2,638 | 2,280 | 286.8 | 48.6 | 22.7 | 13 | 5 |
| William C. Carnegie | 1900, Bath, Me. | 2,663 | 2,380 | 289.2 | 46.3 | 22.4 | 10 | 5 |

# APPENDIX III — HISTORY

## AMERICAN FIVE-MASTED SCHOONERS BUILT ON THE WEST COAST
## WHICH SAILED ON THE EAST COAST

BRIGHT —     Home port was Portland, Maine. After World War One she was acquired by Maine interests and registered from Georgetown and later from Portland. In 1933 she was converted into a barge. She was sunk on September 1, 1940, when in collision with ss "Hawaiian", off Sharp Island Buoy 18-A, Chesapeake Bay.

GERBEVILLER — She was built for the French government. She was sold in the early 1920's and said to have been a rum runner. In 1928-29 she was owned in Montreal, Canada. In 1932 she was laid up in Brooklyn, New York and was slightly damaged by a fire on June 20, 1934. She was eventually abandoned in Brooklyn.

MARIE DE RONDE — Home port was New York, New York. She was originally built with an engine, but this was removed. After being laid up for many years at Rockland, Maine, she was towed to Portland on April 3, 1933 and converted to a barge. On December 19, 1935, she caught fire and was shelled and sunk 55 miles SE. of New York.

NANCY —     Home port was Philadelphia, Pennsylvania. She was a bald-headed schooner with a spike bowsprit. On February 20, 1927, during a heavy gale, she dragged her anchors and went ashore on Nantasket Beach, Massachusetts. She stayed there intact for many years, but was finally broken up.

ROSE MAHONEY — Home port was San Francisco, California. She was listed as abandoned in the 1929 "List of Merchant Vessels of the U. S."

W. H. MARSTON — Home port was New York, New York in 1921. This vessel was originally a Honolulu packet. She carried a spike bowsprit and leg of mutton Spanker, typical of many west coasters. In December, 1927, she was lost in the Gulf of Mexico.


# APPENDIX IV — STATISTICS

## AMERICAN FIVE-MASTED SCHOONERS BUILT ON THE WEST COAST
## WHICH SAILED ON THE EAST COAST

| Name | Year and Where Built | G. Tons | N. Tons | L. | B. | D. | Crew |
|---|---|---|---|---|---|---|---|
| Bright | 1918, Seattle, Wash. | 2,176 | 2,011 | 258.3 | 48.6 | 24.2 | 16 |
| Gerbeviller | 1918, Tacoma, Wash. | 2,128 | 1,976 | 260.0 | 45.7 | 22.5 | |
| Marie De Ronde | 1918, Aberdeen, Wash. | 2,415 | 1,895 | 266.7 | 48.0 | 24.0 | 9 |
| Nancy | 1918, Portland, Ore. | 2,117 | 1,678 | 259.2 | 44.9 | 22.3 | 9 |
| Rose Mahoney | 1918, Benicia, Cal. | 2,051 | 1,933 | 260.7 | 48.3 | 22.4 | 13 |
| W. H. Marston | 1901, San Francisco, Cal. | 1,169 | 1,110 | 219.0 | 42.5 | 17.5 | 12 |

# BIBLIOGRAPHY

Bowker, Francis E., HULL DOWN, Reynolds Printing Inc., New Bedford, Mass. 1963

Bradlee, Francis B. C., PIRACY IN THE WEST INDIES AND ITS SUPPRESSION, The Essex Institute, Salem, Mass., 1923

Brewington, M. V., CHESAPEAKE BAY, Cornell Maritime Press, Cambridge, Md. 1953

Burgess, Robert H., THIS WAS CHESAPEAKE BAY, Cornell Maritime Press, Cambridge, Md., 1963

Burgess, Robert H., CHESAPEAKE CIRCLE, Cornell Maritime Press, Cambridge, Md., 1965

Chapelle, Howard I., THE HISTORY OF AMERICAN SAILING SHIPS, W. W. Norton Co., New York, 1935

Chapelle, Howard I., THE NATIONAL WATERCRAFT COLLECTION, Smithsonian Institution, Washington, D.C. 1960

Chapelle, Howard I., THE SEARCH FOR SPEED UNDER SAIL 1700 - 1885, W. W. Norton Co., New York, 1967

Crowninshield, B. B., FORE AND AFTERS, Houghton Mifflin Co., Boston, Mass., 1940

Desmond, Charles, WOODEN SHIPBUILDING, The Rudder Publishing Co., N.Y., 1919

Fuller, Capt. Thomas, THE LAST PIRACY OF THE SPANISH MAIN, private printing by Capt. Kidd Press, New York, 1903

Gardner, Arthur H., WRECKS AROUND NANTUCKET, The Inquirer and Mirror Press, Nantucket, Mass., 1915

Halcomb, H. Sherman, MAGNUS MANSON AND BENEDICT-MANSON MARINE COMPANY, private printing, Beverly Farms, Mass., 1956

Kittredge, Henry C., MOONCUSSERS OF CAPE COD, The Riverside Press, Cambridge, Mass., 1937

Marvil, James E., M.D., SAILING RAMS, Laurel, Delaware, 1961

McKay, Richard C., SOUTH STREET, A MARITIME HISTORY OF NEW YORK, G. P. Putnam Sons, New York, 1934

Morgan, Charles S., SHIPBUILDING ON THE KENNEBUNK — THE CLOSING CHAPTER, Historical Society of Kennebunkport, Me., 1952

Morgan, Charles S., NEW ENGLAND COASTING SCHOONERS, The American Neptune Pictorial Supplement V, The American Neptune, Salem, Mass. 1963

Morison, Samuel Eliot, THE MARITIME HISTORY OF MASSACHUSETTS 1783 - 1860, Houghton Mifflin Co., 1921

Morris, E. P., THE FORE AND AFT RIG IN AMERICA, Yale University Press, 1927

Packard, Aubigne Lermond, A TOWN THAT WENT TO SEA, Falmouth Publishing House, Portland, Me., 1950

Parker, John P., SAILS OF THE MARITIMES, The Maritime Museum of Canada, 1960

Parker, Lt. W. J. Lewis, USCG, THE GREAT COAL SCHOONERS OF NEW ENGLAND, The Marine Historical Association, 1948

Rattray, Jeannette Edwards, SHIP ASHORE! A RECORD OF MARITIME DISASTERS OFF MONTAUK AND EASTERN LONG ISLAND 1640 - 1955, Coward McCann Inc., New York, 1955

Rice, George Wharton, THE SHIPPING DAYS OF OLD BOOTHBAY, The Southworth-Anthoensen Press, Portland, Me., 1938

Rowe, William Hutchinson, THE MARITIME HISTORY OF MAINE, W. W. Norton and Co., Inc., 1948

Stick, David, GRAVEYARD OF THE ATLANTIC, The University of North Carolina Press, 1952

Talbot, Frederick A., STEAMSHIP CONQUEST OF THE SEA, J.B. Lippincott Co., Philadelphia, 1912

Taylor, Frank H. and Wilfred H. Schoff, THE PORT AND CITY OF PHILADELPHIA, The Local Organizing Commission of The Congress, Philadelphia, 1912

Thomas, Lowell, RAIDERS OF THE DEEP, Garden City Publishing Co., N.Y., 1928

Wasson, George S., SAILING DAYS ON THE PENOBSCOT, Marine Research Society, 1932

Willoughby, Malcolm F., RUM WAR AT SEA, U.S. Government Printing Office, Washington, D.C., 1964

LIST OF MERCHANT VESSELS OF THE UNITED STATES, (years 1884 - 1920), U.S. Government Printing Office, Washington, D.C.

Periodicals:

THE AMERICAN NEPTUNE, Peabody Museum of Salem, Mass.

LOG CHIPS, Dr. John Lyman, Washington, D.C.

NAUTICAL RESEARCH JOURNAL, The Nautical Research Guild, Whittier, California

SEA BREEZES, The P.S.N.C. Magazine, Liverpool, England

SHIPS AND THE SEA, Kalmbach Publishing Co., Milwaukee, Wis.

Newspapers:

THE ELLSWORTH AMERICAN, Ellsworth, Maine
Various articles 1963 - 1964 by Capt. Harold G. Foss

MAINE COAST FISHERMAN, Camden, Maine
Various articles 1950 - 1964

NEW BEDFORD STANDARD TIMES, New Bedford, Mass.
July, 1948

NEW YORK TIMES, New York, N.Y.
February 15, 1917

THE VINEYARD GAZETTE, Martha's Vineyard, Mass.
June 28, 1963, January 17, 1964

Personal Correspondence:

Robert B. Applebee, Stockton Springs, Me.

Francis E. Bowker, Mystic, Conn.

Capt. Harold G. Foss, Hancock, Me.

H. Sherman Holcomb, Salem, Mass.

Daniel S. Poor, Ridgewood, N.J.

Mrs. Allan Robbins, Teaticket, Mass.

Charles F. Sayle, Nantucket, Mass.

Philip C. F. Smith, Peabody Museum, Salem, Mass.

Edouard Stackpole, Mystic Museum, Mystic, Conn.

Giles M. S. Todd, Hingham, Mass.

Andrew F. Willis, Boston, Mass.

# GLOSSARY

ABAFT — back of, behind

AFT — toward the stern or back end of a vessel.

ANCHOR — a heavy hook or weight dropped with rope or chain to the sea floor where it catches or digs in and keeps a vessel from drifting.

AVAST — stop, cease.

BACKSTAY — standing rigging running from upper masts back to the side of the hull.

BEAM — the greatest width of a vessel.

BEATING — sailing against the wind, sailing close hauled.

BECKET — a line used to secure a wheel from turning or a tiller from swinging. Also a fitting on the butt of a block onto which the standing part of a fall is spliced.

BELAYING PIN — a removable rail pin used in making a line fast.

BILGE — the rounded lower part of the hull of a vessel inside or out.

BINNACLE — the structure housing the compass.

BITTS — square timbers going through the deck used for towing or making the vessel fast.

BLOCK — a pulley, usually of wood.

BONNET — an additional length of canvas laced to the foot of a sail.

BOOM — a spar attached to the foot of a sail.

BOW — the front end or forward part of a vessel.

BOWSPRIT — the spar extending horizontally or at an angle, straight out from the bow of a vessel.

BUFFALO RAIL — a low solid rail forward or aft on a schooner.

BULKHEAD — a partition in the hull of a vessel.

BULL'S EYE — a rounded piece of wood (usually lignum vitae) through which runs a piece of running rigging. The round opening in the bull's-eye does not contain a sheave.

BULWARK — the solid side of a vessel above the topside deck.

CAP — an iron band or wooden band around the lower masthead which also holds the lower part of the topmast.

CAPSTAN — a type of verticle windlass placed on deck and turned, usually by crew members walking around and pushing against capstan bars inserted in the head of the capstan.

CARVEL PLANKING — smooth sided ship construction.

CATHEAD — a rectangular timber jutting from the bow on each side which is used in "catting" the anchor, or getting the anchor on board the foredeck or foc's'le head.

CEILING — inside planking in the hull of a vessel.

CHAINPLATE — a metal band bolted to the side of the hull in line with the shroud or backstay it serves.

CLEW — the after, lower corner of a fore and aft sail. The lower corners of a square sail.

CLEW UP — to haul a sail up to a spar by the use of clew lines.

CLINKER BUILT — overlapping planking on the side of a hull.

COAMING — the raised edges or sides surrounding a hatch or skylight.

COASTER — a vessel carrying cargo or passengers from one coastal port to another coastal port in the same country in the same ocean.

COMPANIONWAY — a stairway leading down from the deck.

CROSSTREES — short, flat pieces of timber fastened athwartship above the trestletrees at the doublings of a lower and upper mast.

DAVIT — a crane with a falls at its top end used for raising and lowering a boat.

DEADEYE — a round piece of hardwood through which is drilled three holes. If an upper deadeye, it is fastened to the end of a shroud or backstay. If a lower deadeye, it is fastened to the upper end of a chainplate. Lanyards are rove through the three holes in the upper and lower deadeyes and set tight to support the standing rigging.

DOLPHIN STRIKER — the Martingale; a spar acting as a brace extending vertically from the bottom of the bowsprit.

DONKEY ENGINE — steam engine usually located on starboard side of forward house used for hoisting anchor, sails and cargo and for warping. Later vessels had gasoline donkey engines.

DOUBLE ENDED — a boat that is pointed on both ends.

DOUBLINGS — the area where lower and uppermast overlap.

EYES — the extreme forward part of the hull.

FISH TACKLE — the block and tackle and gear used to pull an anchor on board a vessel's foredeck.

FLY RAIL — an open rail around the poop or quarterdeck.

FOOT — the bottom edge of a sail.

FORE AND AFT SAILS — those sails that are normally set lengthwise on a vessel and secured on their forward edge to a mast or stay or spar.

FORECASTLE — the superstructure at the bow of a vessel, also the forward quarters for the crew.

FOREFOOT — the junction of the stem and keel.

FRAMES — the ribs in the hull of a vessel.

FREEBOARD — the distance between the lowest watertight deck and the water.

GAFF — a spar attached to the head of a fore and aft, four sided sail.

GASKETS — lines used to tie down sails when they are not in use.

GUYS — standing rigging running from the bowsprit to catheads or bow side.

HALYARDS — lines used to raise or lower the sails or spars to which sails are attached.

HATCH — an opening in the deck through which cargo is passed.

HAWSEPIPES — flanged iron pipes in the bow through which the anchor chain passes.

HEAD — the top of a mast or the top edge of a four sided sail. The ships toilet.

HEADSAILS — all triangular sails set before the foremast on headstays.

HEADSTAYS — standing rigging running from the foremast to the bow or bowsprit.

HEAVE TO — to stop way (by backing some of the sails on a square rigged ship).

HELM — the wheel used to steer a vessel.

HOGGED — a sagging in the hull of a vessel.

HOUNDS — that part of the structure on a masthead which projects fore and aft and supports trestletrees.

JAWS — the forked extension of a gaff or boom which fits over and slides up or down a mast.

JIB — name for a triangular sail carried on a stay ahead of the foremast.

JIBBOOM — a boom to which the foot of a jib is made fast — also the spar called the Flying Jibboom, which rests on top of and extends beyond the bowsprit.

KEEL — the backbone of a vessel.

KEELSON — an auxilary keel constructed inside the vessel over the frames and over the keel.

KNEE — an angular piece of wood, heavy and thick, used to brace and connect deck beams and the frames (or ribs) in the hull of a vessel.

LANYARD — Length of light tarred line which goes through deadeyes and is used to pull them together to tighten up backstays and shrouds.

LAZARETTE — the space under the poop or quarterdeck which is entered through a small hatch or companionway.

LAZYJACKS — rigging set up from trestletrees or masthead to the boom on a fore and aft sail which help contain the sail when it is lowered.

LEE — the side away from the wind.

LEECH — the after edge of a fore and aft sail or the leeward edge of a square sail.

LUFF — the forward edge of a fore and aft sail or the weather edge of a square sail.

LUFFING — causing the sails to flap by bringing them too far into the wind.

MAKE FAST — to tie to or tie down.

MAST — upright circular timber used to support sails.

PEAK — the top corner of a triangular sail. The after top corner of a four cornered fore and aft sail. The after high end of a gaff.

POOP — the raised after section on a vessel (higher than a quarterdeck).

PORT — the left side of a vessel when looking forward.

QUARTERDECK — a deck slightly raised over the height of the main deck that is located in the after section of a vessel.

RATLINES — short lengths of line seized across the shrouds, making ladders in the rigging.

REACHING — sailing with the wind close to the beam.

REEF — reducing the area of a sail exposed to the wind.

RIBS — the frames in a vessels hull.

RIG — the arrangement of masts and sails on a vessel.

RIGGING — the ropes used to support the masts and work the sails on a vessel.

RUDDER — the flat verticle plane hung under water from the sternpost with pintles and gudgeons. When swung to either side by Helm or tiller, the rudder changes the course of the vessel when under way.

RUNNING LIGHTS — the red port light and the green starboard light carried close to the sides near the forward part of a vessel.

RUNNING RIGGING — the ropes that control the use of the sails.

SADDLE — support around the lower portion of the mast upon which the jaws of the boom rest when the sail is not hoisted.

SCUPPERS — openings in a vessels bulwarks to let water run off the deck.

SHEAVE — the wheel that turns in the middle of a block or pulley.

SHEER — the curvature of the deck in a fore and aft direction.

SHEET — a rope controlling the position of the aft, lower corner of a fore and aft sail or the lower corner of a square sail.

SHROUDS — the heavy standing rigging that brace the masts athwartship, often fitted with ratlines.

SPAR — a round or oval timber used as a mast, yard, gaff or boom.

SPRIT — a spar used on a type of fore and aft sail that runs diagonally across the sail to support the peak of the sail.

SPRING STAY — the stay on a schooner that runs from one masthead to the next.

SQUARE SAIL — a four cornered sail hung from a yard set athwartship or across ship.

STANDING RIGGING — rigging that does not move or run, that is used to support the masts.

STARBOARD — the right side of a vessel when looking forward.

STAYS — strong ropes or wire that are part of the standing rigging used to support the masts in a fore and aft direction.

STAYSAIL — any sail hoisted on a stay; usually named for the stay on which it is set.

STEEVE — the angle at which something inclines upward.

STEM — the heavy timber in the extreme bow of the vessel that extends from the keel to the forecastle head.

STEP — the square or rectangular hole in keel or keelson made to receive the heel of the mast.

STERN — the back or aft end of a vessel.

STERNPOST — the timber extending from the aft end of the keel upward to the transom or deck depending upon the type of hull.

STRAKE — a fixed width of planking running fore and aft along the hull.

TACK — the lower forward corner of a fore and aft sail, also the rope used in securing it.

TACKING — a process of sailing upwind by means of changing course across the wind.

THROAT — the area on the gaff immediately behind the jaws.

THWART — a seat running crossways in an open boat.

TOPPING LIFT — a part of the rigging on a fore and aft vessel which runs from near the aft end of the boom to the lower mast head and can be used in raising the boom.

TOPSIDES — the part of the side of a vessel that is above the waterline.

TRANSOM — the wide, flat or slightly curved structure at the extreme stern or after end of a vessel's hull.

TREENAILS — (often pronounced and spelled "trunnels") wooden fastenings driven through planking and frames to hold the two together.

TRESTLETREES — heavy pieces of timber bolted fore and aft to the masthead above the hounds as a support for crosstrees and masting above.

TUMBLE HOME — the sloping inward of the vessels sides above the point of greatest beam.

WALE — a thick, heavy strake of planking running the length of the outside hull above the waterline.

212

WAY — the forward motion of a vessel through the water.

WEATHER — the side nearest the wind. To survive or ride out a severe storm.

WEIGH — to hoist the anchor.

WELL DECK — an open main deck below the level of the main rail.

WINCH HEADS — flarred drums on each end of a shaft that are used in hoisting, warping and handling cargo.

WINDLASS — a mechanical device in the forward part of a vessel used to hoist the anchor.

WING OUT — (often pronounced "wung out") sailing before the wind in a fore and aft rigged vessel with some of the sails swung out over the port side and some of the sails over the starboard side. Running before the wind.

YARD, YARD ARM — a horizontal spar carried across or arthwartship on the forward side of a mast.

# INDEX

# INDEX

# INDEX

222

# INDEX